More Than a Lawyer

Robert Chanin, the National Education Association, and the Fight for Public Education, Employee Rights, and Social Justice

Michael Edwards and Mark Walsh

National Education Association
Washington, D.C.

Library of Congress Cataloging-in-Publication Data

Edwards, Michael, 1948-
  More than a lawyer: Robert Chanin, the National Education
Association, and the fight for public education, employee rights, and
social justice / Michael Edwards and Mark Walsh.
     p. cm.
  Includes bibliographical references and index.
  ISBN 978-0-8106-1550-2 (hardcover : alk. paper) -- ISBN
978-0-8106-1551-9 (pbk. : alk. paper)
  1. Chanin, Robert H. 2. Cause lawyers--United States--Biography. 3.
National Education Association of the United States--Officials and
employees--United States--Biography. 4. Educational law and
legislation--United States. I. Walsh, Mark, - II. Title.
  KF373.C3884E39 2010
  340.092--dc22
  [B]
                                        2010009832

Contents |

Foreword |

Ifirst saw Bob Chanin in action at my first National Education Association (NEA) Convention—the Representative Assembly—in 1980, and I must admit I was awed.

Delegates would put to Bob complicated and sometimes convoluted questions regarding the NEA Constitution, Bylaws, or Standing Rules, and he would untangle those questions and render opinions. His opinions were so authoritative, and delivered with such gravitas, that everyone listened and agreed. And even if you, as a first-time delegate like me, couldn't quite follow the winding staircase of logic that led Bob to his judgment, you were convinced he must be right, and therefore the business of the Representative Assembly—debating and deciding NEA's direction for the coming year—could proceed.

Bob Chanin served NEA in many capacities as its general counsel, but I have always thought the contributions he made to the functioning of our annual 9,000-delegate Representative Assembly, possibly the world's largest deliberative body, to be among his most significant.

Nobody ever said democracy was easy, certainly nobody who ever attended our Representative Assembly. Democracy can be a difficult, messy, and often exasperating process. And yet, I am convinced that NEA is what it is today—a strong organization and a powerful union, responsive to the needs of its members—because of our conscientious adherence to democracy. And frequently over the years, it has been Bob Chanin who oiled the gears of our democratic procedures, keeping them from seizing up.

In 1966, NEA and the American Teachers Association (ATA) merged. ATA was the organization that represented black teachers in segregated schools, and at that time, it was the largest black professional organization in the U.S. While the merger agreement united two organizations at the national level, it still had to be consummated in the states where two separate organizations existed—one white and affiliated with NEA and the other black and affiliated with ATA. Merger at the state level was an exceedingly difficult, sometimes contentious, process. But with great diplomatic aplomb and legal prowess, Bob Chanin helped to negotiate many of the state NEA-ATA merger agreements. This enabled NEA to move forward as a fully integrated organization, truly committed to equal opportunity for all.

Another of Bob Chanin's noteworthy contributions to NEA, as this book chronicles, is in the area of unionization and collective bargaining. NEA came late to organized labor, but after the decision was made that NEA had to unionize, it was Bob Chanin whom we threw into the fray. It was Bob Chanin who helped write many of the public employee bargaining laws for the states. It was Bob Chanin who helped bargain many of our local associations' first collective-bargaining contracts. It was Bob Chanin who developed the model collective-bargaining agreements that local associations could follow. And over the years, it has been Bob Chanin who reminded anyone who needed reminding that our members, for all their dedication, are in fact educators and employees, and not missionaries, and therefore, they deserve the very best working conditions, salaries, and benefits we can bargain for them.

Bob Chanin defended the rights of public school employees with great skill. He fought to win legal protections for public school employees, including the right of pregnant women to continue teaching and the right to teach regardless of sexual orientation. He also defended the right of students to a quality public education—a right articulated in most state constitutions. For NEA, Bob has been both an accomplished labor lawyer and a civil rights attorney.

Bob Chanin spent many years fighting against vouchers in state and federal courts, including the U.S. Supreme Court. ("Vouchers" are the mechanism by which the state provides public money to parents so that they can send their children to private schools.) Bob's case before the U.S. Supreme Court involved the Cleveland, Ohio voucher program, and he lost that case by a 5-to-4 vote. But the Cleveland voucher case actually has turned out not to be much of a loss at all because Bob came up with alternative theories for defeating voucher schemes. In the seven years since the Supreme Court decision, only three states have enacted voucher schemes—Colorado, Arizona, and Florida. And in all three states the voucher programs were struck down on state constitutional grounds. Bob handled the cases in Colorado and Florida.

Bob Chanin is the counsel of record in 151 court decisions, an incredible testament to his work ethic. And contrary to the practice of many attorneys, Bob never signed a brief that he was not involved in writing.

Even I, a high school math teacher, always looked forward to reading a new Bob Chanin brief. Admittedly, I skipped the legal references, but I found the brief itself so well crafted and so tightly reasoned, and the story that he told so clear that it truly was a pleasure to read.

I am told there are about 760,000 practicing attorneys in the United States today. Organizations hire lawyers to give them advice and to tell them what they can or cannot do and to take their side in court. We know Bob Chanin could have earned far more as a corporate attorney. We have been fortunate to have him as our legal counsel for over four decades—a period in which we and public education have been under almost constant attack.

The highest accolade I can bestow on Bob Chanin is to say that he has served our members, the hard-working people in America's public schools and colleges, with great diligence and determination.

And lastly, I must say that Bob Chanin has served another lesser known but vital role in NEA. He has been our in-house skeptic when new policy ideas and initiatives surfaced and were discussed by our Executive Committee. Unfazed by the hype that often haloes the education *idea-du-jour*, Bob has helped us to think clearly and rationally about whom we are and what we should be doing; and thanks to Bob, we have evaluated proposed policies on their merits, not their hoopla.

I still have a hard time grasping that Bob Chanin has retired. In many respects, he will be impossible to replicate, and I will miss him tremendously, as a colleague, as a general counsel, as a confidant—and as a friend.

Dennis Van Roekel
President, National Education Association
Washington, D.C.
July 2010

More Than a Lawyer

Prologue |

Finding His Calling

Prologue

Finding His Calling

In 1997, Professor Myron Lieberman, the prominent author of such books as *The Future of Public Education, Education as a Profession*, and *Collective Negotiations for Teachers*, made this comment in *The Teacher Unions*, a treatise sharply critical of the National Education Association (NEA):

> In my opinion, Chanin has had a larger impact on public education over the past thirty years than any other individual, in or out of government.[1]

In 2009, Mike Antonucci, the founder of the research firm Education Intelligence Agency and an author whom *Education Week* has called "the nation's leading observer—and critic—of the two national teachers' unions," wrote that "Chanin was in on [the formation of teacher unions] from the very beginning. If he wasn't the architect, he was certainly the mason, welder, and custodian of the teacher union as we know it today."[2]

These comments about Robert H. Chanin's critical role in the evolution of public education and the development of public education employee unions may be surprising to many readers because he has not been well known outside of union and legal circles, although he served as NEA's general counsel for more than forty years.

To Professor Lieberman, it was no accident that Chanin had a low public profile compared with perhaps the best-known figure in American education-employee unionism, Albert Shanker, the late president of the American Federation of Teachers (AFT). Shanker, Lieberman wrote, actively sought the limelight, while Chanin preferred to work behind the scenes. "It was in Shanker's interest to generate favorable publicity; in Chanin's, to avoid publicity," Lieberman said.[3]

Chanin began representing NEA in 1963, and served continuously as NEA general counsel from 1968 until he retired at the end of 2009. In addition, he served as NEA deputy executive director from 1973 to

1980, was a professor at George Washington University Law School from 1972 to 1980, and was a partner in the Washington, D.C., law firm of Bredhoff & Kaiser from 1980 to 2005.[4]

This book highlights NEA's crucial participation in some of the groundbreaking developments of the past half century and Bob Chanin's pivotal role in advising the Association and plotting its legal, policy, structural, and operational strategies during this time of dramatic change. These developments include the rise of public-sector collective bargaining; the civil rights movement, including continuing efforts to desegregate the public schools and promote and defend affirmative action for students and employees; landmark court cases protecting the rights of public employees, women, and gay and lesbian Americans; and the transformation of NEA, with more than 3.2 million members, into one of the nation's most effective advocates for public education, school employees, and social justice.

As is the case with every large organization, as crucial as specific individuals are, accomplishments are almost always the result of team efforts. This has certainly been true of NEA. As Bob Chanin himself often noted, a great many other individuals guided him, assisted him, and helped make it possible for the Association to achieve what it has over the past five decades. "As in the Verizon cell phone commercial," he would say, "there has always been a team behind me."

It should also be noted that this book is not a comprehensive history of NEA or of the full array of issues with which it has been engaged. To be sure, it does trace significant parts of NEA's history, though it does so primarily to place the work and accomplishments of Bob Chanin in their proper context. It is, in fact, the story of how a particular individual helped shape NEA and, in so doing, some of the most defining and challenging movements of our time. NEA has often been referred to as "more than a union" because of its important role in promoting not only improved compensation and working conditions for education employees, but also quality public education and social justice. In the same way, Chanin has been much "more than a lawyer," contributing in a wide variety of ways to historic progress, both within public education and in society at large.

Robert Howard Chanin was born in Brooklyn, New York, on

December 24, 1934. Known as Bob from his early childhood, he was the second of two sons of Frank and Irene Chanin. His brother, Irv, was five years older than he.

Bob's father had arrived in New York City from Russia in 1901, when he was six years old. A high school graduate, Frank Chanin did not attend college, and at the age of 18 entered the workforce. With his brother and several other members of the Chanin family, Frank started a business manufacturing children's coats. The Chanin Children's Coat Company had begun to prosper in the 1920s, but the business, like so many others, was devastated by the 1929 stock market crash. By the time Bob was born, the company had given up its Manhattan factory and was operating out of the basement of a house in Brooklyn that was owned by Frank's sisters.

Bob's mother was a native New Yorker whose parents had come from Russia to New York City several years before she was born. Like her husband, Irene graduated from high school, but did not go to college. Following her graduation, she worked as a secretary, which she continued to do until Bob's brother was born and she stayed home to care for him.

Bob grew up in the Flatbush section of Brooklyn. His family lived in a rented apartment on the ground floor of a two-family house in a working class neighborhood—"lower middle class" in the sociological parlance of the day.

By 1934, the Great Depression had reached its depth. Money was scarce, and the Chanin family's circumstances were typical of the times. Bob's father worked long days, leaving the house well before his sons were awake and arriving home late in the evening, as he strove to keep his family afloat in the nation's struggling economy. Frank was a talented designer of children's coats who was highly regarded in the garment industry, and he received several job offers from larger, more prosperous businesses that would have improved his family's financial situation. He turned these offers down, however, because he knew that without him the Chanin Children's Coat Company—which provided a livelihood for his brother and other family members—could not survive. Nursery school and other forms of organized day care were not the norm in those days, and Bob's mother stayed home to take care of her children.

Frank and Irene Chanin both came from observant Jewish families, and they brought the religious traditions with them into their own home. The family kept faithfully to kosher dietary laws, and observed the Sabbath and other Jewish holidays. Bob remembered the Sabbath with particular fondness: because observant Jews are not allowed to work from sundown on Friday until sundown on Saturday, his father spent the day with his family in the synagogue and resting at home. "Were it not for the Sabbath," Bob recalled, "I am sure my father would have worked seven days a week." During their growing-up years, Bob and his brother reflected the work ethic and values of their parents, receiving religious training several days a week as well as on Sundays.

At a time when few homes had even one television set, and when personal computers and video games were many decades in the future, young people still found much to amuse themselves after school. There were no ball fields or organized sports leagues for kids who grew up in Bob's neighborhood, but there were street games—like stickball (which was a spin-off of baseball, played in the street with a rubber ball and a broomstick for a bat, and with the fenders of parked cars as convenient stand-ins for bases), and two-hand touch football (in which the quarterback would call plays such as "go straight, cut right at the Buick, and stop just in front of the Ford"). Such games were generally a safe pastime, because there was little traffic to worry about, and the street lights allowed the games to go on well after sunset.

There were more things to do, however, than play street games. A Boy Scout troop provided one of the few organized activities to keep the neighborhood boys out of mischief and teach them teamwork. Headquartered in the synagogue Bob's family attended, the troop he joined offered a supportive "Jewish environment" for boys of observant families like his. Being motivated from early childhood by tenacity, a competitive spirit, and a desire to excel in everything he undertook, Bob became one of the most decorated Scouts in New York City, amassing medals, religious and secular, ascending to Eagle Scout, and being inducted into the Order of the Arrow at Scout Camp.

Looking back, Bob would come to view his early self as avidly competitive—so competitive that he would pore over his books, not as much for the joy of acquiring knowledge as for the high grades he could achieve through intensive study. In the same spirit, he accumulated Boy Scout merit badges not necessarily because he was interested in the subject matter of the badge, but simply so that he could have more badges than anyone else.

Somewhat ironically for a man who during his adult career came to be known for his consummate rhetorical skill—from articulate speech-making and persuasive negotiating to arguing before the U.S. Supreme Court—as a child Bob was burdened with a speech impediment. With a perseverance that was to become a hallmark in future years—and the help of a caring elementary school speech teacher who worked with him on her own time after school—he succeeded in overcoming this burden.

In order to earn spending money, like many other youngsters during World War II, he collected newspapers "for the war effort" and sold them at a nearby collection center. The going rate for papers was sixty cents per one hundred pounds, and the proceeds were saved for special things such as his first two-wheel bicycle, a Columbia, which he bought for eighteen dollars after months of collecting papers. He also used his proceeds for purchases that expressed his identity and family values. In the early 1940s, anti-Semitic graffiti could be seen on walls and sidewalks, and some of the people Bob came in contact with would on occasion openly express their admiration for the Nazis. Without knowing how Chanin was spelled, some people pronounced his family name "Shannon" like the fabled river in Ireland, and they assumed that with the "non-Jewish" first name Robert and his dark curly hair and fair skin, he must be Irish. When he heard someone defend what the Nazis had done to the Jews, or had to listen to anti-Semitic slurs, Bob wanted to make his true identity clear to them. So he took some of the money saved from collecting newspapers and bought himself a Star of David pendant to wear around his neck. It was not merely a young boy's bravado, but also his way of letting others know who he was and what his family believed. He continues to wear that same Star of David to this day. The anti-Semitism that Bob witnessed—and personally experienced—gave him the bitter taste of discrimination against people of different religions and cultures.

When Bob moved on to high school, he carved a path different from that of his brother and friends, who went to the local public high school, Erasmus Hall, well known for its high academic standards. Bob, who had inherited his father's artistic ability and flair for design, decided that he wanted to attend the High School of Music and Art in upper Manhattan. He aced the entrance examination and began an intensive program that he found agreeably challenging, both academically and for the development of his skill in the arts. M&A, as it was called, was one of a handful of early magnet schools in New York City, comparable to the Bronx High School of Science, Peter Stuyvesant High School and the Brooklyn Technical High School. All of these schools were well-known in New York City as solid stepping stones to careers and preparation for college and later studies at graduate and professional schools. Bob's choice, M&A, eventually merged with the High School of the Performing Arts to form LaGuardia High School, which was featured in the play and movie, *Fame*.

The commute from Brooklyn to another borough was difficult and tiring, even for an energetic teenager. Bob spent more than two hours on the subway every day, leaving home at 6:30 in the morning, and rarely returning until 6:30 in the evening. In comparison, his relatives and friends only spent half that time—between 8:00 a.m. and 2:00 p.m.—in their classes at Erasmus. But the desire to be "different" from his peers paid off. It gave him both an academic and artistic base from which to choose a career path.

The secondary education provided at M&A expanded Bob's experience. For the first time, he found himself in a racially integrated social environment, with well-educated minority students, many of whom were to become celebrities in the arts. While other teenage boys were absorbed in playing sports, Bob and his classmates, in addition to engaging in sports, were visiting museums, attending plays and concerts, and learning about broad areas of culture to which their peers in non-magnet schools might only be introduced much later, if at all. His high performance throughout his four years at M&A, resulted during his senior year in his selection as art editor of the school yearbook—a true accomplishment in such a supremely gifted student body. Art and academics were combined with the realities of daily life, so to earn spending money while in high school, Bob had begun to work week nights and Saturdays as a stock boy at Ohrbach's department store in Manhattan, a position "inherited" from his brother, who had filled the job before him.

On graduating from M&A in 1952, Bob faced a dilemma: he excelled in art and graphic design and could have gone on to one of the celebrated New York City art schools—Cooper Union or Pratt Institute, both of which had offered him scholarships, but neither of which provided a bachelor's degree. The idea of art school, however, did not sit well with his parents. It would not have fulfilled their ambition for him to become a professional—a lawyer or doctor or teacher. Bob's brother Irv already had a bachelor of science degree, was working on a master's degree, and was soon to be enrolled in medical school on his way to becoming a vascular surgeon. He agreed with the elder Chanins and advised Bob to keep his options open by taking a college degree that would prepare him for graduate work or a professional school. He could always return to his artwork later or continue it in his spare time.

Bob, too, had doubts about making an "irrevocable commitment to art" by continuing studies that might lead to a diploma, but not to a bachelor's degree. He knew talented M&A graduates who were employed in art or advertising agencies under the supervision of art directors with far less talent who held their positions simply because they had a degree in business administration. Bob concluded that talent alone did not guarantee future success.

Despite their desire for Bob to attain a college degree, his family could not afford to pay his college tuition or living costs. The way out of that quandary was for him to go to a college that would provide him with a degree without the cost of tuition or room and board. The answer was Brooklyn College, from which his brother had recently graduated. It was close enough to the Chanin home for Bob to commute to classes, and the only tuition cost was a matriculation fee of $7 or $8 a semester. Other expenses were easily met; for example, used textbooks could be borrowed or purchased for a nominal sum. Bob's application to Brooklyn College was accepted on his high school record alone; he met the admission requirements without having to take the standard entrance examination.

Brooklyn College, which along with the City College of New York, Queens College, and Hunter College later became part of the CUNY system, offered both academic and art programs of extremely high quality, and many of its alumni held positions of responsibility in public service and government, as well as at academic and cultural institutions. Bob found that he could still pursue his art studies, along with other academic work by taking classes taught at the college by such eminent artists as Mark Rothko. As he progressed through college and moved away from the concentrated "art culture" of his high school years, his outlook about his future changed and he began to think in terms of one of his family's preferences—law school.

In June 1956, Bob received his bachelor's degree from Brooklyn College, with a dual major in art and political science. He graduated *summa cum laude* and was offered scholarships by the law schools of Yale, Harvard, Columbia, and New York University. He decided to go to Yale Law School on a full scholarship, drawn by its relatively small class sizes.

That June, too, Bob became engaged to Rhoda Paley, whom he had been dating for four years. They had met during the summer of 1952, when Bob worked as a counselor at Secor Lake Camp near Mahopac, New York. Bob was seventeen when he met sixteen-year-old Rhoda, who lived with her family in their summer home on Secor Lake, and also worked as a counselor that summer at the camp. For the next four years, when Bob visited Rhoda in New York City, he would take the long subway ride from the Church Avenue Station in Brooklyn to the Gun Hill Road Station in the Bronx near her family's apartment, an even longer journey than his commute to M&A High School had been. Rhoda's family owned a paint and wallpaper store, and by Bob's standards the Paleys were people of wealth, because—in contrast to his own family—they had a second home in which to get away from the city during the summer, owned a car and a television, occasionally ate out at restaurants, and could afford to send Rhoda and her brother Marty to NYU.

Now officially engaged to Rhoda, Bob left for Yale Law School in

September 1956. It was the beginning of an arduous and uncomfortable year for him. Not only was he away from Rhoda, but he was also apart from his family. For the first time in his life, he lived in a dormitory with other students. Although his tuition and lodging were taken care of by his scholarship, he had little spending money, and between adjusting to law school and the demanding first year curriculum, a part-time job that would provide some income was not an acceptable option. One of the many distressing aspects of the new environment was the difficulty he found in keeping to a kosher diet. The dining hall kitchens were only supplied by non-kosher butchers, so for Bob, an observant Jew, meals had to be meatless. As he said years later, "1956-57 was a tough year all around."

Rhoda, an education major, graduated from NYU in February 1957, so she and Bob made a plan for the immediate future. They would marry in June, and Rhoda would get a position teaching in the New Haven Public Schools for the two years left for Bob to complete his law degree. She would be the major breadwinner, though Bob would earn as much as he could with part-time jobs. The plan worked well to begin with. After their wedding, the couple—with Rhoda at the wheel, because Bob, whose family had no car, did not know how to drive—drove to New Haven in the used DeSoto they had purchased in the Bronx for $75. They rented a basement apartment which, as Bob recalls, "Had its bad points and good points"—dark because of its location, but warm during the cold New Haven winters because of the exposed heating pipes that ran across the ceiling. The windows, only very slightly above ground, allowed them to glimpse the feet of passing pedestrians, so they were able to keep up with the comings and goings of their neighbors by observing the footwear that passed by. With a kitchen of their own, and a kosher market nearby, Bob was able to eat regular meals again.

Meeting expenses was an immediate problem while they waited out the weeks until September when Rhoda would begin teaching second grade. To make the most of the months before his law classes began, Bob sought a job at Malley's department store in downtown New Haven, which had a policy of not employing Yale students for the summer because, after the store had gone to the expense of training the students, they would leave when classes began in the fall. Bob was determined to get a job at Malley's, so he took a few facts and fabricated them into a believable story for the personnel department: he and his wife had just moved to New Haven; he already had department store experience at Ohrbach's in New York; and he was interested in a career in retailing. He never mentioned Yale, and he got a job as a floor walker. Meanwhile, both he and Rhoda extended their quest for gainful employment by selling *World Book Encyclopedias* door-to-door, an enterprise at which neither proved a smashing success—even if someone answered the door, it was virtually impossible to get a foot inside the house to present a convincing sales pitch. Although Rhoda did manage to sell a few *World Book* sets, Bob was a total failure at the job, perhaps because he liked to get straight to the point and was not adept at salesmen's chit-chat. They kept up their discouraging activity long enough, however, to earn a free set of *World Book*, which proved useful later when their children were in school.

During these months Rhoda's parents worried about whether their daughter and her husband had enough to eat—which might not have been too far from the truth—so they would surreptitiously check the pantry whenever they came to New Haven to visit Bob and Rhoda. Aware of the Paleys' well-meaning—if annoyingly paternalistic—habit of snooping, the newlyweds would prep for these parental visits by borrowing food from their neighbors and proudly exhibiting the goods in conspicuous places around their tiny apartment, a veritable cornucopia of tuna fish and canned vegetables. After the parents had departed, secure in the knowledge that the "children" were not starving, Bob and Rhoda would quickly gather up the provisions and return them to their rightful owners, ever grateful for the temporary handout.

By the end of that first summer, the Chanins' two-year plan was showing promise of viability, especially after Bob read a notice on a university bulletin board advertising for an instructor in psychology at New Haven College. Bob applied for the position, highlighting the fact that he had done well in the few psychology courses that he had taken in college, and was offered the job. The next question was whether he could fit teaching into his law school class schedule, which he did by instructing college students in the morning before his law classes and in the evening. In retrospect Bob likes to say that he got the job by overstating his qualifications and kept it by managing to stay one step ahead of the students. That he succeeded as a psychology instructor was proven by the fact that he held the job during the two succeeding school years until he graduated from Yale Law School and left New Haven for New York City in June 1959.

Very early in those two years, however, the Chanins' plan, which despite minor snags had begun to unfold so well in the summer, ran off the rails completely. In October 1957, Rhoda discovered that she was pregnant. New Haven, like most public school systems at that time, did not countenance visibly pregnant teachers in the classroom. Such a policy is unthinkable in the 21st century, but whether guided by excessive modesty or fear of harm to tender young minds, in the mid-20th century, most school districts in the United States had zero tolerance for pregnant teachers. If a teacher became pregnant during the school year, she had to stop teaching when she "began to show." Her employment was generally terminated without maternity leave or without the option of a transfer to a position in which she did not interact with children. New Haven's school policy would allow Rhoda's employment to continue until March, and then Bob would be compelled to take over as primary breadwinner, while continuing his studies. Between his second-year law school classes and his need to outpace his psychology students, he had little time for another part-time job, and Rhoda's parents stepped in to ease the financial burden. At the end of the 1957-58 school year, with their first child expected within weeks, Bob and Rhoda returned to the Bronx to live with the Paleys for the summer.

Bob found a job driving a bus for a day camp. Although Rhoda had taught him how to drive during the previous year, he had no experience with a manual transmission, so on the weekend before camp began, Rhoda's father instructed him in the mysteries of driving a stick-shift bus. Always a quick study, Bob learned his lesson thoroughly, and on July 22, 1958, when their son Jeff was entering the world around 8:00 a.m., instead of pacing the floor outside the delivery room in accordance with the mid-20th century stereotype of a first-time father, Bob was at the wheel of his bus, picking up campers and delivering them to their day's activities. The Paleys' apartment seemed exceptionally crowded during the succeeding five weeks with the senior Paleys, their son Marty, the Chanins, and their new baby. With something of a feeling of relief, Bob and Rhoda returned to their New Haven apartment that September.

Bob graduated from Yale Law School in June 1959. In the late 1950s, Yale Law School was promoting interdisciplinary courses, taught jointly by law school professors and professors from other departments of the university. He had found one such area—a combination of law and psychology—particularly interesting. Not only had it fitted in with his teaching at New Haven College, but the courses that he had taken had suggested that a background in psychology along with a law degree from Yale would make him more marketable to law firms. Hence, with the encouragement of some of his professors, Bob decided that his next step would be to take a PhD in psychology to enhance his marketability.

The old problem of finances loomed over his plan, however, and was more threatening now that he had a family to support. He reasoned that if he could find a job on the staff of a university that would provide sufficient income for the needs of his family, he would be able to attain a PhD in psychology because of the tuition waiver allowed a university employee. Columbia University offered just such an opportunity. Bob applied to the Columbia Law School Project for Effective Justice, a research endeavor designed to address problems of judicial administration, such as court delays. He was hired as one of two full-time lawyers on the project, each of whom received an annual salary of $6,500, a wage comparable to salaries that most reputable law firms in New York City and other major U.S. cities were then paying starting attorneys. Although the cost of living was much lower at that time, $6,500 could scarcely cover expenses for a young family in New York City. It was a placeholder, however, the right job at the right time.

The Project for Effective Justice—which was directed by Professor Maurice Rosenberg, with Professor Michael Sovern, who would go on to become president of Columbia University, as associate director— gave Bob the opportunity to work on his analytical and writing skills.

Rosenberg was an ideal mentor, and Sovern became a close colleague with whom Bob collaborated in preparing several project reports. The project was a full-time job, so Bob took his psychology courses at night. By the end of the 1960-61 school year, he had completed most of the work toward a PhD. Although he still needed to take a few additional courses and fulfill other minor requirements to complete the program, the primary remaining obligation was his doctoral dissertation. His topic, already approved, was to be the use of psychological tests and methodology in jury selection. Well ahead of its time then, the concept was later developed and perfected as part of the work of the American Jury Project.

Completion of Bob's doctorate posed another dilemma, however. His family was growing; with the birth of his daughter Stacy on March 26, 1961, three others were now dependent on his income. The dissertation, he knew, would require at least a year to research and write and it would not be possible for him to continue working full-time. In addition, he had discovered that the bundling of law and psychology was not as marketable as some of his professors at Yale Law School had led him to believe. The prevailing view then—as it is now—was that lawyers should practice law, and if a case called for the skills of a psychologist, a firm would hire one. Bob concluded that there was no point in continuing his schooling.

In 1962, Bob converted his doctoral work into an MA in social psychology. This meant that he had acquired his BA at Brooklyn College, his LLB (JD) at Yale Law School, and his MA at Columbia, all at no financial cost whatsoever to himself or his family—a feat of which he remains very proud.

Realizing that the time had come to end his student days and begin practicing law, Bob consulted Michael Sovern about law firms to approach. Sovern had spent a summer working at Kaye, Scholer, Fierman, Hays, and Handler—a large Manhattan law firm with an active management-side labor law practice—and he offered to speak with senior partner Milton Handler, who taught part-time at Columbia Law School. Handler, who was head of the firm's antitrust department, was impressed by Bob's record and the recommendations he received from Rosenberg and Sovern. That meeting was the first step toward an offer to become an associate at Kaye Scholer, which Bob accepted.

In the summer of 1962, Bob began work at Kaye Scholer. Taking Sovern's advice, he expressed an interest in labor law, and after a few months was assigned to that department. He found many of his assignments challenging and absorbing, and he was working with interesting and influential clients, including, among others, Republic Aviation, Jonathan Logan, Fairchild Hiller, Mack Trucks, and Continental Grain. But his upbringing had led him to have empathy with employees and unions, and representing management caused him some discomfort.

Bob's work and his beliefs came into direct conflict in 1963 when he went with one of the law firm's partners to upstate New York to implement the closing of a washing machine plant. Kaye Scholer had been brought in to negotiate with the union over the employees' severance arrangements. As Bob later recalled, the company had authorized the lawyers to spend up to a specified amount on the total severance package. By utilizing well-honed negotiating skills and their superior bargaining position, Bob and the partner worked out an agreement with the union that gave the workers substantially less than had been authorized, thus saving the company a tidy sum.

Once the agreement was signed, the final step was to hand out the severance checks. Because the plant was located in a small town in which managers and employees shopped at the same stores, were members of the same churches, and attended many of the same social functions, they had gotten to know each other well. During the severance payout, Bob sat at a table with the director of personnel and a secretary while the workers moved forward in a somber line to receive their final checks. In a scene that repeated itself as each employee approached the table to sign for his or her severance, Bob overheard the conversations between the personnel director and the workers:

"I'm sorry," the personnel director would say in a tone of sincere regret. "What are you going to do now?"

"I don't know. What can I do?" the worker would ask. "I gave this company forty years of my life. I'm sixty years old. This town doesn't have a lot of options." After pausing a moment, he would add, "Not for someone my age."

After the last worker had picked up his check and trudged out of the plant into the fading daylight, it was time for the corporate officials and lawyers to celebrate at an elaborate reception in the executive dining room. No expense was spared. Still flush with the success of the day, one of the executives gave a rousing speech, not about what the day meant for the people now out of work, but about what a great job Kaye Scholer had done saving the company so much money. "I'd like to toast your *outstanding* work," he announced admiringly to the lawyers.

For Bob it was a transformational moment. He had spent the afternoon listening to the workers' bewildered talk about the hard times they now faced. While part of him wanted to savor the moment and enjoy the praise for a job well done, he felt chagrin at his part in the day's activity. He knew that the money Kaye Scholer had helped the company save could have been better used by the employees and their families than by the company that had shut down the plant. He knew, too, that he did not have the stomach to continue working as a hired gun for management.

The trip back to New York City was quiet, and it gave Bob an opportunity for some soul-searching. By the time he arrived home, he knew what he wanted to do. Somewhat apprehensively he said to Rhoda, "It's time for a change. I'm working for the wrong side." His realization presented an old dilemma, however. He had a bright future at Kaye Scholer, with excellent financial prospects. The Chanin family had grown with the birth of their third child, Lisa, on April 5, 1963, and going to work for a law firm that represented unions would have meant a substantial cut in income.

The answer to Bob's dilemma was found in the fact that a few months earlier Kaye Scholer had acquired a new client. Public employees throughout the nation, from firefighters to sanitation workers, were unionizing and battling fiercely for the right to engage in collective bargaining. A leading group in this public employee movement was school teachers, and the National Education Association, with three quarters of a million members, was the largest and most influential organization of teachers in the nation. But NEA styled itself a "professional association," and had no experience with collective bargaining. Knowing that Kaye Scholer had labor law expertise—albeit representing management—NEA had sought the firm's help in navigating these uncharted waters. Kaye Scholer had agreed to represent the Association.

With the memory of the sad scene he had witnessed at the washing machine plant still fresh in his mind, Bob asked to work with the new client, and his request was granted. So Bob Chanin found his calling and NEA found its champion. Thus began a 45-year fight for public education, employee rights, and social justice.

Part I |

A Movement is Born

"Union gives strength." —*Aesop*

Chapter 1

A Wake-Up Call for NEA

The forty-three educators who founded what would become the National Education Association were individuals of enormous determination and vision. They came to Philadelphia in August of 1857 in the most difficult of times . . . as a troubled nation moved closer and closer to almost certain civil war. They were steadfast in their belief that no matter what the circumstances, education was the key to the nation's future. The organization they established—then called the National Teachers Association—had at its core two fundamental principles: "to elevate the character and advance the interests of the profession of teaching and to promote the cause of popular education in the United States."[1]

Over the next one hundred years, the Association would grow to become the nation's preeminent educational organization, with a membership of more than 700,000 and a vast record of accomplishment. During that time, it had become the face and voice of America's teachers—if not of education itself. Indeed, when NEA celebrated its 100th anniversary in 1957, President Dwight Eisenhower and Vice President Richard Nixon joined in the celebration, a nationwide hook-up of television stations broadcast the event, and the United States Post Office issued a stamp commemorating the occasion and paying tribute to the organization.

Inside the organization, however, changes were brewing.

NEA's structure and internal dynamics reflected the world its members knew and within which they worked: the American school system. This was a world dominated by school boards and school administrators, where classroom teachers had little voice in the decisions that affected them and virtually no recourse should they not agree with those decisions. School administrators were nearly all male, while almost all teachers were single women who were expected— in some places by custom and in other places by law—to leave the classroom if they married.

So, too, the Association was dominated by school superintendents, principals, college presidents, and professors of education. This was not because of their numbers. Classroom teachers were by far the largest category of NEA membership. It was because of the positions the administrators held. And while they may have shared with classroom teachers a commitment to educational quality and improvement, as well as to specific policy goals such as increased funding for education, they were steadfastly opposed to giving teachers more voice in decision-making. And they were certainly opposed to the idea of teachers forming unions—an idea that had been simmering for almost six decades.

In the 1890s, a surge of interest in unionization among American manufacturing workers, particularly in the largest cities, was inspired by the American Federation of Labor (AFL), which had been founded in 1886 by Samuel Gompers, and which was, by the last decade of the 19th century, the largest coalition of industrial unions in the country. Encouraged by the example of manufacturing workers, teachers in Chicago formed their own organization, the Chicago Teachers' Federation (CTF), which was unique in a number of ways.[2] It was organized by and for women teachers in elementary schools. Its leaders were female at a time when the leadership of both NEA and AFL was virtually all male, and when women in America were still more than two decades away from winning the right to vote. It was the only teachers' organization in the country that was affiliated with a local council of labor unions. And it used grassroots organizing strategies that were unheard of among teachers or other female workers at the time.[3]

In 1897, teachers Catharine Goggin and Margaret Haley led the CTF in a campaign to raise teachers' salaries, which had been stagnant for 20 years. When the school board turned a deaf ear, more than half the teachers signed a petition, an act of courage in an era in which challenging school board authority could easily lead to dismissal.[4]

The Chicago school board ultimately responded to this pressure by signing an agreement to provide raises in 1897, but then reneged on the deal, claiming it had no money in its budget for pay increases. Haley and others conducted their own research and used public records to prove that major corporations in the city had been allowed to avoid ten million dollars per year in taxes they owed—more than the combined budgets of the public schools and public libraries. When the teachers went public with the information, the leader of the Republicans in the Illinois House of Representatives told Haley, "When you teachers stayed in your school rooms, we men took care of you, but when you go out of your school rooms as you have done, and attack these great, powerful corporations, you must expect that they will hit back."[5]

In 1903, having demonstrated that funds were available, the teachers, represented by a legal team that included the famous civil liberties and labor lawyer Clarence Darrow, went to county court successfully to enforce their agreement.[6] Darrow is perhaps best known for defending Tennessee school teacher John Scopes in 1925, when Scopes was put on trial for teaching students about the theory of evolution at a time when state law required teaching the creation story as told in the Bible.

Word of the Chicago teachers' victory spread to other cities, and teacher activists began to develop a two-pronged strategy for getting more organizational and political support for their efforts to improve pay and working conditions. They worked within NEA to change its policies and leadership, and at the same time asked the AFL to charter a national teachers' union. A national teachers' union would be chartered in 1916 by the AFL: the American Federation of Teachers (AFT).

By 1904, NEA leaders apparently were feeling enough pressure from teachers that they agreed to let Haley address the Association's annual meeting in St. Louis. Her speech, more than fifty years ahead of its time, was titled "Why Teachers Should Organize."

To the consternation of the administrators who led the Association, Haley raised a controversial issue that would still be raging six decades later when Chanin began working with NEA: Should the organization be a professional association that deals only with education policy, or should it also be a labor union that brings pressure to bear on employers to achieve better pay, benefits, and working conditions for teachers? Teachers needed both, Haley argued. They were being told then what their successors would still be told in Chanin's time—that it was "unprofessional" to insist on better pay and working conditions instead of putting children's welfare first. Haley argued that the two goals were not mutually exclusive, and that working conditions affected both teachers and students; working conditions such as:

1. Greatly increased cost of living, together with . . . practically stationary and wholly inadequate teachers' salaries.

2. Insecurity of tenure of office and lack of provision for old age.

3. Overwork in overcrowded schoolrooms, exhausting both mind and body.

4. And, lastly, lack of recognition of the teacher as an educator in the school system, due to the increased tendency toward "factoryizing education," making the teacher an automaton, a mere factory hand, whose duty it is to carry out mechanically and unquestioningly the ideas and orders of those clothed with the authority of position, and who may or may not know the needs of the children or how to minister to them.[7]

The solution to these problems, Haley argued, was for teachers to form unions and join forces with industrial workers who were doing the same. Together, they could confront the "corporation lobby" that controlled the legislatures, the taxing bodies, and even the courts that "defy the law they were elected and sworn to uphold."

"Two ideals are struggling for supremacy in American life today," Haley observed. "One, the industrial ideal, dominating through the supremacy of commercialism which subordinates the worker to the product and the machines; the other, the ideal of democracy, the ideal of the educators, which places humanity above all machines, and demands that all activity shall be the expression of life. Those two ideals can no more continue to exist in American life than our nation could have continued half slave and half free. It will be well indeed if the teachers have the courage of their convictions and face all that the labor unions have faced with the same courage and perseverance."[8]

Haley was not alone in her desire to forge a national teachers' union. There was a growing movement within NEA that shared her concerns and her approach. But it had little impact on NEA's leadership, made up of school administrators reluctant to cede power to classroom teachers, and even more reluctant to countenance collective bargaining. Then, in 1910, the Association's "progressives" won their first major victory when Ella Flagg Young was elected president of NEA.

Young had become superintendent of the Chicago schools the previous year, the first female superintendent of a major city school system. Her work in support of teachers had very quickly gained nationwide notoriety. She had ended Chicago's subjective teacher performance evaluations, enhanced the educational curriculum, expanded kindergarten, instituted the teaching of "sex hygiene," increased vocational training, improved teacher compensation, and created a set of "grade teachers' councils" to involve the city's school teachers in the educational decision-making process. It was said that she had personally met virtually all of Chicago's 6,000 teachers and remembered a good many of their names.[9] Her support among Chicago's teachers was extraordinary. CTF leader Margaret Haley, along with Grace Strachan and Katherine Blake of New York, led a campaign to elect Young president of NEA. Riding a wave of remarkable popularity, she was nominated from the floor of the 1910 NEA convention, defeating Z. X. Snyder, the presidential candidate selected by the Association's nominating committee. It was the first time in fifty years that a nominating committee's choice was rejected.[10]

The election of Ella Flagg Young gave NEA its first female president. It was an historic event. Women's suffrage was still an ideal, not a reality, in the United States. In fact, women would not gain the vote for another decade. Yet here a woman was chosen to lead America's largest, most prestigious, and most visible educational organization. Within the Association, Young's policies and positions on the inclusion of teachers at every level of school decision making helped dissipate some of the growing conflicts within NEA, but they did not put them to rest. First, her term was only a single year. And second, she was, after all, the superintendent of the Chicago schools, not a teacher, and despite her positions and policies, she did not fully represent the teachers' voice when it came to pay and working conditions. It would be three more years before NEA established a Department of Classroom Teachers designed to focus specifically on the needs of those members. Led by

Haley, Mary O'Connor of Buffalo, and other outspoken teachers, the Department soon adopted "vigorous" resolutions denouncing arbitrary teacher evaluation systems, calling for advisory councils of teachers to give expert professional advice to school boards and administrators, and advocating for better salaries, pensions, and tenure.[11] Even this was not sufficient in the progressives' view. There still needed to be a fundamental change in the Association's outlook and structure. And there had to be real and lasting attention paid to improving teachers' pay and working conditions.[12]

Haley and her supporters continued to press for such changes. Each year, when NEA held its annual meeting—open to all educators—in a major industrial city with an active labor base such as Pittsburgh or Milwaukee, Haley and others would organize teachers from that area to attend in large numbers to push for NEA support for campaigns to improve pay and working conditions for teachers. But as the 1920s began, that tactic was no longer a meaningful option. The NEA leadership scheduled its 1920 annual meeting in Salt Lake City, a location that would be difficult to reach for teachers from the industrial heartland. At that meeting, the leadership won approval from the attendees to change the rules for future NEA annual conventions. Instead of being open like a town hall meeting to any member who chose to participate, the gathering would be a "Representative Assembly" made up of delegations from the state associations.

In some ways this was a major step in enhancing democratic decision-making within the organization and, in subsequent years, the Representative Assembly would come to symbolize the democratic and representative nature of NEA. But others at the time, perhaps justifiably, saw the choice of Salt Lake City and the ensuing rule changes differently. To them this seemed little more than a strategy to limit the voice and influence of the dissidents specifically and (given that the state delegations were controlled by administrators) of rank-and-file teachers generally. An article in *The Journal of Education* at the time reported that "Salt Lake City had been selected because it would be impossible for the 'Holy Terror' [Margaret Haley] to issue an S.O.S. call to the grade [school] teachers of any large city as was done at Milwaukee, and city and state officials had assured the panic-stricken [NEA] officials that they could keep the teachers of Salt Lake City and all of Utah under control."[13]

While continuing to pressure NEA, some teachers who wanted to form a union to work for better pay and working conditions also turned their attention to the fledgling AFT, formed by teachers from the Chicago federation and similar groups in a handful of other cities. But AFT was unable to build a national movement. All unions in the United States were facing fierce repression, and AFT and its affiliates were no exception. In many communities, teachers had to sign pledges not to support a union, or they would not be hired.

Even in Ella Flagg Young's Chicago school district, the union was under siege. While she was away on vacation during August 1915, Chicago Board of Education president Jacob Loeb proposed a policy forbidding any Chicago teacher from joining a union. By the time Young returned, the so-called "Loeb Rule" had been adopted. She fought the subsequent dismissal of teachers who were union members, but disheartened by the negative direction of events, she retired the following summer at age 71.[14] Little effective opposition to this policy remained. Before the 1916-17 school year began, the Chicago school district fired 38 officers and activists in the CTF, which had become Local 1 of the AFT, formed just a few months earlier. Before their firing, all of the teachers had been given good evaluations by their supervisors. In order to get their jobs backs, CTF had to agree to withdraw from the Chicago Federation of Labor and AFT.[15]

In other cities, school administrators began to pressure teachers to join NEA as a way of involving them in an administrator-controlled, professional organization instead of a union. Although the AFL might have provided resources to help the teachers' union fight back, it had little interest in helping female teachers gain influence and power. Its primary concern was protecting the status of workers in male-dominated crafts such as the construction trades. In fact, the top leaders of NEA and the AFL developed such an unlikely but close working relationship that in 1929, AFL President William Green told AFT he could not attend its convention because he would be speaking at NEA's Representative Assembly, which was taking place simultaneously. Even then, the labor federation recognized that NEA was a major force in its field. AFT President Mary Barker wrote in fury to the AFL's secretary-treasurer that "the affinity between [the leaders of] the AFL and the NEA has finally dawned on me. Autocratic, complaisant, monopolistic—antisocial, fear ridden, illiberal inherently."[16]

Already small and isolated throughout the 1930s, AFT was further weakened by internal battles between its more conservative and left-leaning elements. The charters of several local chapters were taken away entirely because of alleged "communist infiltration."[17]

For much of their early history, the teachers' unions were not able to engage in collective bargaining on behalf of their members. This continued to be the case through the 1950s. But by the 1960s, the world was beginning to change. Three pivotal dynamics gave rise to the movement that brought about collective bargaining by teachers.

In the 1930s, as part of the New Deal that was President Franklin D. Roosevelt's response to the Great Depression, Congress enacted the National Labor Relations Act (NLRA), which gave private sector workers the right to bargain collectively with their employers and established the process for doing so. Under the NLRA, if a majority of the employees of a private company votes to unionize, the union has exclusive jurisdiction to represent those employees, and management cannot negotiate with any other employee organization. The law requires an employer whose workers have chosen a union to negotiate in good faith on a collective-bargaining agreement, or contract that covers "wages, hours, and other terms and conditions of employment." Once the collective-bargaining agreement is reached, management has a legal obligation to abide by it. If an employer violates the law, the union may file unfair labor practice charges with the National Labor Relations Board (NLRB), the federal agency responsible for administering the NLRA.[18]

At the time it was enacted, however, public-sector workers, including teachers, were specifically excluded from the rights the new law was intended to guarantee. Many Americans could not envision public employees, such as firefighters or police officers, engaging in a collective-bargaining process that might result in a strike, with workers refusing to provide the protection the public counted on. Many people could still remember a well-publicized police strike in Boston in 1919 that was crushed by Massachusetts Governor Calvin Coolidge, an event that eventually helped propel him to the U.S. presidency and sent a lasting message to all public-sector workers. President Roosevelt himself opposed providing the same rights to public employees that he championed for private employees. "Militant tactics have no place in the functions of any organization of government employees," he wrote. "Such action, looking toward the paralysis of government by those who have sworn to support it, is unthinkable and intolerable."[19]

Passage of the NLRA was followed by the rise of a new labor federation known as the Congress of Industrial Organizations (CIO). Unlike the AFL, which generally organized workers into separate unions for discrete skilled crafts, such as those practiced by electricians or plumbers, the CIO united all workers in an entire industry, leading to a massive increase in unionization among private sector workers, including formation of the United Auto Workers (UAW), the United Steelworkers, and the other major industrial unions of the 20th century.

This discrepancy between the rights of private- and public-sector workers gradually created a significant gap in their pay and benefits. By 1955, when the AFL, headed by George Meany, who had come out of the United Association of Plumbers and Pipefitters, and the CIO, headed by Walter Reuther of the UAW, merged to form the AFL-CIO, one out of three private-sector workers in America was covered by a collective-bargaining agreement, while virtually no public-sector workers were.[20] As an example of the income disparity between public- and private-sector workers, in 1960, the average wage for urban school teachers—well-educated professionals without bargaining rights—was 20.4 percent lower than the average wage for workers in the heavily unionized trucking and warehousing industry.[21]

The second major dynamic laying the groundwork for the collective-bargaining movement by teachers and other public employees in the 1960s was embodied in the economic and social consequences of World War II. The federal government had imposed wage and price controls during the conflict, and when those were lifted, prices that all workers had to pay rose much faster than wages. Discontent over this led to many legal strikes in the private sector, and a few illegal ones by public employees. Even though they had no legally established right to collective bargaining or to strike, teachers in at least twelve states walked off the job in the 1946-47 school year over pay and other issues.[22]

"For the first time in the history of this country school teachers in substantial numbers have gone out on strike or are threatening to strike," *The New York Times* reported on February 14, 1947. "Since the opening of school last September, there have been twelve major strikes involving more than 2,000 teachers and 50,000 pupils."[23] The story mentioned strikes in Norwalk, Connecticut; St. Paul, Minnesota; and Buffalo, New York, among a host of smaller communities. "The strike spirit has spread. Scores of key cities and hundreds of rural communities face a revolt of teachers," primarily over low salaries, the newspaper said. It noted further NEA's then-policy of opposition to strikes, and continued, "In a recent statement, the NEA urged group action rather than strikes. . . . The NEA proposes that a salary committee, chosen by the entire faculty, receive full authority to represent and act for the local education association."[24]

After the war, the composition of the teacher workforce began to change. Many returning servicemen went to college, thanks to the G.I. Bill's tuition subsidies, and many of those chose to go into teaching. Contrary to the way female teachers had traditionally been perceived, the new male teachers were more widely acknowledged as the principal breadwinners for their families, a responsibility they could not easily fulfill on wages that were substantially lower than those earned by unionized factory workers.[25]

World War II also increased the expectations of female teachers regarding pay, working conditions, and respect on the job. Millions of women worked outside the home during the war, bringing in their own paychecks as they kept the economy operating while the men were away in the military. For the first time many held factory jobs with union wages. They were encouraged to venture outside their traditional homemaker roles through advertising campaigns featuring "Rosie the Riveter," a woman who did her patriotic duty by producing weapons and industrial goods to sustain the war effort. After the war, many women wanted to continue to have their own work lives. By the end of the 1950s, the percentage of families in which the woman worked outside the home had more than doubled since before the war.[26]

In addition, the expectations of female teachers rose because of changes in the economy that gradually created better paying positions for women in white collar and service fields. In 1956, slightly over a decade after the war ended, America for the first time had more white-collar workers than industrial laborers.[27] Teaching generally paid less than other white-collar professions requiring similar education and skill levels, so women who were committed to staying in teaching became more likely to demand better pay.

The third factor setting the stage for collective bargaining in education was a dramatic national shift from small schools and school districts to larger schools and consolidated school systems with many more students and staff. In 1965, the United States had only one-fifth the number of school districts that it had in 1940.[28] This meant that school systems were more bureaucratic and top administrators more distant, making it even harder for teachers to have input or ensure fair treatment without an organization of their own. It also meant that many school districts now had greater resources that potentially could be tapped for better teacher pay and benefits.[29]

Teaching was becoming a harder job under more difficult conditions. Class sizes grew as the return of servicemen after years away led to the post-World War II baby boom. Continued migration of African American families from the South to industrial centers also added to school populations and to pressures on teachers in major Northern cities.[30]

Perhaps the demand for change was inevitable. In any case, pressure was indeed building, and AFT and NEA remained the two logical organizations to which teachers might turn. In 1960, AFT had about 60,000 members nationwide, most of them concentrated in large cities where there was already a strong labor union presence as well as the most unrest among teachers.[31] Believing that a strong presence was needed directly where its members lived and worked and where the day-to-day decisions were made by school boards and administrators, it based its structure at the local community level.

By contrast, NEA and its affiliates had more than 750,000

members and a vibrant presence in nearly every state. NEA had built its organizational structure on the concept of strong state—not local—affiliates. This stemmed from its recognition that the primary responsibility for education rested with state governments and that a strong presence was essential at that level to affect the course of American public education.[32] NEA and its affiliates had gained some remarkable successes through this approach and saw no reason to change it. Through their prestige, strong state presence, broad public relations campaigns, research reports, and insider lobbying and relationships, NEA and its affiliates won major advances in pensions, laws providing tenure to experienced teachers, civil service procedures that provided some protection from unfair treatment, and increases in school funding. The NEA leadership was justly proud of these accomplishments, and the notion that they—through their knowledge, experience, relationships, and power—were the ones who brought them about ran deep within the organization's hierarchy. Indeed, like the school districts where most leaders and top staff of NEA and its affiliates had been administrators, the Association had a culture of benevolent paternalism that was based on the idea that teachers did not need collective bargaining or the right to strike because those in charge would take care of them.[33]

NEA's culture was exemplified by its executive secretary, William Carr. "Dr. Carr," as he expected to be—and was—called, joined the NEA research department in 1929, having taught school for one year before obtaining his PhD from Stanford University. By 1952, he had risen to what was then the most powerful position in the organization, given that the executive secretary typically served for many years and directed the work of the NEA staff, while the president was a teacher or administrator who served for only one year, and did not take full-time leave from his or her employment or move to Washington, D.C.

In a nation that would have no federal department of education until 1980, NEA in many ways filled that void, providing vital research as well as policy proposals to Congress and the White House. Hence, Carr was a key leader of the education establishment. When presidents, Democrat or Republican, needed the most prestigious experts from the education field for a committee or conference, he was invited to attend. He was a major architect of the United Nations Educational, Scientific, and Cultural Organization (UNESCO), after World War II. At NEA's 100th anniversary celebration in 1957, President Dwight D. Eisenhower joined Carr and other NEA leaders at the ceremony and presided over the cutting of a birthday cake for the occasion. Comfortable in his insider role, Carr believed that it was in the best interests of teachers to let him and other officials drawn from the ranks of school administrators achieve gains for all educators. It was no secret that he was convinced that public opinion would turn against teachers if they formed unions, engaged in strikes or other militant action, or became affiliated with organized labor as part of the AFL-CIO.[34]

Carr had strong support for these tenets from the executive secretaries of the state education associations that were affiliated with NEA and held most of the power within the national organization. Domination of the Association by the state affiliates was accentuated by the fact that most local education associations in the school districts lacked the resources necessary to represent teachers effectively. In 1959, according to an NEA study, more than 93 percent of the organization's local associations had no paid staff. The few that did often employed just a secretary. Only a quarter sent a representative to all meetings of the board of education, and only one out of six sent more than two written letters to the school authorities during the entire year.[35]

Not surprisingly, a study conducted in 1958 in the state of Massachusetts found that 74 percent of school board members said they felt pressure from parents during the year, but only 44 percent from teachers and 5 percent from the labor unions in the area. (The study did not differentiate between NEA, AFT, or other nonteacher labor unions.) School boards reported being four to five times more likely to hear from business or commercial organizations, economically influential individuals, and old-line families in the community than from local labor unions.[36]

As the 1950s drew to a close, the growing gap in pay and benefits between private-sector workers and public employees generated pressure for collective bargaining among public-sector workers. This national groundswell surfaced in New York City, where a local affiliate of an AFL-CIO union called the American Federation of State, County, and Municipal Employees (AFSCME) conducted a series of militant demonstrations and illegal strikes under the leadership of a young firebrand organizer named Jerry Wurf, seeking to win the right to collective bargaining that so many private-sector workers in the city already enjoyed. As a result, New York City Mayor Robert F. Wagner Jr., the pro-labor son of the U.S. senator who authored the NLRA in the 1930s, issued an executive order[37] in 1958 granting most city workers the right to choose a union as their exclusive representative to engage in collective bargaining with the city.[38]

Mayor Wagner's order, however, did not provide for collective bargaining by employees of the city's school system. With no legally established process for winning pay increases, 800 night school teachers who were paid only twelve dollars per night conducted an illegal strike in January 1959. The strike resulted in a doubling of their pay, showed teachers in the city what collective action could achieve, and added pressure to establish collective bargaining for teachers.[39]

By the beginning of the 1960s, the potential for adding thousands of teachers to the ranks of organized labor attracted the attention of Walter Reuther, head of both the UAW and the Industrial Union Department of the AFL-CIO. Only about three percent of the rapidly growing white-collar work force in America, both in the public and private sectors, was unionized. Having been one of the pioneers of private-sector unionism, Reuther could see that collective bargaining for teachers and other public employees was labor's next frontier. "The importance of a growing, active teachers' union to all of organized labor cannot be too greatly stressed," Reuther said. In addition to the expanded membership and increased power teachers could bring to the union movement, they could serve as examples to other white-collar workers. As one of Reuther's key organizing lieutenants wrote, "How long will a file clerk go on thinking a union is below her dignity when the teacher next door belongs?"[40]

According to *The Brothers Reuther*, a memoir written by Reuther's brother Victor, Walter Reuther channeled more than $1 million to AFT over a period of several years to help that AFL-CIO affiliate gain exclusive representation rights for teacher groups.[41] A substantial part of that aid was targeted to New York City. As a result of AFL-CIO funding, Dave Selden, the national AFT organizer who was in charge of the campaign to win teacher collective bargaining in New York City, was able to hire an assistant named Albert Shanker.[42] The two of them would go on to play significant roles in the development of education-employee unionism for decades to come.

In November 1960, the AFT affiliate in New York City, the United Federation of Teachers (UFT), which had about 4,500 members among the 45,000 schoolteachers in the city, called a strike seeking the right to collective bargaining. Although only a minority of teachers risked firing to take part in the illegal walkout on November 7, Mayor Wagner immediately offered to establish a committee to look into the question of collective bargaining for teachers if UFT would call off the strike, which it did on November 8. Wagner was not neutral in his approach. Indicative of his pro-labor sentiments, the committee was stacked in UFT's favor, its three members being major labor leaders connected to the AFL-CIO, with which UFT and AFT were affiliated. David Dubinsky, the national president of the International Ladies' Garment Workers Union (ILGWU) and Jacob Potofsky, the national president of the Amalgamated Clothing Workers of America (ACWA), each led an important AFL-CIO union, while Harry Van Arsdale was the head of the powerful local labor council composed of the AFL-CIO's affiliates in the city.[43]

Not surprisingly, the committee's report recommended an election, which was scheduled for June 1961, to decide whether teachers wanted collective bargaining. UFT campaigned hard for a "yes" vote. NEA and its New York affiliates, which did not believe in collective bargaining, urged teachers to vote "no."[44]

If there was any doubt that teachers were ready for collective bargaining, the New York City vote answered the question. Out of about 45,000 teachers, there was an unusually large turnout of more than 75 percent, with nearly 27,000 voting in favor and fewer than 9,000 opposed.[45]

The next step was to hold a mail-ballot election in which teachers would choose their exclusive collective-bargaining representative. The city's Department of Labor set the election for December 15.[46]

Three options were on the ballot: UFT; the NEA-supported Teachers Bargaining Organization, which included the Elementary School Teachers Association, the Secondary School Teachers Association, and the New York City-National Education Association; or the Teachers Union, a former CIO affiliate until it had been dropped by that organization on charges of communist domination and had been banned by the New York City Board of Education in 1950 for the same reason.[47]

Although NEA's efforts to win the hearts of New York City teachers were low-pressure, the campaign was hard fought by the UFT. In his memoir, *Teacher Rebellion*, Dave Selden admitted that his union had paid the building manager of the NEA campaign headquarters to report on strategy meetings and conversations that took place there.[48]

As the ballots went in the mail, AFT and the AFL-CIO were able to draw on their political connections to arrange endorsements for UFT by Eleanor Roosevelt, President Roosevelt's widow and a leading independent activist in her own right; A. Philip Randolph, the founder of the Brotherhood of Sleeping Car Porters and the most prominent African American leader in the labor movement; and other well known New Yorkers. Their endorsements appeared in an advertisement in *The New York Times* that was also mailed by UFT to teachers' homes.[49]

Although NEA sent in organizers and mailed out materials, the Association did not give the campaign the same priority that AFT and the AFL-CIO did. Top NEA leaders were confident that New York City teachers would choose a professional association as their representative, rather than a union affiliated with the same labor federation that included blue-collar and industrial workers.

When the ballots were counted, however, 20,045 teachers had voted to make the AFT affiliate their exclusive collective-bargaining representative, while 9,770 voted for the NEA-supported Teachers Bargaining Organization, and 2,575 voted for the Teachers Union. Charles Cogen, the president of UFT, told *The New York Times* that he expected that AFT's New York City victory would "set a pattern for the teaching profession in schools throughout the nation."[50] In contrast, NEA's Carr still did not see unionism and collective bargaining as the wave of the future for teachers. At the 1962 NEA

Representative Assembly held a few months after the New York City vote, he reiterated his belief that NEA must continue to be a professional association in which teachers maintained their independence from organized labor and its "policies on a variety of controversial economic and social issues" advanced through "political alliances and commitments." At a time when AFT was attacking NEA because it included in its membership ranks the very school administrators with whom teachers would be negotiating if they achieved collective-bargaining rights, Carr emphasized the importance of maintaining the key role that administrators played in the Association. "Teachers and school administrators are colleagues, not opponents," he said. "They do not occupy a master-and-servant or boss-and-hired-hand relationship."

Carr went even further, telling the NEA delegates that school boards throughout the nation had a responsibility to help ensure that teachers would choose NEA rather than AFT. "The issue of unions versus independent professional associations is not one to which any [school board] can be indifferent," he said. "There are real and important differences in public policy between the two approaches. School boards cannot meet their responsibilities by calling down an impartial plague on both houses."[51]

Given the outcome in New York City, it was clear to some of NEA's state and local affiliates, particularly in major urban centers where AFT had its strongest base, that teachers in America were indeed ready for collective bargaining, and that if NEA did not help its affiliates respond, teachers would choose AFT. Leaders of some of those affiliates pressured Carr to devote significant resources immediately to building the capacity of state and local associations to compete with AFT for exclusive representation rights in city school districts across the country. Carr responded by establishing an "Urban Project" to provide support to urban affiliates. The Project could easily have turned into just another bureaucratic committee that after many months would issue a report and do little more. But state and local associations from the more industrialized states with significant private-sector unionization wanted prompt, meaningful action. Recognizing that many state associations, run by school administrators, were opposed to collective bargaining, the NEA Board of Directors mandated that the Urban Project should "work with and through state associations when possible, but should not be delayed if the state association is unable to cooperate."[52] This represented a sea change in NEA culture as it was the first time in the Association's history that the power and prerogatives of the state affiliates had been challenged.[53]

NEA's urban local affiliates expected that Carr would appoint someone who came from one of the major cities to lead the new initiative. Many of them were sorely disappointed when he chose instead as his special assistant and director of the Urban Project a soft-spoken former school administrator, a Mormon from Utah named Allan West, who had been the executive secretary of the Utah Education Association for sixteen years.[54] Despite his conservative background, however, West, who joined the NEA staff in 1961, soon demonstrated to the urban affiliates that he had the vision and determination to make the project a success. He saw that collective bargaining was the future in the education field and that NEA had to undergo a dramatic change or become irrelevant to hundreds of thousands of teachers. He also realized that NEA's state and local associations were ill-equipped to work with legislators to achieve state laws allowing collective bargaining, deploy the financial and human resources needed to win elections for exclusive representation rights, or negotiate first contracts with school boards.[55]

West also knew that NEA itself did not have the capacity or expertise to help state and local affiliates make the shift from being primarily professional associations to becoming unions that promoted and supported collective bargaining as well as the highest level of educational practice. NEA employed no lawyers with experience in drafting labor legislation or negotiating collective-bargaining agreements with management. Nor were many outside lawyers with public-sector labor law experience available because the field was too new. Virtually all private sector union-side labor lawyers had clients that were AFL-CIO affiliates, creating a potential conflict of interest since NEA would be competing with AFT, itself part of the AFL-CIO.[56]

The task of selecting a law firm to represent NEA fell to West. In 1980, he wrote a book in which he discussed his retention of Kaye Scholer:

I met with Frederick R. Livingston, a senior partner with
the New York firm of Kaye, Scholer, Fierman, Hays,
and Handler to explore the possibility of establishing a
relationship as counsel to the NEA for labor relations.
Livingston invited his partner, a Donald H. Wollett, to
join us. Wollett had been a member of the law faculty
at the University of Washington and at New York
University before joining the firm. We reviewed the NEA's
problems associated with the adaptation of the collective-
bargaining process to negotiations with school boards.
I stressed the Association's desire to do some innovative
thinking to make the process compatible with the nature
of the teaching profession and the public service. Both
men appeared to welcome the challenge of developing
modification of collective bargaining to the new frontier
and the public sector. I left them with the understanding
that they would discuss the possible association with the
NEA with the partners of the firm and then contact me
[in] Washington.[57]

NEA's proposal presented Kaye Scholer with something of a
dilemma. One did not have to be omniscient to recognize that public-
sector labor law was about to explode nationally and here, knocking
on Kaye Scholer's door as a potential client was a well-heeled sleeping
giant that was about to awake. By the same token, however, Kaye
Scholer was strictly a management-side labor firm that did not represent
unions.

Wollett, who was later to serve as Chanin's mentor, prepared a
paper for the law firm explaining why taking NEA as a client would
not present any conflict. After all, Wollett pointed out, NEA operated
in the public sector and, in any event, was not really a union: it was
simply a professional association that acted like a union. Other partners
in the firm readily agreed, and in 1963, NEA became a client of Kaye
Scholer, with Don Wollett as partner in charge.[58]

One of the first steps West and Livingston took was to approach
Walter Reuther to see if they could persuade the AFL-CIO to withdraw
the resources it was pouring into AFT organizing. As West later
recalled, "We also wanted to remind him of the successful cooperation
of the AFL-CIO and NEA on national legislation and the possible

effects of his actions on its continuing. If feasible, we were prepared to explore new areas of cooperation on matters of mutual concern in lieu of continuing the competition for membership begun in New York City." Reuther failed to show up for the first scheduled meeting, sending aides instead, but Livingston caught up with him on the beach during a break in an AFL-CIO convention held in Florida. The answer was not what NEA had hoped. "Reuther's plans were too far along to be changed," West later recalled. "The battle for America's teachers had begun."[59]

Chapter 2

In the Trenches

Frederick Livingston set up a small group of lawyers within Kaye Scholer to handle the new NEA work. Chanin, reflecting his self-doubts over representing management in episodes such as the washing-machine factory closing, asked to be assigned to it. The group was directed by Wollett, a partner in the firm's labor law department. Fifteen years older than Chanin, Wollett had been a law professor and had served as director of the Arthur Garfield Hays Civil Liberties Program at New York University Law School before joining the firm.

Wollett, Chanin, and the other lawyers learned in depth about the problems teachers were facing. The great majority of teachers entered and stayed in the profession because of their commitment to education and the young people in their communities. They were responsible not only for students' academic training but for their social development as well. In each classroom, teachers had to cope with a wide variety of student learning styles, emotional baggage many students brought from home, and, in some cases, students' disabilities. Yet, teachers often were not provided the support and resources they needed to be successful. Teaching was a depressed sector in which many were paid so little that they had to have a second job to make ends meet. In most school districts, teachers were not paid for planning time, so they had to do lesson preparation, grading, and other essential tasks on their own time. If they wanted additional training to improve their skills, they had to pay for it out of their own pockets.

When teachers brought proposals for improvements to their local school boards, those officials were free to ignore them—a situation that Chanin and others would come to describe as "collective begging" rather than collective bargaining. At the individual school level, teachers often were subject to arbitrary and abusive treatment from insensitive administrators and had virtually no say in determining the conditions under which they spent every day of their professional lives.

Wollett saw how hard teachers' jobs were when he sat in on a class after his son started in public school. He watched the teacher skillfully handling outbursts by a series of children, including his son, and wondered how she could do it day after day. He had served as a management lawyer in tense negotiations with a steelworkers' local union over the quality of the raw materials with which workers were expected to meet production quotas. The obstacles the steelworkers faced, serious though they were, were nothing, Wollett said, compared with the difficulties created by the uneven "raw materials" with which teachers had to work.[60]

Chanin started off doing the basics—helping to write legal memoranda and researching legal arguments—but Wollett soon moved him into the field. This was a very different world from sitting in a cubicle in a New York law office. Here Chanin saw the direct connection between the work he was doing and the lives of the men and women working in America's schools. For him, these weren't academic exercises; they were life-changing experiences.

He soon took the lead in working with NEA state affiliates to develop and enact collective-bargaining laws and negotiate first contracts. It was exciting work not only because of the personal contact involved but because the Kaye Scholer lawyers were breaking new ground, writing new laws and establishing what those laws meant, not just implementing statutes that had been on the books for years. By this period, in the mid-1960s, doing legal work for private-sector unions often meant making incremental refinements in established contracts that in many cases already provided middle class wages and benefits. Older labor lawyers told Chanin that the new public-sector legal work had the excitement they recalled from the 1930s, when private-sector collective bargaining was in its infancy.

Chanin and the rest of the Kaye Scholer team could not simply base public-sector laws and collective-bargaining agreements on private-sector precedents and case law. Thirty years of private-sector experience had to be evaluated to determine what would or would not apply to the public sector and be advantageous to teachers. This would be a significant change not only in law, but in political and economic terms as well, and Chanin and his team had to think creatively.[61] Federal employee unions set an important precedent in 1962 when they achieved the right to collective bargaining. The enabling executive order signed by President John F. Kennedy affected several thousand teachers employed in Department of Defense schools run for military families, as well as those run on American Indian reservations by the Department of the Interior. Although it did not directly affect the majority of teachers, the executive order nonetheless "signified a change of attitude toward negotiations in the public sector," Chanin and Wollett later observed.[62]

The first step for the Kaye Scholer lawyers was to identify states with the best prospects for getting teacher collective-bargaining laws passed and implemented. When it came to choosing the right targets, the stakes were high because a failure in one state could be a major setback with implications that reverberated throughout the nation. Moreover, opponents of collective bargaining within NEA were ready to pounce on any failure of the new Urban Project strategy. Consequently, targeted states had to possess several essential ingredients. The NEA state affiliate had to have a commitment and the necessary resources to lobby for a collective-bargaining law and to support its local affiliates in winning representation elections and in negotiating contracts. There also had to be a strong private-sector union movement in the state so that unions and collective bargaining would already be familiar concepts to many teachers and their families. Often, a state was targeted in part because it had a governor and legislature with which the NEA affiliate already had a strong relationship.

Until the late 1970s, NEA efforts to win collective bargaining involved only teachers and not education support employees such as aides, custodians, or bus drivers. Only then, in most parts of the country, did NEA organizing begin to extend beyond teachers to include these other employees, which the Association now refers to as education support professionals, or ESPs.

Over several years, Chanin helped to draft and lobby for the enactment of laws that gave teachers bargaining rights in states across the country, including Connecticut, Hawaii, Illinois, Maryland, Massachusetts, Minnesota, New Jersey, New York, Pennsylvania, Rhode Island, and Vermont. These laws became the models for other states in which Chanin played a less direct role in securing bargaining rights for teachers but where the lawyers he trained, NEA staff he mentored, and NEA affiliates he inspired took up the fight.[63]

Whenever he went into a state, Chanin had to determine whether it was possible to coordinate NEA activities with those of other public-employee unions that often were working for collective-bargaining laws as well. In company with state Association officials, he would meet with leaders of the firefighters, police, and other public-sector unions to determine whether the NEA affiliate could collaborate with the unions to bring about enactment of a state law providing collective bargaining for all public employees, or whether the NEA affiliate would have to go it alone and seek a collective-bargaining statute just for teachers.

It was through this coordination that Chanin got to know many of the leaders of America's labor movement. One with whom he would work particularly closely in future years was Jerry Wurf of the American Federation of State, County, and Municipal Employees (AFSCME). In 1964 Wurf rose from his position as head of the AFSCME affiliate in New York City to become its national president. Like Chanin and AFT's Al Shanker, Wurf came from Jewish-immigrant roots in New York City. He had overcome a childhood bout with polio and the lifelong limp that resulted to become one of labor's most dynamic leaders, as well as one of the most irascible.[64]

While most other unions were tightly focused on the more skilled professions in the public sector, AFSCME under Wurf tied labor organizing to the civil rights movement and became the voice of low-paid laborers, many of them black workers who were segregated into the most hazardous or physically demanding jobs. Probably the most famous example of AFSCME's combination of labor and civil rights activity was the sanitation workers' strike in Memphis, Tennessee, in 1968. Two black workers in their thirties were crushed in a garbage truck that the city had failed to maintain properly, even after complaints from the union. The incident provided the spark for about 1,300 workers to walk off the job on February 12, demanding that the city engage in collective bargaining with AFSCME. Key issues on which the workers—virtually all of whom were black—wanted to negotiate included safe equipment; an increase in their wages, which were then below $70 per week; and pay even for rain days—a right that was provided to supervisors, all of whom were white. As the strike dragged on into April, the Reverend Dr. Martin Luther King Jr. came to Memphis to support the strikers. While there, he was assassinated, and tragic as was his death, it strengthened the bond between the labor and civil rights movements.

A combination of the resulting national media attention, a march by tens of thousands of people led by Coretta Scott King, the civil rights leader's widow, and an effective black boycott of white businesses in downtown Memphis forced the city to agree to recognize the union. Workers won a small pay increase, a commitment to basing promotions on seniority and competence rather than race, and a procedure for challenging violations of workers' rights. So strong was the white power structure's opposition, however, that the agreement did not establish the legal requirements and procedures for collective bargaining that public employees were achieving by state law in many northern states.[65]

In some states where a collective-bargaining law could not be achieved, NEA affiliates tried to convince school boards to engage in collective bargaining voluntarily, asserting that such bargaining between a school district and a local education association was legal as long as the legislature had not said that it was not. Chanin successfully argued this issue before several state supreme courts.[66]

Actually passing a collective-bargaining law settled the question of whether bargaining was legal in a particular state and established procedures, rules, and, in most cases, a state agency the union could go to if school boards were not following the law. The next step was to hold elections to determine which union would be the teachers' exclusive bargaining representative.

NEA's geographic reach was a tremendous asset since in many areas it was the only organization to which teachers could turn. But in some areas, it faced stiff competition from the AFT. Consequently, a vote had to be conducted in those areas so teachers could choose between the local affiliates of NEA and AFT. The two organizations developed highly pointed critiques of each other. AFT said teachers should not be represented by NEA because it was dominated by administrators. It was a "tea and crumpets" society or a "company union," AFT leaders would often say. Teachers, AFT said, needed a real worker-controlled union experienced in collective bargaining. On the other hand, NEA said that it was the right choice because it was independent of organized labor and dedicated only to education issues. AFL-CIO unions, it claimed, were for blue-collar workers, not professionals.

The idea of separating what NEA had to offer from that of the rest of organized labor became a centerpiece of NEA's efforts. AFT proudly used the traditional union term "collective bargaining." NEA staff tried to fashion new terminology to describe its approach to representation.

At one point, NEA considered using the term "cooperative determination," but soon found it to be too cumbersome a phrase to be effective among the membership. Indeed, the phrase smacked of the very academic jargon the younger members were trying to escape. "Professional negotiations"—a phrase coined by NEA staffers Martha Ware and Jack Kleinman—fit the bill more neatly. It differentiated NEA's approach from that of other unions, highlighted the "professional" nature of the undertaking, helped alleviate the concern that courts might inappropriately apply private-sector union precedents to the public education sector, and responded to the sensitivity of some NEA affiliates and members who disliked being associated with trade unionism. It would not be the only euphemism in NEA's vocabulary. Strikes were not strikes in some NEA parlance; they were "job actions," "walk outs" or "professional leave days."[67] To some within NEA even the term "union" was an anathema, the preferred characterization being "association" or "employee organization."

The language used in the field often depended on the state. Chanin would deliver the same speech in different states, but while using traditional union terms in a heavily unionized state such as New Jersey, he would rely on euphemisms in a state such as Tennessee.[68]

The battles for representation accelerated at a staggering pace. From the beginning of 1963 through the summer of 1965, 36 bargaining elections were held involving more than 50,000 educators. Although NEA won 23 of these elections compared with AFT's 13, AFT prevailed in many of the larger school districts, and the number of supporters of each organization was roughly the same.[69] But the challenges continued. And for the next three decades, NEA and AFT would battle it out in state after state, local after local.

One difficult issue that had to be settled before a representation election could be held was the composition of the bargaining unit— the group of employees who would be covered and could vote. In most situations in the private sector, there was traditionally a clear dividing line between rank-and-file workers, who would be in the union bargaining unit, and supervisors, who would not be in it. Among public-sector groups such as teachers, firefighters, or police, however, managers and those they supervised were accustomed to being united in the same professional organizations. At first, units for collective bargaining in some school districts were constructed to include both teachers and administrators, but difficult contradictions arose on issues such as evaluation, supervision, and discipline where the interests of the two groups were not the same. Ultimately, it became the norm for teachers to have their own unit for purposes of collective bargaining, even if, as fellow NEA members, they continued to coordinate with administrators on common professional concerns. The tensions caused by mixing commonalities and bargaining issues remain even today, however, when the interests of the two groups diverge.[70]

Once collective-bargaining laws were passed and NEA affiliates won exclusive representation rights, Chanin and the other lawyers tackled the job of negotiating collective-bargaining agreements with school districts. Since these agreements dealt not only with wages, hours, and working conditions but also with issues involving the teaching and learning process (such as class size and textbooks) that differed greatly from issues in the private sector, many of the provisions had to be developed from scratch. The first agreements were particularly important because they established precedents that could then be used as templates for negotiations in other districts and states.[71]

A few superintendents and school boards worked cooperatively with the Association, but most saw collective bargaining as a threat to their authority. As Chanin and Wollett would later observe, "The unarticulated reason for resistance by many school boards to voluntary acceptance of a structure of collective negotiations is obvious.

Collective negotiations means bilateral decision-making in respect to policy matters traditionally within the sole control of school boards. It means that teachers will gain power at the expense of those who now have power."[72]

From a national perspective, no group was more concerned about this shift in power than the National School Boards Association, which was founded in 1940 to represent the interests of the thousands of local boards of education, the traditional and most basic unit of governance for American elementary and secondary schools.

Writing in the March 1963 issue of *The American School Board Journal*, a member of the Portland, Oregon, board of education lamented the growing movement among teachers to assert their interests through collective bargaining, strikes, and other tactics. "Efforts of education organizations to develop legal and extra legal means of pressuring school boards and communities for economic and other benefits would appear to be attempts to improve the status of these groups rather than to express great concern for the welfare of children," said the board member, Howard L. Cherry, an orthopedic surgeon.

He reminded NSBA members that the traditional method of arriving at salaries was to have teachers or their representatives make their case to the school board or the superintendent. "After hearing all presentations and appraising its resources, the board then has set a salary scale and/or provided other benefits for the staff," Cherry noted with approval. And he reminded readers of the NSBA's policy opposing school board negotiations with teachers, which the association had just strengthened early that year. "School boards . . . shall refrain from compromise agreements based on negotiation or collective bargaining," the policy said. "They shall also resist by all lawful means the enactment of laws which would compel them to surrender any part of their responsibility."[73]

But the surrender of responsibility was well underway. When it was time to meet with the teachers' representatives to negotiate an agreement, most school boards expected to sit in their normal places up on a dais while the teachers sat down below, as they would at a board meeting or hearing. Chanin had to educate many a school board that negotiations would be held across a table, with the two sides sitting as equals. This seemingly small change held enormous psychological significance for teachers, who, for the first time in their professional lives, felt that they had to be listened to and respected. Even so, it was often difficult at first for teachers to realize that they were legally protected when they were speaking to school boards and administrators, not as employees, but as legally recognized representatives of all teachers in the district.

Chanin and other negotiators had to establish precedents on another question: On which subjects did management have a legal obligation to negotiate in good faith? Which subjects were "mandatory" under a state's new collective bargaining law; which were "permissive" but not required; and which were "prohibited" and not legally subject to negotiation at all? Most of the state statutes adopted some form of the language in private-sector labor law that mandated negotiations about "wages, hours, and other terms and conditions of employment." But where was the dividing line between terms and conditions of employment and educational policy?

In Huntington, New York, for example, a dispute arose over contract clauses covering such issues as reimbursement to teachers for job-related personal property damage; partial tuition reimbursement for teaching-related graduate courses; and arbitration of disputes over disciplinary action against tenured teachers. The Huntington school board's refusal to recognize the validity of the clauses, which had been part of a fact-finder's recommendations under New York State's 1967 law on teacher collective bargaining, went to the state's highest court. This was one of several such cases that Chanin argued, and in March 1972, the New York Court of Appeals found that the challenged contract provisions dealt with mandatory subjects under the teacher bargaining law.

The president of the New York State Teachers Association at the time, Thomas Hobart, praised Chanin's work and said, "Boards of education and other public employers will no longer be able to hide behind the cloud of 'legality' when facing tough bargaining agents who want to negotiate dismissal procedures, the length of the work day, agency fee, lighting—virtually anything that has to do with the terms and conditions of employment."[74]

Although many school boards could accept a mandate to provide teachers with increased pay and benefits, which their districts generally could afford in the booming economy of the 1960s, they had a harder time agreeing to proposals that included teachers in decision-making that had previously been the sole prerogative of school district management. Long before the national "education reform" debates of the 1980s and 1990s about increasing teacher involvement in educational policy and the learning process, Chanin worked with many NEA affiliates to develop and achieve contract language that made teachers stronger partners in decision making on issues such as class size, textbooks, planning time, professional development, evaluation procedures, promotions, class schedules, and time off for professional meetings, as well as more traditional issues such as sick leave, health insurance, lunch time without other duties, transfer rights, vacations, pay for extra duties such as coaching, due process for discipline, and fair layoff procedures. The question of which of these categories were mandatory subjects for bargaining had to be worked out every step of the way, from the drafting of the state collective-bargaining laws to the development of case law and the negotiation of the first contracts.

Chanin also worked on developing mechanisms to resolve impasses in collective bargaining—another major area requiring new ground to be broken because the dynamics and legal framework differed from those of the private sector. In his view, any effective process for impasse resolution had to result in greater, less desirable consequences of continuing at impasse than of reaching a negotiated agreement. In private-sector collective bargaining, the strike threat created a strong incentive to reach agreement because both management and workers would lose money if a walkout occurred. In the public sector, however, strikes cost employees money but actually saved money for the employer, so the two sides did not share the same incentive to negotiate in good faith to reach an agreement without a strike. In any case, public employee strikes were illegal under most state laws, and there was little chance of changing those laws.

A state law that provided for binding "interest arbitration" by a neutral third party to resolve outstanding issues created a mutual incentive to bargain in good faith, because most school boards would prefer to negotiate an agreement than let an outsider determine the settlement. That option was not always available, however, in part because it was not always clear whether letting a neutral outsider rule on outstanding bargaining issues would be considered an illegal delegation of the state government's authority. Mediation was used successfully in some cases, but if the school district dug in its heels, that process did not create any incentive for management to reach a settlement. A more effective method an association could develop was fact finding by a mediator, local religious leader, or some other neutral third party. Once a fact finder issued a public report recommending solutions that were perceived as fair and impartial, that often helped create a political environment in which it was harder for elected officials to stonewall.[75]

NEA's strategy was to find states and school districts in which the political climate was conducive to negotiating favorable collective-bargaining agreements that could then serve as models for other states and districts. After one of the first state collective-bargaining laws passed in Connecticut in 1965, for example, Wollett and Chanin identified what they called "lighthouse districts" in that state. The two lawyers helped the local associations in those districts negotiate their first collective-bargaining agreements, and then made those agreements the models that NEA affiliates in other districts could follow. New Haven and Stratford were two of the first lighthouse districts. In New Haven, the first agreement doubled starting salaries and established for the first time that a teacher could not be fired if she became pregnant. Winning that provision was particularly satisfying for Chanin because his wife had been forced to give up her teaching job in that same district in 1958 when she became pregnant with the first of their three children.[76]

In Michigan, where the collective-bargaining law also passed in 1965, the first lighthouse district Chanin worked in was Midland, a town about twenty miles west of Lake Huron. In session after session of negotiations on the first collective-bargaining agreement, the Midland school district's representatives did little more than listen, repeatedly saying they would "take under advisement" the proposals Chanin put forward on behalf of the teachers.

Chanin learned an important lesson in Midland—that it was often impossible to separate the labor and bargaining issues from the broader political, social, and economic dynamics of the community. He already knew that whenever he went to a new school district, he first needed to ask teacher leaders and Association staff, "Who's the real power behind decisions in this school district?" It could be the superintendent, one particular member of the school board, another elected official, or someone in the business community.

When he asked that question in Midland, he was told, "You're negotiating with the wrong people. Midland is the headquarters of Dow Chemical. You can talk all you want at the bargaining table, but in the end Dow Chemical has to be comfortable with the settlement, because it affects taxes and the image of the town." Knowing that Dow Chemical was an antitrust client of Kaye Scholer senior partner Milton Handler, Chanin asked Handler to make a call to Dow to arrange for him to meet with company officials.

At a brief meeting arranged with one of the Dow executives, Chanin and the president of the local NEA affiliate explained that a strike was possible if a reasonable agreement with the school board could not be reached. The executive said that a highly visible strike would not be helpful to Dow's efforts to recruit engineers and other skilled professionals, whose first two questions usually were: "What is the salary?" and "How good are the schools my children would go to?"

With Dow engaged, word must have gotten back to the school board to negotiate more seriously. When Chanin went to the very next negotiating session, the board's attitude had suddenly become cooperative, and before long an agreement was reached.[77]

Another lighthouse district in Michigan was Saginaw, where the key decision maker was school board member Walter Averill, a leader of the state school board association and a vocal opponent of collective bargaining, which he equated with "letting unions take over management of the schools." One of the provisions Chanin sought in the agreement with Saginaw was a grievance procedure ending in binding arbitration by a neutral third party to resolve disputes over the interpretation of the collective-bargaining agreement. Without that "grievance arbitration" process, management alone could decide what each part of the agreement meant, or it could simply refuse to comply with it. That would force the local association to go to court every time a provision of the agreement was violated, a process that would be expensive and would result in long delays. School boards that were used to wielding complete unilateral power had a hard time accepting that they would have to abide by a neutral party's interpretation and enforcement of the agreement. But eventually Averill agreed to that provision, which led other school boards to do so as well.[78]

The factors that produced smooth negotiations sometimes varied by region of the country. In 1966, NEA asked Chanin to go to Paducah, Kentucky, to help resolve a strike. He had never heard of the town. A travel agent arranged for him to fly into the Alben Barkley Regional Airport, named after Paducah's most famous resident—the vice president under President Harry S. Truman and the last American president or vice president born in a log cabin.

When Chanin arrived, he rented a car and called the local NEA affiliate to find out where the meetings would be.

"The Alben Barkley Hotel," he was told.

"How will I find it?" he asked.

"It's the big building downtown."

Chanin, who worked on the fifteenth floor at 55th and Park Avenue in New York City, soon discovered that the "big building downtown" in Paducah meant that the hotel was two stories tall.

Chanin met first with the teachers from the local association, who warned him to be careful while in town. "We've been on strike now for a week," said one. "The public is not amused."

"The public is never amused," Chanin said. "That's nothing new."

"Well, this public that is not amused has shotguns and rifles," the teacher said.

Chanin looked around town. Sure enough, there were men standing on street corners carrying guns. They were not happy that their children were out of school, and they wanted the strike settled. A settlement was always Chanin's objective, but this case offered a little extra incentive.[79]

As Chanin's reputation as a negotiator spread, he found that he could use it to the advantage of the local associations. He would often get a call from officials of a local affiliate saying they had reached an impasse with the school district. He would tell them that he would be there for the next negotiating session and that they should let the local media know the day before he arrived that NEA's high-powered lawyer was coming to town. They were to build him up, touting the landmark settlements he had negotiated in other states. The idea was to enhance his effectiveness in the minds of school board members, getting them to feel more insecure and defensive, and giving him a psychological edge in the negotiations. These "mind games" often worked, and after he had met with members of the school board and gotten them to agree to contract provisions they had previously rejected, the local people would tell him, "It's amazing! We made the same proposal to them last week and weren't getting anywhere." Often, what mattered was not just what was said in the negotiations but who said it.[80]

Sometimes, the local power structure itself did Chanin the favor of building up his image to almost mythical proportions. In Manchester, New Hampshire, he worked with the Manchester Education Association (MEA) in 1968 to persuade the school board to agree to collective bargaining even though the state had not yet passed a bargaining law. The association made it clear that, unless the board agreed to collective bargaining, teachers from other parts of the state would be told that Manchester was not a desirable place to work and current Manchester teachers would be helped to find jobs in other communities. Chanin led a march down the city's main streets, and was firm at the bargaining table in a way that the school board was not used to.[81]

In response to the MEA's unprecedented campaign, the local newspaper, *The Union Leader*, which was one of the most notoriously anti-labor papers in the country, ran a cartoon depicting Chanin as "Super Duper Negotiator" in a Superman outfit, smashing the school board. Another cartoon depicted him King Kong-size, towering over the frightened school board members. The paper tried to portray him as an "invader" using NEA's power to intimidate not only the school board but also "Responsible Teachers" who supposedly were content with their pay and working conditions. But the effect of this characterization of Chanin as a super-hero was the exact opposite of what the paper intended. Most teachers who saw those cartoons became even bolder because it was so clear that the seemingly all-powerful establishment in Manchester was threatened by NEA's clout.[82]

Along with the cartoons, *The Union Leader* ran lengthy, hysterical editorials under headlines such as "The Battle of Manchester." "Manchester is a city under siege," began one. Chanin's battle plan, the newspaper warned gravely, "is to destroy it economically if it refuses to hand over its local government to the invaders from without, the National Education Association."

The answer, the paper said hopefully, was that "Manchester citizens, unlike their city cousins in New York, say, are too strong willed to succumb to bullying tactics. We predict a complete rout of 'General' Chanin and the emergence of new, responsible leadership from within the ranks of the Manchester Education Association."[83] The paper's prediction proved wrong. MEA held firm, and eventually Chanin negotiated an agreement with the school board to engage in collective bargaining, which led to the district's first contract with its teacher association.[84]

Experiences like that of the Manchester campaign convinced many school boards and superintendents that they were overmatched in dealing with Chanin and other NEA-affiliated lawyers and trying to handle collective-bargaining negotiations by themselves. Soon they began to hire their own lawyers, and the strategic maneuvering became more sophisticated.

Normally, collective bargaining was conducted in private to allow an honest exchange, as traditional practice had been in the private sector. But in some cases school boards or their lawyers believed that they could outsmart Chanin by asking that the negotiations be opened to the public. The public interest would be affected by the outcome, they said, but in reality they thought that by opening the negotiations to public view they could sway community opinion by showing that teachers were primarily interested in improving their own salaries and benefits and not the quality of education.

Chanin was happy to agree to sessions that were open to the public. Collective bargaining between teachers and the school board was usually big news, especially in small towns. Reporters would attend, often with television cameras. In one New England town, Chanin took advantage of the presence of the media to publicize the problems teachers and students actually faced. Here, as in other such situations, his forays into publicity were always convincing. "This teacher has a class of twenty-eight students," he might say. "She has a total of eight textbooks, and those are outdated. The students have to wear coats in class because there are holes in the roof and the snow comes in. We're asking for proper conditions so the teachers can teach and the students can learn." Most school boards soon reconsidered and decided that private negotiating sessions were better after all.[85]

While his initial role was to be the teachers' lawyer and negotiator, Chanin often had to be an organizer, strategist, and publicist as well. Part of his job was to help keep the teachers united, because they were frequently under pressure from the school board and some of the parents, especially if a strike was feared. Since he was always the chief spokesperson in negotiating sessions, he did not have time to take notes, so he would ask one member of the collective-bargaining team to take notes and would give another a special assignment to take down any offensive or degrading comments made by the superintendent or school board members, or their lawyer. If someone on the management side of the table said, for example, that teachers did not work full time because they went home at three o'clock and had summers off, or that female teachers were just the second wage-earners in their households and did not have to support their families, he asked that the specific words be taken down. Then, when he spoke at rallies or teachers' meetings in communities where negotiations were at an impasse, or a strike was looming, Chanin would pull out the notes and say, "Let me read you what they think of you."[86]

In many cases, such disrespectful remarks from administrators were what motivated teachers to take risks. Would they participate in an illegal strike for a pay increase or a half-hour of planning time? Maybe. But when they were reminded of the lack of respect and demeaning attitude they lived with every day, many were persuaded to say, "I'm not going to stand for that anymore." Chanin worked with many veteran female teachers, referred to by some as "little old ladies in tennis shoes," who had put up with disrespect from management for decades and were determined to see a change before they retired. And not only veterans, but all teachers wanted not just better salaries but also the security of knowing they would not face adverse treatment on the job because they made a complaint.

When Chanin would cross-examine the superintendent or a school board member in a fact-finding hearing, an arbitration, or a lawsuit, he would meet with the teachers afterward to explain the legal issues he had brought out to advance their case. Many times, that wasn't what the teachers were focused on. "Boy," they would say with pride, "you sure brought that son-of-a-gun down a peg!"[87]

Even the local news media in some towns noticed the changing dynamics between teachers and school boards. After a bargaining session between the school board and the local education association in Pittsfield, Massachusetts, a local newspaper, *The Berkshire Eagle*, published a profile of Chanin that began, "There was a time when Pittsfield's public school teachers would crawl before the School Committee like peasants before a tsar. But with the advent of collective bargaining rights this year, the whole psyche of the teacher-school board relationship has changed. The educators now sit as virtual equals, carrying a pride in their manner and a rigidity in their demands that were totally lacking a year ago."

This change was occurring, the paper said, "under the tutelage of Robert H. Chanin, a New York attorney who, since early September, has been serving as chief negotiator for the Pittsfield Teachers Association."

"Chanin," the paper reported, "has a slick manner that appeals to most, but annoys others. One school committeeman said, 'He's a lot smarter than I wish he were, but he's not as smart as he thinks he is.'"

"With Chanin in charge," the profile continued, "the Association has demanded things it never dared ask for before, including a salary package that would bring an estimated $1 million increase over last year's $6.2 million budget and the right for teachers to negotiate things like maximum class sizes and textbook allotments. The attorney has won the admiration of his charges by doing unprecedented things such as verbally dissecting a school committeeman during a bargaining session."[88]

When all other approaches to getting a collective-bargaining agreement failed, teachers who saw no progress sometimes decided that they had no alternative but to take some days off together—even though striking was illegal. If circumstances permitted, which was not always the case because of school calendars and budget cycles, such actions were strategically timed to have the greatest impact. So the end of summer or the conclusion of Christmas vacation, when parents were eager to have their children back in school, were good times for teachers to apply this pressure.[89]

From Chanin's perspective as a lawyer, a strike generally represented a failure of the process of collective bargaining, which is meant to work out problems to achieve an agreement both sides can accept. Whenever he had a chance to be in on the planning of a campaign from the beginning, he took pride in the fact that he was always able to work out a fair settlement without a strike. Sometimes, that meant that on the first day of school teachers were lined up by seven in the morning, holding up their signs, ready to begin picketing as soon as the school bell rang at nine. "But we'd reach a settlement by quarter to nine," Chanin recalled.[90]

At other times, however, he was called in to help a local association when a strike was inevitable or had already started. In such situations, strikes often had a positive effect, uniting teachers and making them more committed union members. There was nothing like walking a picket line in the middle of winter to build bonds of camaraderie. It was a difficult decision for a teacher to go on strike and even risk going to jail for violating an injunction to return to work. While brief stays in jail or convictions for illegal striking represented a permanent blemish on teachers' records, they usually emerged from the experience with a new sense of unity and dedication to the cause.

Within NEA the use of strikes was a major philosophical and strategic issue that had to be resolved in the mid-1960s. In the winter of 1966, the New Jersey Education Association (NJEA) supported a brief illegal strike by teachers in Newark. Chanin and Don Wollett were called in by NJEA to provide legal counsel to the strikers.

William Carr, who as executive secretary of NEA was still reluctant about collective bargaining itself, was furious that a major state affiliate and the attorneys NEA had retained would join forces to support such a militant action. He called a meeting in Washington that included Allan West, Wollett, and several leaders of NJEA, including the NJEA executive director, Dr. Fred Hipp. Although Hipp had a background as a school administrator, he had made a complete turnaround, becoming a strong advocate of unionism and collective bargaining. Despite the change in his attitude, he was a revered, influential, and powerful leader both within his own state and throughout the nation. Jack Bertolino, a former teacher and later NJEA director of field services, also attended the meeting. He had become a member of the Association in the 1950s, when he was recruited, not by a fellow teacher but, rather, by his school principal, who had told him that joining NEA was "the professional thing to do." Hired at age 27 by the state association, he was devoted to bringing collective bargaining to New Jersey.

As Bertolino later recalled, Carr said he was going to fire Kaye Scholer for supposedly inciting teachers to use tactics they would never engage in on their own. He also informed the New Jersey association leaders that they were going to be brought up on NEA ethics charges if they continued to promote strikes and other "unprofessional" behavior.

Fred Hipp listened to what Carr had to say and then gave him an ultimatum in return: if NEA did not support NJEA's efforts on behalf of its members, the New Jersey association would consider disaffiliating from the national organization. Moreover, if NEA decided not to supply Kaye Scholer's services to NJEA anymore, NJEA would retain the firm on its own.[91] Realizing that NEA would split apart if he took action against major state affiliates that were pro-collective bargaining, Carr did not pursue charges against NJEA, nor did he try to fire Kaye Scholer. But he did make his case to the 1966 NEA Representative Assembly a few months later, where, using Newark as a point of reference, he argued that "the use of strikes by the teaching profession for the economic advantage of the teacher will impair, and ultimately destroy, the confidence of the public in the teacher."[92]

The Representative Assembly rejected Carr's view and voted instead to commend the action taken by the Newark teachers. The following year Carr retired. He had reached the then-mandatory retirement age of 65 and the end of his contract. But it was more than that. As even he could clearly see, it was the end of an era.

William Carr was replaced as NEA executive secretary by the Association's research director, Sam Lambert. His appointment was a compromise between those who supported and those who opposed collective bargaining and unionism.[93] Lambert was deeply challenged by the position. A mild-mannered, well-liked, down-to-earth staff member, he was in many ways Carr's opposite. Where Carr would often lunch with dignitaries at Washington's elite Cosmos Club, Lambert would grab his lunch at a neighborhood drugstore around the corner from the NEA building. Where Carr was always sure of himself, Lambert was often indecisive. The chain-smoking Lambert was in a perpetual state of worry, always shying from conflict. And he was torn by the currents running through the Association. On one hand, he had great sympathy for—and identified with—the young men and women who were now gaining prominence within NEA and the teaching profession. He understood their experiences, their hopes, their needs, their fears. But he also had a deep regard for NEA's history and an unyielding belief in the "professional" approach which it had taken for more than a century. For the next five years, he would have to try to reconcile these conflicts and oversee the Association's transformation.[94]

In 1967, at a time when both NEA and AFT affiliates were becoming more militant, the Representative Assembly adopted a policy that the Association would support affiliates that went out on strike by providing money, staff support, and legal advice. While the policy called for "every effort" to be made to avoid a work stoppage, it recognized that strikes will occur "under conditions of severe stress," and it declared that in such situations, NEA would provide affiliates with "all the services at its command."[95]

The prohibition of teacher strikes was one of the many issues that had to be interpreted by the courts as collective bargaining became established. One key case in which Chanin and the local lawyers he worked with sought to plow new legal ground was *School District for the City of Holland v. Holland Education Association*, decided by the Michigan Supreme Court in 1968. Teachers in that Michigan community walked out because collective bargaining had broken down, and the school district obtained an injunction ordering them back to work based solely on the fact that the strike was against state law, as teacher strikes were in every state at the time.

The Association appealed based on two issues. The first was that public employees had a right to withhold their labor under the free-speech and free-association clauses of the First Amendment of the U.S. Constitution, as well as the Due Process Clause of the Fourteenth Amendment. The Association also threw in a claim under the Thirteenth Amendment, arguing that the statutory ban on strikes violated the post-Civil War amendment's prohibition against involuntary servitude. The Association lost on those questions in the Michigan case.[96] But Chanin was proud that his 13th Amendment argument was accepted by two members of the Michigan Supreme Court, although they were in the minority, and he later told a Michigan Education Association meeting that "they were the first and last justices to do so."[97]

The Association's second argument, however, was more successful. When teachers engaged in an illegal strike, the school district had the right to ask a court to issue an injunction, ordering the employees back to work. Many courts were issuing such injunctions immediately after strikes began, putting striking teachers and their associations in the position of facing stiff fines or even jail time for violating a court order. Chanin and other Association lawyers reminded the state supreme court that injunctions could only be issued after an evidentiary hearing—which could often take many days—to determine whether the party seeking the injunction had met the two traditional prerequisites for a court's exercise of its equity power.

The first prerequisite was whether the party seeking the injunction could show that "irreparable harm" would result if the strike were allowed to continue until the case was decided on the merits.

The school district argued that the teachers were causing irreparable harm to the children who were missing school. But Chanin and the other lawyers were ready with a counter argument. Was there irreparable harm when the schools closed for the football playoffs? Or for the opening of hunting season? Or for a farm products festival? How could it be that the school board did not consider that those closures caused irreparable harm to students, yet it wanted the courts to prevent supposed irreparable harm when teachers missed a few days of work to achieve a collective-bargaining agreement?

By a four-to-three vote, the Michigan Supreme Court agreed with the Association's argument. "The mere failure of a public school system to begin its school year on the appointed day cannot be classified as a catastrophic event," the court said. "There has been no public furor when schools are closed down for inclement weather, or on the day a presidential candidate comes to town, or when the basketball team wins the state championship."[98]

The second prerequisite to the issuance of an injunction, NEA said, was that the party seeking it must come into court with "clean hands," which in this context meant that the school district must have negotiated in good faith and not have engaged in conduct that, in effect, had precipitated the strike. The court agreed.

Holland was a landmark decision that dramatically changed the collective-bargaining dynamic in Michigan, putting school districts and associations on a more level playing field. Trial courts in Michigan from then on were required to hold an often-lengthy evidentiary hearing on the irreparable harm and clean hands issues before granting an injunction ordering teachers back to work. This meant that the strike could at the very least continue for some time, and school districts, in turn, had more incentive to reach an agreement.

Moreover, when a strike did take place, the *Holland* decision provided a sound analytical framework that lower courts could use in deciding whether or not to issue an injunction. And, following the *Holland* decision, several trial courts in Michigan did deny school district requests for injunctions, but they did not necessarily do so based on the analytical framework set forth in *Holland*. One example was the October 28, 1968, decision by a Michigan trial court in the *Chippewa Valley* case, in which the court offered the following explanation for denying the school district's request for an injunction:

> I cannot grant it. I cannot find anything in the law which says that I should. I know that I can and there is no point in your thinking that I can't. I don't have to be particularly

liberal. That would be running away from something. I can grant a restraining order for so many things that it isn't funny. I can ruin people by granting one. But it's a question of power and authority. I have a great deal more power than I do authority to use that power and while here I feel that I have the power, I don't find the authority to use it. I cannot grant the restraining order.[99]

Because the injunction was denied, Chanin was pleased with the result. But, as he recalls thinking at the time, "the precedent value of that line of reasoning is mind-boggling."

In the first years of public-employee collective bargaining, it was possible to achieve dramatic improvements in compensation through the collective-bargaining process. Salaries and benefits such as health care were so modest to start with that there was plenty of room for improvement, and many school districts had built up substantial rainy day funds upon which they could draw. School boards had never faced potential strikes before and were afraid of the political fallout if they were held responsible for causing students to be at home when parents needed to be at work. Many local newspapers supported the Association because teachers were negotiating for improvements that would benefit students as well as faculty. Thus, according to the National Center for Education Statistics, from 1960 to 1973, the real purchasing power of the average teacher's paycheck after inflation rose by 39.8 percent. In the thirty years that followed, however, it rose only another 3.8 percent.[100] Opposition from many school boards stiffened as the economic boom times of the 1960s gave way to a series of recessions in the 1970s and subsequent decades. Elected officials began to worry more about the political impact of raising taxes to pay for better salaries and benefits than about having students home because of a teacher strike. While many school districts had previously agreed as part of strike settlements to let teachers make up the missed days at the end of the school year, they began rejecting such settlements, realizing that it took away an economic incentive for teachers not to strike, or to end strikes that did occur. In fact, some states passed statutes outlawing the practice.[101]

The changing political environment was brought to light during the 1967-68 school year when, without consulting NEA, the Association's state affiliate in Florida attempted the first-ever statewide strike. Since school districts were heavily dependent on funding from the state, there were limits on what could be gained at the local level without persuading the state legislature to provide more money for kindergarten programs, special education, and other needs. When the Florida legislature appropriated increases that were inadequate, and Republican Governor Claude R. Kirk Jr. said he intended to veto even those appropriations, the state affiliate planned a statewide walkout.[102]

The strategy proved to be difficult to execute. It is hard enough to get teachers in one school district to engage in an illegal strike, but even more of a challenge to maintain unified action by teachers in dozens of school districts at once. The Association leaders in Florida also underestimated the response from the governor and members of the legislature, who were determined not to be seen as giving in to an illegal strike.

Don Cameron, who would go on to become executive director of NEA from 1983 to 2001, was the executive director of a local NEA affiliate in Michigan, and with dozens of other Association activists, he headed to Florida to aid the strike. "However noble its intention, the Florida Education Association (FEA) was in over its head," Cameron later observed. "It was no more equipped to handle such an undertaking than a troop of Boy Scouts."[103]

State and local leaders began to put the squeeze on to break the strike. The walkout took place during the Vietnam War, when many male teachers had received deferments from the military draft. But now draft boards notified striking teachers that, if they were not teaching, they were subject to losing their deferments. In addition, many lawyers who were representing individual local associations were being told by their corporate clients that they had to choose between defending an illegal teacher strike and their bread-and-butter business. Allan West asked Chanin to go to Florida to see if he could help FEA find a way to bring the strike to a resolution, but at that point there was little to be done except damage control.

After three weeks, the strike began to crumble. The Dade County Classroom Teachers Association, without consulting FEA, made a deal with the Miami-Dade County school district to return to the classroom without any dismissals of striking teachers. Several other local associations followed suit.

Ultimately, FEA called off the strike with a tacit understanding that the governor would let the original increases passed by the legislature go into effect without his signature. Teachers, meanwhile, suffered serious adverse consequences. Many school districts used the opportunity to clean house, getting rid of the more vocal teacher activists. Teachers who did not get their jobs back had to go into another line of work or move to another part of the country.

Sam Lambert would later lament that the national Association provided FEA with nearly $2 million—money that NEA could not really afford, Lambert said—and the effect was to help the Florida association "and three or four of its reckless leaders practically destroy FEA." As Lambert told the 1972 Representative Assembly, "Regardless of what any of us said about Florida at the time, [the strike] was a financial and organizational disaster."[104]

As a result of the Florida experience, the strategy of conducting statewide strikes to get more state funding never gained momentum, although in many states teachers have conducted marches at the capital to pressure the legislature, often with the unspoken approval of local school districts. For Chanin, the Florida affiliate's strike underscored an important lesson—before launching a strike or other tactic, there has to be an exit strategy in case the plan does not work.[105]

By the late 1960s, the transformation of NEA from a professional association to a force in teacher collective bargaining was being documented in the press. "School and college teachers across the country, fed up with lagging salaries and a lack of voice in policy-making, are looking more and more to strikes, sanctions, mass resignations and similar tactics to change matters," *The New York Times* declared on June 11, 1967. "Teacher organizations and school boards are increasingly facing each other across the bargaining table in an effort to resolve their differences."[106]

The *Times* and *The Wall Street Journal* noted the heightened competition between AFT and NEA. "Each organization is striving to outdo each other in the race for teacher allegiance," the *Times* said.

To be fair, both newspapers had written extensively throughout the 1960s about the growth of collective bargaining in education. "The National Education Association, . . . pressured by union competition and growing militancy among its own members, is turning toward the tools of trade unionism," the *Journal* declared as early as 1963.[107] Five years later, the same newspaper reported in a front-page story that "the AFT's success in using militant tactics to organize big-city school systems in the 1960s has forced a transformation of the NEA from a genteel giant, oriented toward research, into an aggressive group that sounds and acts like a union, though it still rejects the label."[108]

By that time, the National School Boards Association, which early in the 1960s had hoped to cling to its policies against negotiation and collective bargaining, also recognized that the transformation was complete. *The American School Board Journal* published a cover story in November 1968 titled, "The Tough New Teacher: How he got that way, and the run he's giving school boards for their money and their decision-making authority." "It's all happened in the last eight years: From docile public servant to fisted militant, the American teacher has emerged determined to have the principal say in public education," said the story, which focused on the teachers' "voice and big stick, the National Education Association."

"NEA has shed its image of an aging sisterhood of spinster teachers and has come alive to the will of its members, 80 percent of whom are teachers, a group that is getting younger and bigger all the time," the *School Board Journal* observed. "How was the change accomplished? Carefully and completely: through a series of aggressive policy maneuvers—sparked mainly by NEA's teacher members—that has seen NEA change gradually from an association unwilling to concede that the word 'strike' was part of the language to an action organization that backs its striking locals with money and muscle."[109]

Chapter 3

General Counsel

By late 1967, it was apparent to Allan West that to function effectively in the collective-bargaining era, NEA needed a full-time in-house counsel at the headquarters in Washington, not just the legal support it was getting from Kaye Scholer in New York City. There was a need for a full-time presence to help the Association develop its policies and provide on-the-spot legal advice. The soft-spoken West—who was now NEA's assistant executive secretary for field operations—also wanted a forceful ally at his side in NEA's high-level strategy meetings.[110]

West and Wollett agreed that Chanin was the logical choice. He had the requisite ability to lead an in-house legal operation. Further, because of his accomplishments in collective bargaining, he had achieved a kind of folk-hero status to organizers and teachers in the field. West asked him if he would consider making the move to the nation's capital.[111]

Chanin and his wife had a difficult decision to make. Except for a brief stay in New Haven when he was attending Yale Law School, New York was the only home they had known. Moving meant they would see their parents far less often, and that their three young children would be separated from their grandparents.

Chanin asked Wollett, "What do you think?"

"You'll be right in the middle of the action," Wollett said. "You'll be doing what you love to do. It's only four or five hours away. If you don't like it, you can always come back after a few years. And it certainly won't hurt your résumé."[112]

Chanin agreed to take the job, starting on March 1, 1968. At 33 years of age, he was certainly one of the youngest lawyers ever to become general counsel of a large national union.

The news of Chanin's arrival was received less than enthusiastically by some NEA officers and staff who had been there for years, before the move toward collective bargaining had begun. They were troubled that NEA was spending more and more of its budget supporting collective bargaining by its affiliates. Not only was the Association hiring on its national staff teachers, local association leaders, and state and local association staff who had worked on collective-bargaining campaigns in the field, but it was also placing a union-oriented lawyer right at the center of the operation. The badge of honor for staff members was no longer the title they had once had in a school system, or their advanced degree in education, but whether they had been involved in a strike, or perhaps had even gone to jail.

Sam Lambert, ever fearful of conflict or controversy, had some advice for Chanin, telling him, "If you are coming down here you've got to be under control. . . . We don't want you encouraging the state and local associations to go out and stir up trouble." The advice was disingenuous at best, as if Lambert truly thought Chanin was not going to do what he was supposed to do as general counsel. And, in any event, such advice came at least five years too late, Chanin believed. Despite Lambert's caution, however, the job of spreading collective bargaining continued with Allan West's active support.[113]

A linchpin of this effort was the establishment of a three-member organizing team that would become known as "The Flying Squad." By 1968, AFT had made some significant inroads in the eastern states and West and others realized that a concerted effort to engage urban affiliates in collective bargaining was needed to stop this trend from spreading throughout the nation. The team was headed by Ken Melley, whose union-organizing work had started when he was a high school biology teacher in 1957 in his home state of Connecticut. He had gone to a meeting of the local education association where the leadership proudly announced that the school board had decided to give teachers an across-the-board annual raise of fifty dollars. "Isn't that generous of the board!" the association leaders said. Melley, who was supporting a young family with a couple of kids, stood up and said, "Actually, it's not." The local leaders were so taken aback by the opposition they faced that they resigned and said to Melley and other rebels that if they thought they could do any better maybe they should try leading for a while. The insurgents did, rallying the teachers and community and winning a one hundred dollar raise instead. Soon thereafter, Melley had joined the Connecticut Education Association staff and had played a crucial role in advancing collective bargaining in that state.[114]

With Melley on the Flying Squad were Chuck Bolden from Iowa and Chip Tassone from Michigan. They set up shop in Des Plaines, Illinois, minutes from Chicago's O'Hare International Airport. The team operated as NEA's "special ops unit," providing expertise and resources needed to stem AFT's expansion and win bargaining elections for NEA state and local affiliates.

The Flying Squad's first assignment was in St. Louis, Missouri, but after a month on the ground, it was apparent that the situation was lost and the team would not be able to make a real difference. Its next stop was Denver, Colorado.

In 1969, the Denver Classroom Teachers Association wanted to engage in collective bargaining even though there was no state bargaining law in place. The Colorado state association director, Dr. Robert Johnson, was a former school administrator who did not believe in collective bargaining. Melley, who had gotten to know Chanin in 1965 during the campaign that first achieved collective bargaining in Connecticut, understood that there were important legal issues at stake in Denver and that a lawyer could play an important role there. He asked Chanin to become involved.

Melley later recalled that he and Chanin had to walk a tightrope between the local association in Denver and the Colorado state association. Johnson would call Lambert to complain about NEA's involvement, yet West told the national staff to continue to assist the Denver association, by far the largest local in that state. Ultimately, Chanin and others guided the Denver association through the process of organizing an election to establish an exclusive bargaining representative, winning the election against an AFT affiliate, and then negotiating a collective-bargaining agreement. Soon thereafter, Johnson resigned, one of many former school administrators who no longer felt in tune with the Association in an age of collective bargaining.

The Flying Squad would go on to help win representation elections in such diverse communities as Wilmington, Delaware; Portland, Oregon; Buffalo, New York; Phoenix, Arizona; and the state of Hawaii.[115] But it was clear a far more comprehensive approach to providing collective-bargaining support for NEA affiliates was needed.

The opportunity for this emerged from the 1968 Representative Assembly, when urban affiliates agreed to support an increase in NEA dues from $15 to $25 if a program of local service were initiated to help them see some direct added value for this increased cost. The task of developing the concept and the subsequent structure was assigned to NEA's field services division and, not surprisingly, to Chanin. Together they crafted a program of "specialized service to local associations, with special emphasis on the areas of negotiation, grievance administration, member consultations, coordination of state and national resources, public relations, and legislative and political activities."[116] The initiative was based on the idea that while teachers had expertise in their professions, teaching was a full-time job. There needed to be staff support and expertise to conduct the business of the Association. Trained NEA representatives would assist local affiliates with contract negotiations, leaving lawyers to handle legal issues for which only they were qualified. Staff would also handle other policies and programs of the local associations, such as business management, the development of political action groups, and providing the classroom teacher with the latest research on the improvement of instruction.

The proposal was given the name by which it remains known today—UniServ, short for Unified Service. It was presented to the NEA Executive Committee in November 1969 and was adopted by the 1970 Representative Assembly. It was an historic undertaking, the goal of which was to have one staff member in the field providing direct and continuing service for every 1,200 NEA members. The national, state, and local education associations would pool resources to finance, train, and assist these staff members. The result would be the creation of a vast, nationwide infrastructure to serve NEA members and advance the Association's goals.[117]

UniServ would fill another purpose as well. Throughout most of NEA's history, a teacher could select which level of the Association to join—local, state, or national, or any combination of the three. Since the early 1940s, there had been discussions of the need to "unify" the membership, but little had actually occurred to bring about unification. Before 1968, only nine state associations required members to belong to all three. The UniServ program could be a major vehicle in moving unification forward, solidifying the Association, and greatly enhancing its effectiveness in advocating for its members and their interests.

Gary Watts, NEA's director of Field Services, and his deputy, Ralph Flynn, knew that Ken Melley was the right person to direct and implement this effort. Melley, in turn, brought his former Connecticut Education Association colleague, Vincent Kiernan, on board, and together they set about making the UniServ Program a reality.

The first step was to gain state-by-state agreements to participate in the program. Chanin carefully crafted guidelines and a model document and Melley met with state affiliate leaders to negotiate their agreement and to iron out any problems. In most cases, the affiliate accepted Chanin's language without question.

In the fall of 1970, 220 UniServ representatives took to the field. A year later, the UniServ staff had grown to more than 500. By 1973, the number was more than 750. And the program continued to grow. By 2008, UniServ had more than 1,900 full-time staff members nationwide. They were the face of NEA.[118] NEA's field staff, the business magazine *Forbes* once suggested, constitutes "the largest field army of paid political organizers and lobbyists in the U.S., dwarfing the forces of the Republican and Democratic national committees combined."[119]

With the added incentive resulting from the UniServ Program, by the 1975-76 school year every state affiliate but one had adopted the unification requirement. The single stand-out was Missouri, which was then disaffiliated because of its failure to unify and was replaced by a newly chartered state affiliate. The result of unification was to significantly increase membership strength, resources, and capacity-building at all three levels and make NEA an even more powerful national organization on political and legislative issues.

Chanin had spent most of the previous five years traveling five or six days a week to work on the passage of collective-bargaining laws, on the negotiation of the first agreements, and on litigation in the states. It was clear that this much travel could not continue, given his new responsibilities for establishing and managing the Association's legal operation and being involved in broader policy making. It was time to turn much of the field work over to the developing cadre of public-sector labor lawyers and staff working for NEA and its state and local affiliates.[120]

To assist in this transition, and to provide support for state and local counsel and association staff, Chanin worked with Don Wollett to produce a major treatise, *The Law and Practice of Teacher Negotiations*, published in 1970. The book provided a practical guide to strategy and tactics. It included nearly a thousand pages of detailed advice on collective bargaining, drafting and implementing statutes, and model contract language. Drawing on eight years of work by at least a dozen lawyers, the book included sample letters to school boards for use in specific situations, as well as arguments and counter-arguments on the issues that typically came up between association negotiators and school districts.

The book became the standard reference for lawyers, Association staff, and teacher activists. Chanin would get calls from people who had the book open to a certain page and would say they had done what it said there but weren't sure of the next step. He would refer them to another section where it explained what their next move should be, often with a sample memorandum they could adapt to fit local needs. One longtime staff person said she kept the book next to her bed so if she thought of a question during the night she could quickly look up the answer.[121]

Chanin and Wollett made it clear to readers that building teacher unity and winning over public opinion were essential steps that made legal victories possible. Using as an example an Illinois court decision that overturned decades of precedent to allow collective bargaining, they commented, "Perhaps it is not impertinent to suggest that legal niceties, the skills of advocacy, and the use of source materials are simply irrelevant to the question of why the Illinois court decided as it did. Perhaps the decision was based upon judicial notice that the press for collective negotiations by public employees had reached the point in Illinois where its denial by resort to conceptualism and the 20-year history of legislative inaction was no longer socially tolerable."[122]

According to the publisher, the Wollett-Chanin book sold "satisfactorily, but not spectacularly"—which meant that the authors did not make much money from it.[123] As Chanin pointed out, however, making money was not the reason he and Wollett had written the book. "To be perfectly frank," he explained, "the purpose was to establish ourselves as the gurus of public-sector labor law generally, and teacher collective bargaining specifically." In this regard, the book was eminently successful.

Reynold Seitz, who was at the time a professor at Marquette University Law School and the president of the National Organization on Legal Problems in Education, reviewed the book in the Fall 1971 issue of the *Oregon Law Review*. He wrote:

> The authors have succeeded to an admirable degree in presenting a practical working tool, but the "how to do it" features do not detract from the evident scholarship involved. Some suggestions may not be accepted by advocates for one side or the other, *but the authors have shown no bias*.[124] (Emphasis added)

Chanin and Wollett were pleased with Professor Seitz' favorable review, but in light of that last line, Chanin remembers asking Wollett "what book Seitz had read."

A more accurate assessment, in Chanin's opinion, appeared in the Winter 1971 issue of the *Connecticut State Bar Journal* by a professor at the University of Connecticut Law School:

> Messrs. Wollett and Chanin have done a thoroughly credible and exhaustive job of presenting recent court decisions and rulings of administrative boards. But any suggestion that this is an unbiased presentation of the developing law in this important area should be rejected out of hand. This is not an objective legal treatise. It is rather the *mein kampf* of teacher unionism.[125]

The book not only confirmed Chanin and Wollett as recognized authorities on public-sector labor law, but it also gave NEA added credibility. The authors were closely identified with the Association, and the fact that they had written the book sent a message that NEA had been transformed and was firmly committed to collective bargaining.

At a 1990 tribute to Wollett, Chanin recalled a personal anecdote about the book's publication, saying that he had proposed that their names appear in alphabetical order: Chanin and Wollett. Wollett, on the other hand, proposed that his name appear first, because of his greater experience, because of his national reputation in labor law, and because as a partner of Kaye Scholer, his position had been superior to that of Chanin, who at the time they drafted the book was still working as an associate at the firm. Chanin added, "I found this last argument compelling, and we went with Wollett and Chanin."[126]

Unlike some other fields of law, teacher collective bargaining was constantly evolving during this period, with new statutes enacted and cases brought forward almost daily. By the time the book was printed and distributed in 1970, some sections were already out of date, so the authors had to produce a revised edition almost immediately. The updated book was published in 1974.

Meanwhile, Chanin recognized a need for greater cooperation among teacher association lawyers. He established an association of lawyers representing NEA and its affiliates to coordinate strategy, share information, and provide training on the rapidly exploding new field of teacher collective bargaining. The first meeting took place in Washington in the fall of 1968. Fewer than twenty people attended. Some state associations had no one to send, while others were still not committed to collective bargaining. Most, if not all, of the attendees were much older and more experienced lawyers than Chanin, but few had a background in labor law, much less public-sector labor law. Each of the organization's conferences at that point mainly consisted of Chanin and Wollett lecturing on teacher collective bargaining and public-sector labor law.

Over the years, the group mushroomed to the point that its meetings included hundreds of lawyers from nearly all 50 states, and even some lawyers from other unions. As new computer technology became available, the group developed a year-round information-sharing network through which a lawyer in one state could ask counterparts in the rest of the country for their advice on dealing with a particular topic or situation.

The organization Chanin established became a model for coordination by lawyers throughout the union movement. Originally, it was called the National Association of Teacher Attorneys, but then NEA and some of its affiliates began to include education support professionals, so a name that referred only to "teachers" was no longer acceptable. Chanin held a contest at one of the meetings to change the name, with a bottle of cheap wine as the prize. One of the favorites was Federation of Employment Experts, which could be shortened to its acronym, "FEE." Another suggestion was the National Association of Unified School Education Attorneys, or "NAUSEA." The winner, however, was the much tamer National Organization of Lawyers for Education Associations, or NOLEA, which remains the group's name today.[127]

Chanin also built up NEA's own in-house legal capacity. He hired David Rubin to be NEA deputy general counsel. An expert on constitutional law, Rubin had been acting general counsel of the U.S. Commission on Civil Rights and a Justice Department attorney in President Lyndon B. Johnson's administration. With President Richard M. Nixon taking office in 1969, many of the more liberal-minded government lawyers left federal employment, and it was a good time for organizations such as NEA to recruit them. Chanin also needed to line up some top outside firms to handle work for which the small in-house staff would not have time or resources. First among these was Kaye Scholer, with the continued involvement of Don Wollett and Fred Livingston. But the relationship between Chanin and the firm had now changed.

Livingston had always viewed Chanin the way senior partners in a typical law firm view the firm's associates. In meetings, deference was generally given to the views of the partners; associates' opinions carried far less weight. But after Chanin moved from the firm to be NEA counsel, with control over assigning the Association's work, Livingston treated his comments during meetings with a new-found respect. Chanin went home after one of those meetings and told Rhoda, "I don't know how, but now that I'm the client I have become brilliant all of a sudden!"[128]

It was becoming increasingly difficult, however, for Kaye Scholer to continue its past role from its base in New York. In the late 1960s, neither e-mail nor fax machines existed for rapid communication. The commute for face-to-face meetings was time consuming and expensive, and talking on the phone was not the same as being able to hash out a question of strategy over lunch.

Chanin turned to the Washington law firm founded in the 1950s by Arthur Goldberg, then the nation's most prominent labor lawyer. He also used the services of Shea & Gardner, another Washington law firm that included Steve Pollak, former assistant attorney general for civil rights under President Johnson.

Subsequently known as Bredhoff & Kaiser, Goldberg's firm was one that would figure in Chanin's life and work for the next quarter century. Goldberg had been general counsel both of the CIO under Walter Reuther and of the United Steelworkers before being appointed by President John F. Kennedy to be U.S. secretary of labor and, later, an associate justice of the U.S. Supreme Court. Chanin would become a partner at Bredhoff & Kaiser in 1980 and would remain with that firm until 2005, all the while continuing to serve as NEA's general counsel. Typically, he would spend Mondays, Tuesdays, and Wednesdays at NEA's headquarters on 16th Street, and Thursdays and Fridays at the law firm. On his days at Bredhoff & Kaiser, he would park his car in the NEA garage and take the ten or fifteen minute walk to the firm's offices.

By 1973, Chanin was not only general counsel with the duty of supervising NEA's legal staff, but he was NEA's deputy executive director as well. With the Association's rapidly burgeoning growth and his own responsibilities increasing, he found that his time was spent more and more on administrative functions. Joining Bredhoff & Kaiser and shedding his deputy executive director position seemed like the right solution. He could continue as NEA's general counsel, reduce the amount of time he had to put into purely administrative matters, and even explore additional legal work. "I wanted the environment of a law firm," Chanin said. While he had hoped to get involved in some of the legal work of Bredhoff & Kaiser's other labor clients, there was so much NEA work that such opportunities were rare during the long association. Not only did Chanin spend virtually all of his time on NEA matters, so did several of the firm's other lawyers.[129]

The advent of teacher collective bargaining led to an explosion in the number of legal cases involving defense of teacher activists. NEA had in place an employment defense program called the DuShane

Fund—named after former NEA president Donald DuShane—that was established after the Association won reinstatement for Kate Frank, a teacher in Muskogee, Oklahoma. Frank had been fired in 1942 for helping to organize a campaign to unseat several school board members.[130]

In the collective-bargaining era, however, a much larger legal program was needed. Hundreds of teachers per year were facing firings, discrimination, or other adverse actions because they were engaging in union activity. In addition, the Association began funding lawsuits involving teachers' due-process rights and the rights of women, people of color, and gays and lesbians in the teaching field under the U.S. Constitution, or state and federal law. Since teachers were employed by the government itself, NEA cases often dealt with their rights under the First and Fourteenth Amendments to the U.S. Constitution. The First Amendment guarantees freedom of speech and association. The Fourteenth Amendment guarantees "equal protection" of the law and "due process of law." As Chanin correctly predicted in a law journal article published in 1972, "The United States Constitution will play a considerably greater role in public sector negotiation than it has in private sector negotiation. As a result, much of the traditional legislative responsibility for fashioning labor relations policy will shift to the courts, and constitutional litigation will provide a major vehicle for ordering the relationships among public employers, public employee organizations, and individual public employees."[131]

To respond to the expanding need for employment defense for teachers, NEA established in 1976 what became known as the Kate Frank/DuShane Unified Legal Services Program (ULSP). The program was jointly administered and funded by NEA and its state affiliates. It provided money, based on a matching fund formula, for state affiliates to work with local associations for employment defense. By 2008, the ULSP budget had grown to $23 million per year. The ULSP created an incentive for state affiliates that did not have a legal defense program to create one.

The ULSP also ensured that cases NEA and its affiliates took to federal court would be selected and handled in the best way to protect and expand the rights of all education employees. Under the federal court system, complaints initially are filed in the U.S. district court that covers the particular geographical area. If an appeal from the district court decision becomes necessary, the case can be taken to one of the thirteen U.S. Courts of Appeals that cover different regions of the country. If a party to the case wants to appeal from there, it can ask the U.S. Supreme Court to review the case. The Supreme Court, however, only accepts about one-and-a-half percent of the cases it is asked to review. If the high court chooses not to review the case, then the appeals court's ruling stands and establishes a precedent in all the states covered by that appeals court. If the Supreme Court does review the case, its ruling establishes a precedent for the entire country.

Under the ULSP, NEA pays the entire cost of pursuing a federal court appeal, but only after reviewing the case to ensure that there are sound strategic reasons to take it forward. If a decision is made to appeal a federal district court decision to a federal appeals court, NEA provides not only the funding but the lawyers, and the same is true at the U.S. Supreme Court level. The reason for this system is that precedents established by the appeals courts or the Supreme Court affect other teachers or education employees, not just those within the limited jurisdiction of a particular federal district court.

NEA also pays for and uses its lawyers for some important and potentially precedent-setting cases in state courts.

While collective-bargaining laws had been enacted in thirty states by the mid-1970s, it was becoming clear that such laws were unlikely ever to be adopted in many of the southern and western states. NEA decided to make it a priority to work for the enactment of a federal law that would provide for public-sector collective bargaining in the entire nation. It was obvious that persuading Congress to pass such a law would require collaboration with other public-sector unions.

This was a turning point for NEA. The Association had long been a fiercely independent organization, clearly differentiating itself from the rest of organized labor. When, in 1968, proposals began to surface suggesting a possible merger between NEA and AFT, NEA President Elizabeth Koontz responded on behalf of the NEA Board of Directors by rejecting the idea outright and inviting AFT to end its relationship with the AFL-CIO and join NEA and its affiliates instead. Indeed, NEA would have clear and unequivocal policies prohibiting any affiliate from joining the AFL-CIO or any other labor organization well into the 1990s. These weren't just paper policies. NEA disaffiliated one of its largest locals—Miami-Dade—and subsequently its entire Florida state affiliate over this issue in 1974. And a 1970s poll of NEA members showed that 61 percent of NEA members would drop their NEA membership and quit the Association if NEA affiliated with the AFL-CIO. For decades, NEA battled the AFT and at times other labor unions over representation rights and labor issues. It had made a cause out of its independence.[132] Now there was a need to act cooperatively.

In 1973, Chanin helped develop the vehicle to accomplish this: the Coalition of American Public Employees, known as CAPE.[133] The two largest organizations forming CAPE were NEA and AFSCME. Other coalition members included the National Treasury Employees Union, the American Nurses Association, and the National Association of Social Workers.

AFSCME's president, Jerry Wurf, had given a stirring speech at NEA's Representative Assembly in 1972, calling for public-employee unity. On the surface, it might have seemed that AFT would have been a more logical coalition partner for AFSCME, since both were affiliated with the AFL-CIO, while NEA was not. But Wurf and the AFT's Al Shanker had been rivals for years, apparently going back to their competition for influence in their home base of New York City. Also, NEA and AFSCME shared similar views on many major social and political issues.

After decades of following a policy of independence from the rest of the labor movement, it was a breakthrough for NEA to work in a formal way with other unions through CAPE. The CAPE unions coordinated legislative priorities in some of the states, but the main focus became lobbying for a federal public-sector collective-bargaining law.

Laying the groundwork to try to achieve that goal became one of the major reasons that, in 1976, NEA for the first time in history endorsed a presidential candidate, the Democratic nominee, Jimmy Carter. Through his running mate, Senator Walter Mondale, one of the most pro-labor members of Congress, NEA persuaded Carter to support a federal collective-bargaining law for state and local public employees, even though Carter himself had no experience with public-sector collective bargaining as there was no such statute in Georgia, where he had served as governor.

At first, not all of the NEA state associations—particularly in northern, heavily unionized states—were united behind the concept of a federal law. Such a law would preempt existing public employee collective-bargaining statutes in their states. If federal standards and enforcement were worse than what the states had, federal preemption could be a step backward for them, even if it were an improvement in southern and western states that had no state law. Further, state affiliates might suffer a loss of political influence if control of collective bargaining shifted from state courts and labor boards to federal authorities. Nevertheless, most of the affiliates came on board, at least officially, when Chanin drafted a federal bill providing that state laws, where they existed, would still prevail as long as they met certain basic federal standards. But some of the state associations still feared that their state law would eventually be brought down to those minimum federal standards. They were not disappointed when a 1976 U.S. Supreme Court decision, *National League of Cities v. Usery*,[134] suggested that a federal bill would be unconstitutional, giving Carter and Mondale the cover to drop the concept altogether.[135]

The *National League of Cities* decision held that Congress exceeded its powers under the Constitution's Commerce Clause when it extended federal minimum-wage and maximum-hours provisions to previously uncovered public employees. The decision was overruled by the Supreme Court in 1985, in *Garcia v. San Antonio Metropolitan Transit Authority*.[136] But, as Chanin observed, 1985 was not 1976. With Ronald Reagan in the White House by that time, and Republicans in control of the U.S. Senate, a new effort to enact a federal collective-bargaining bill would face stiff political winds.[137]

Lobbying for the federal law, however, did produce one benefit: while the debate was going on, a few more states passed collective-bargaining laws, preferring to determine their own bargaining rules rather than come under possible federal guidelines. That, in turn, reduced some of the pressure to enact a federal law. As of 2010, education employees in sixteen states still did not have a statute giving them the legal right to engage in collective bargaining.

During the 1970s, NEA and its affiliates also grappled with another major issue related to collective bargaining. The surge in teacher collective bargaining that began in the early 1960s had, for the most part, left behind education support professionals (ESPs) who worked alongside teachers in the schools and in higher education—cafeteria workers, custodians, secretaries, paraeducators, clerical workers, bus drivers, and others.

For more than a hundred years, NEA had been an association of administrators, teachers, and other educators who largely believed that including support staff as fully participating members in the same organization would diminish their own image as professionals. Some teachers also felt there was a conflict of interest between themselves and ESPs. According to this view, the two groups competed for resources within the school district budget. If the ESPs got a raise or better benefits, that meant less money for teachers. Others had a different view, believing that raising pay and benefits for ESPs would prevent a school board from arguing that it could not also provide raises or benefits to teachers.

In a few places, ESPs were covered along with teachers when collective bargaining was achieved. But for years, many ESPs turned to competing organizations such as AFT, AFSCME, the International Brotherhood of Teamsters (IBT), or the Service Employees International Union (SEIU).

One of the reasons other unions sometimes had more success representing ESPs in the 1970s was that NEA did not allow those members to participate in the Association's governance. NEA justified the restriction by calling ESPs "associate members" and charging them only half the dues that teachers were charged. Other unions then asked ESPs why they would want to join an organization where they would be treated like second-class citizens.[138]

In the mid-1970s, Chanin helped write amendments to NEA's constitution and bylaws for consideration by the annual Representative Assembly that would have given equal status and equal voting rights to all members, including ESPs. For years, those amendments did not pass. Some teacher delegates said they were concerned that if ESPs became full members and could run for office, such support workers might gain leadership positions in local or state affiliates or even the national association.

A court decision in 1979, however, led to a resolution of this issue. The decision was based on the Labor-Management Reporting and Disclosure Act (LMRDA) of 1959, a federal law that requires unions to treat all members equally and to provide every member with full rights to participate in the union's governance. The law, also known as the Landrum-Griffin Act, was passed by a pro-labor, largely Democratic Congress in response to misconduct in some private-sector unions revealed in the 1950s, such as embezzlement of union funds, kickbacks to union leaders, and the denial of rights of union members.

The LMRDA did not cover public-sector unions unless they represented workers in the private sector as well. As NEA affiliates gained members who worked for private universities and other private-sector education employers, a question arose as to whether the LMRDA applied to NEA. When the Association was first contacted by the U.S. Department of Labor in 1963, it took the position that it represented only a small number of private-sector employees and was not covered by the act. The Labor Department did not seriously contest the issue, but scrutiny by the department intensified in 1976 and 1977 as NEA's first presidential endorsement dramatically raised its political profile. Under threat of a lawsuit by the Labor Department, in 1977 NEA filed a pre-emptive suit contesting the department's position that the Association was covered under the act. In 1979, a federal district court ruled that, in fact, NEA was covered by the LMRDA. Rejecting arguments that the Association came under a *de minimis* exception— that it was not covered because it had only a small number of private-sector employees—the judge said that NEA "cannot be a little bit pregnant."

There was no appeal of the district court decision—not only because it was likely to be affirmed, but also because it provided a means to an end that Chanin and certain other NEA leaders had been seeking. The Board of Directors voted to take steps to comply with the ruling, and Chanin rewrote the Association's bylaws to give all members, including education support professionals, full rights as the LMRDA required. Then, he explained to the 1980 Representative Assembly that NEA had three choices. It could continue to represent private-sector employees and be subject to the federal law, which would mean giving ESPs full governance rights. Or, the Association and its affiliates could stop representing any private-sector workers, making it exempt from the act, and deny full governance rights to ESPs. Or third, NEA and its affiliates could continue to represent private-sector employees and be subject to the act, but exclude ESPs from membership in the Association.[139]

Chanin was confident about which choice the RA would make: he did not believe the delegates would vote to stop representing private-sector workers (who comprised a significant percentage of NEA's higher education constituency) or to exclude from membership the already large and potentially much larger number of ESPs. The question facing the delegates sparked fervent debate, however, with pragmatic and even elitist views expressed. A teacher from California argued that "conflicts of interest are built into an all-inclusive membership. Unlike industries, which can raise prices when necessary, school district budgets are finite. A bargaining team attempting to represent both educators and non-educators fairly will face constant conflict between instructional needs and non-instructional costs."[140] A teacher from Oregon said that "we can ill afford allocating our resources and our dues dollars to fight the myriad of battles that need to be fought even for us, let alone for [ESPs]." A delegate from San Francisco added that "the united teaching profession must continue to be controlled by professionals." Non-certified staff, she said, "will outnumber certified personnel. With all-inclusive membership, non-teachers could easily control Association policies and programs."

Taking the opposite view, a Maine delegate reported that ESPs had been members in his state for the past six years. Working together as equals, he said, teachers and ESPs "have been able to accomplish gains in salaries, working conditions, and public support for schools—gains that would not have been as great if we had been competing as separate units." A delegate from New Jersey reported that teachers and ESPs in his state also were united for everyone's benefit: "School support members work with teachers for children. NEA's whole history has been a fight for justice. Now it is time to extend that support to all who support and work for better education."

Those who wanted to keep ESPs in the Association and comply with the court decision by providing them full membership rights carried the day. Today, NEA has an active program to help education support professionals achieve collective bargaining as well as improved rights and compensation. More than half a million ESPs belong to the Association, but many more of the nearly 2.8 million ESPs in the nation, making up more than 40 percent of the elementary and secondary school work force, lack representation. Nearly nine of ten ESPs are female. Eight of ten work full-time. They make an important contribution to the educational environment for America's students, yet, as of 2007, their average annual salary in the public schools was less than $26,000—barely above the official poverty line for a family of four.[141]

In the 1970s, there was a rough division of labor in the NEA Office of General Counsel. Although Chanin was responsible for supervising and coordinating all of NEA's legal work, his personal focus during those years was on collective bargaining and other aspects of public-sector labor relations. These were largely matters of state law and most of the cases he handled were in state court. While he was also actively involved in cases arising under the U.S. Constitution and other federal laws, such cases came within the primary area of expertise of NEA deputy general counsel David Rubin, who had much of the day-to-day responsibility for them. This changed in 1979, when Rubin was diagnosed with a brain tumor. He underwent surgery, but although the tumor was benign, it had impaired his ability to continue in his position, and he retired in 1980. Other attorneys in the Office of General Counsel picked up Rubin's work, but after his departure Chanin assumed more direct control over NEA's federal court litigation. And two years later, in 1982, he made the first of his five appearances before the U.S. Supreme Court, arguing a case called *Perry Education Association (PEA) v. Perry Local Educators Association (PLEA)*.[142]

Under the law establishing public-sector collective bargaining in the state of Indiana, the teachers in the Perry school district had voted to make the NEA-affiliated local association their exclusive representative. That meant the school board could only recognize and negotiate with PEA and not the competing association, PLEA, which had lost the representation election. PEA then negotiated a collective-bargaining agreement with the school district covering a certain period of years. PEA, in turn, was legally obligated to provide fair representation to all teachers, whether they chose to become Association members or not. If a majority of teachers decided that they preferred exclusive representation by another organization instead, they could vote to make that change around the time that the contract expired—with equal access in that election guaranteed to all competing unions. In the meantime, however, PEA had exclusive access to such means of communication with teachers as posting material on bulletin boards in the faculty meeting areas and putting fliers in each teacher's mailbox at school. The losing organization challenged that exclusive access, saying its rights under the First Amendment's free-speech clause and the Fourteenth Amendment's guarantee of equal protection of the laws were infringed. Chanin handled the case for PEA on the national Association's behalf.[143]

A federal district court ruled for PEA. The losing association, PLEA, took its case to the U.S. Court of Appeals for the Seventh Circuit, which ruled that the school district was unconstitutionally showing preference for one group over another, as well as interfering with PLEA's free-speech rights. The U.S. Supreme Court agreed to review the case.

On October 13, 1982, Chanin stepped to the lectern to deliver his first Supreme Court argument. "Mr. Chief Justice, and may it please the Court," he said, intoning the traditional opening statement. "This case arises in a public school district in Indiana. Indiana has enacted a statute governing the labor relations of its public school teachers."

He went on for more than nine minutes, detailing the facts and procedural background of the case, before being interrupted by a question from the justices. (Speaking for so long uninterrupted would be highly unusual before today's Supreme Court, in which oral arguments are marked by very active questioning from the justices.)

Once they did start asking questions, the justices quickly became engaged in the issues, and even playful. At one point, Chanin was explaining his view that the school district could limit the use of school mail facilities to "school business," which in his view would also include information from the union recognized as the bargaining representative. Justice John Paul Stevens asked him for "some examples of communications from your client to the teachers that would be school business as you describe it?"

> **Mr. Chanin:** I can tell you what this union and other unions typically include in their communications. They send information about the implementation of the collective-bargaining agreement, about the settlement and disposition of grievances, about working conditions that they are dealing with the school board about.
>
> **Justice Thurgood Marshall:** And what a stinker the other union is.
>
> **Mr. Chanin:** Pardon me, sir?
>
> **Justice Thurgood Marshall:** And what a stinker the competing union is.
>
> **Mr. Chanin:** I think that may come in occasionally.[144]

The Supreme Court argument was also noteworthy in that conservative justices such as Warren Burger and William Rehnquist, who normally were not friendly to unions, made it clear by their questions that they were likely to uphold the school board's recognition of PEA's exclusive representation rights. Their apparent intention to vote in PEA's favor reflected their general inclination to uphold the actions of a school board or other governmental entity unless there was a constitutionally compelling reason not to do so. The skeptical questions Chanin faced came from usually reliable allies of labor, such as Justices William Brennan and Thurgood Marshall, who were most concerned about the losing association's free speech rights under the First Amendment.

On February 23, 1983, a five-member majority made up of Chief Justice Burger and Justices Rehnquist, Byron White, Harry Blackmun, and Sandra Day O'Connor ruled in PEA's favor. The preferred access to the district's internal mail system for the association with bargaining rights was reasonable, the court concluded, because it was consistent with the district's interest in preserving the system for its dedicated purpose, in this case internal school communications. The PLEA had alternative channels for communicating with teachers, and under state law had complete access during representation elections, the court noted.[145]

Justice Brennan wrote a dissent, joined by Justices Marshall, Lewis Powell, and John Paul Stevens, stressing his view that the exclusive access granted by the district represented viewpoint discrimination.[146]

Chanin would go on to argue four other Supreme Court cases in the following two decades. His next case was in 1985, when he represented an education employee who had sued her school district, alleging that the district had discriminated based on sex by failing to promote her to an administrative position. The sole question before the High Court in *Springfield Township School District v. Knoll* was a technical one: whether the worker's civil rights suit was filed within the proper time period. After hearing oral arguments, the court on April 17, 1985, issued a short, unsigned opinion sending the case back to a lower court for further consideration in light of another case the justices decided the same day.[147] In that case, *Wilson v. Garcia*,[148] the court ruled that certain federal civil rights lawsuits were akin to personal injury actions and that a longer statute of limitations period should apply for filing suit. The Wilson decision was essentially a victory for the education employee in the Springfield Township case, and for Chanin, as well.[149]

Chanin's third Supreme Court case was also somewhat technical, but it has had a more significant effect on civil rights litigation. The underlying case again dealt with a teacher association's access to school facilities to communicate with its members. The Garland Independent School District in Texas had a regulation that prohibited employee organizations' access to school facilities during school hours and proscribed the use of school mail and internal communications systems by employee organizations. In addition, teachers were barred from discussing Association matters among themselves on school premises, even during lunch or other non-class time. These restrictions were challenged by the Garland Education Association (GEA) and the Texas State Teachers Association (TSTA) as violations of the associations' as well as teachers' First and Fourteenth Amendment rights. The associations lost in federal district court and on some issues in the U.S. Court of Appeals for the Fifth Circuit. But the appeals court ruled for the associations on other issues, finding that the prohibition on teacher speech promoting union activity during school hours was unconstitutional. It also found that there was a distinct possibility that the school district would discipline teachers who engaged in any discussion of employee organizations during the school day, and that such a policy had a chilling effect on teachers' First Amendment free-speech rights. Finally, the Court of Appeals held that the prohibition on the use by individual teachers of internal mail and billboard facilities to discuss employee organizations was unconstitutional.[150]

The associations then sought to recover attorney's fees from the school district under a federal statute, the Civil Rights Attorney's Fees Awards Act, which authorizes such payments to "prevailing parties." Both the district court and the Fifth Circuit denied the associations' motion, concluding that they did not succeed on the central issue in the suit, (the Association's access to the mail facilities). The GEA and TSTA, Chanin told the Supreme Court during the March 1, 1989, oral argument, "succeeded in having the regulation struck down as it applied to teacher-to-teacher communications and as it applied to the [school district's] communications facilities by the teachers themselves." While the associations were unsuccessful in striking down the prohibition against communications by outside representatives, they still considered the partial victory to be significant, Chanin stated. And so did the school district, judging by its "vigorous efforts" to overturn those parts of the ruling on which it lost. "They left no stone unturned in seeking to reverse this ruling," he said.[151]

On March 29, 1989, Justice Sandra Day O'Connor delivered the opinion for a unanimous court in *Texas State Teachers Association v. Garland Independent School District*, reversing the lower courts and ruling for Chanin and the associations. "Petitioners here obtained a judgment vindicating the First Amendment rights of public employees in the workplace," O'Connor wrote. "Their success has materially altered the school district's policy limiting the rights of teachers to communicate with each other concerning employee organizations and union activities. . . . They prevailed on a significant issue in the litigation, and have obtained some of the relief they sought, and are thus 'prevailing parties' within the meaning" of the Federal Attorney's Fee Awards Law.[152]

The High Court's decision in the *Garland* case remains an important precedent in the area of attorney's fees for prevailing parties in civil rights litigation. Chanin argued two other Supreme Court cases: *Lehnert v. Ferris Faculty Association*, a 1991 case about union "agency fees" that is discussed in Chapter 8; and *Zelman v. Simmons-Harris*, a 2002 case about the constitutionality of religious school vouchers, which is discussed in Chapter 9.

While he took on an increasingly wide range of responsibilities involving NEA strategies and policies, Chanin also continued to be directly involved in collective-bargaining cases with particularly high stakes or precedent-setting issues. Perhaps none had a greater financial impact for education employees than *Board of Education for the City School District of the City of Buffalo v. Buffalo Teachers Federation (BTF)*, a lengthy dispute between the NEA affiliate in Buffalo, New York, and the city's school board.

In September 1990, negotiating teams for BTF, the bargaining representative for some 3,800 teachers, and the school district signed off on a new collective-bargaining agreement that included pay increases for teachers. Under the duty to bargain in good faith encompassed by New York State law, the negotiators for each side had an obligation to urge ratification of the agreement by their respective parties. The union negotiators did so, and the BTF membership voted to ratify the agreement. But when the school board met to consider ratification, the school district's chief negotiator criticized the agreement he had just negotiated. As a result, the school board voted it down. BTF filed a charge with the state's Public Employment Relations Board (PERB), accusing the school district of bargaining in bad faith. A year later, in September 1991, the state board upheld BTF's charge.[153]

With the contract still not implemented two years later, the Buffalo school board passed two resolutions in September 1993. The first purported to comply with the PERB order by approving the 1990 agreement, but the second refused to actually fund the pay increases that agreement contained. The school board put forward a new legal theory to justify its action. Under New York State law, public employee collective-bargaining agreements that require appropriation of additional funds are valid only when the appropriate legislative body has provided those funds. For the first time in the history of collective bargaining in the Buffalo schools, the school board, which was both the employer and the relevant legislative body, claimed that after it approved an agreement, it had the legal right to take a second vote on whether to allocate the money necessary to fund the salary increases to which it had just agreed.

Chanin flew to Buffalo to argue the case. He was prepared for all the legal arguments, but what he had not taken into account was the Buffalo winters. "If you are coming up to Rochester or Buffalo to argue in the courts in the wintertime, you have to be prepared," BTF President Phil Rumore would later say in recounting the incident.[154] "Well, there we were leaving the hotel because we were going to walk over to the court. It was snowy. It was mushy. Did he bring his boots? No. He had his designer shoes on. And there he was sloshing through the snow to the court. He walked up to argue the case—*squoosh, squoosh, squoosh, squoosh*—and there he stood in a puddle of water arguing our case. They didn't take pity on him."

Indeed, two lower courts in New York State upheld the school board's claim, and the case then went to the New York Court of Appeals, the state's highest court.

On October 10, 1996, an appropriately shod Chanin argued the case for the Buffalo federation. This time he made sure there weren't any distractions. "You should have seen it," Rumore recalled, "he took complete control over the situation."[155] On December 19, the New York Court of Appeals overturned the lower court rulings. To allow the school board to take a second vote on whether to fund the agreement it had already approved would give the board "a bait-and-switch escape hatch from negotiated, agreed-upon contract terms," the court found.[156]

The court ordered the school board to comply with the 1990 agreement and its salary increases, retroactive to 1990. That meant the board owed well over $150 million in back pay—believed to be the largest court-ordered payment for public employees in American history. Teachers celebrated in the schools when the news was announced, but it would take four more years of negotiation to fully resolve the issue. Payment of the full amount that was owed would have forced the school district into bankruptcy and put its employees' jobs in jeopardy. Ultimately, the state legislature enacted a major appropriation that, together with school district funds, made possible a settlement of $73 million. More than 3,800 teachers received payments of up to $22,000 each. The money made a real difference in teachers' lives, whether they used it to pay off mortgages, make college tuition payments for their children, or other purposes. The victory also reaffirmed the principle that school boards must negotiate in good faith and live up to their legal obligations to their employees.[157] "It was," Rumore concluded, "one of the biggest victories in labor law history and it was thanks to Bob Chanin."[158]

The collective-bargaining movement helped bring about a profound democratization of NEA itself. The organization had been structured as a professional association dominated by school administrators, and organized around numerous departments and curricular subjects. The new NEA was focused on the organization of teachers, collective bargaining, and civil rights issues.

In 1971, more than a thousand delegates from local and state associations met in Fort Collins, Colorado, for a special constitutional convention (called Con-Con) to discuss a new national constitution that would govern NEA and its affiliates, and describe the relationship between them. The event reflected the empowerment of the Association's rank-and-file members, with only a handful of NEA staff present. Delegates' nerves frayed as they worked long hours for two weeks while staying together in dormitory rooms at Colorado State University, isolated from the rest of the world like a jury debating a difficult court case. But the delegates also experienced the exhilaration of trying to develop a new set of governing documents to fit a new era.

Convention delegates—mostly classroom teachers—worked in committees responsible for preparing new constitutional language on a particular subject. The committee documents were then strung together in one package—without time for a full opportunity to determine how the pieces fit together. Con-Con's proposal for a new Constitution and Bylaws was defeated at the 1972 Representative Assembly, primarily because delegates were not prepared to adopt an entirely new and sometimes incoherent document as a package. But the Con-Con delegates' work did not go to waste. NEA set up "a Committee of Twelve" made up of presidents and executive directors from some of the affiliates, with Dr. Fred Hipp from New Jersey as the chair and Chanin as adviser. Instead of presenting the next Representative Assembly with another complete replacement for the existing Constitution and Bylaws, the committee decided to identify the Constitution and Bylaws changes that needed to be made to implement Con-Con's goals. Chanin then drafted the necessary amendments, which were adopted at the 1973 Representative Assembly.[159]

These changes transformed NEA into the most democratic, member-controlled national union in America. The annual four-day Representative Assembly—now made up of about 10,000 elected delegates chosen through a process of open nominations and secret ballots—is often termed the largest democratic deliberative body in the world. Any 50 delegates can bring an issue to the floor by signing a petition to do so. Delegates vote on the basis of one delegate, one vote, so there is no block voting controlled by a handful of officials. Elections of NEA officers are held during the assembly without slate voting. Election of officers is determined by secret ballot, as is voting on amendments to governing documents.

Other changes that enhanced member control were made as well. Ethnic minorities were guaranteed representation at every level of the organization. Power was shifted from the executive director to the elected leaders, and in order to give NEA presidents more influence and ability to carry out a program, the time a president could hold office was extended beyond the traditional single year to two two-year terms. (It would later be extended further to two three-year terms.)

Subsequent Representative Assemblies have maintained the spirit of the 1973 RA. The delegates are teachers, education support professionals, and other NEA members who volunteer many hours of their time during the school year to work for NEA, state associations, and local associations in representing members, resolving problems at work, negotiating collective-bargaining agreements, and engaging in political action on legislative priorities, preparing school budgets, and other issues affecting students and staff. The Representative Assembly each year is in part a reward for such active members, not only to make decisions and set policy for the Association, but also to connect with their counterparts from the rest of the country, to experience firsthand NEA's national strength, and to take back home to other members the collective spirit generated at the meeting.

Meanwhile, changes in the leadership at NEA not only hastened the organization's transformation but institutionalized it as well. At its 1972 Representative Assembly, Sam Lambert gave a fiery speech warning that the Association was moving away from representing an independent teaching profession and toward greater unionism and the potential of an eventual merger with AFT or membership in AFL-CIO. "After I have said what I must say, I may be unemployed," Lambert told the delegates, and, indeed, it was not long before he and NEA parted company.

The organization turned to Allan West as NEA's acting executive director. West enjoyed enormous respect throughout the organization. He had been instrumental in developing NEA's collective-bargaining activities, and his quiet and purposeful leadership had always kept things in equilibrium and given credibility to the movement. He managed the forces of change exceptionally well. "He had a kind of silent intelligence," Ken Melley would say.[160] "He thought everything out thoroughly before he spoke or acted. Everything was done with deliberation. Even his manner of writing—with each letter meticulously formed—demonstrated his care. He was the transition."

If Allan West was the transition, Terry Herndon was the future. After West's tenure as acting executive director ended in 1973, the NEA Executive Committee began to look for a successor who would continue the movement. When it deadlocked between Gary Watts, NEA's director of field services, and Bob Phelps, the executive director of the Pennsylvania State Education Association, the committee turned to the 34-year-old Herndon, a native of Michigan.

In contrast to Drs. Carr and Lambert, who had come out of the

Association's research department, Herndon had been a school teacher and local association activist and, in 1969, had become executive director of the Michigan Education Association. Despite his youth, he was an experienced union organizer and negotiator. He was bold, creative, and an inspiring speaker. But he also understood the nuts and bolts of politics and organizational dynamics.[161]

Herndon moved quickly to solidify the focus of the staff on collective bargaining and unionism by asking Chanin, whose political savvy and strategic thinking he admired, to be deputy executive director and expand the areas of decision making in which he was involved. Chanin agreed, with the understanding he would continue to serve as general counsel as well.[162]

Chanin never had any desire to lead NEA, though the quality of his leadership was widely recognized. Myron Lieberman, the scholar who referred to Chanin in 1997 as having a larger impact on public education than had any other individual in the past thirty years, once noted that "were it not for the fact that NEA members were very unlikely to vote for an attorney as NEA president, Chanin might have been the Albert Shanker of the NEA."[163] As a negotiator for the Mount Vernon, New York, school district in 1966, Lieberman had encountered Chanin for the first time. "In just a few seconds, I realized I was in over my head," Lieberman later said. "Although this was my first experience in bargaining at the table, two hundred contracts and 25 years later, I would say that I have yet to face a more sophisticated and more formidable negotiator."

Lieberman's views on teachers' unions evolved over time, from encouragement of the union movement in the 1950s and 1960s to a view by the 1970s that collective bargaining was harmful to U.S. public education. "The most important reason for my change of position was the realization that collective bargaining in public education is inconsistent with democratic, representative government," Lieberman wrote in his book *The Teacher Unions*.[164] "In teacher-union bargaining, school board representatives, that is, government officials, negotiate public policies with one special interest group in a process from which other parties are excluded."

But Chanin and many other observers believed the movement for collective bargaining left a more positive legacy of change in public education and NEA itself. It transformed teaching from a depressed industry to a self-respecting profession. It enhanced the ability of teachers to shape their work and education policy, replacing the plantation mentality that had prevailed previously in the schools. It changed NEA and its affiliates from a top-down association to a bottom-up, democratic union with 3.2 million members, 16,800 affiliates, and closer ties to other unions. Collective bargaining for public employees in general created what has become the largest and most influential segment of the American union movement. While union membership has dropped below one in twelve among private-sector workers, it remains above one in three in the public sector. While most of the industrial unions have lost half their membership or more, public-sector organizations such as NEA, AFSCME, AFT, and SEIU have continued to grow and are now the major union groups in America.[165]

Chanin's passion for the movement consumed him for years, requiring long hours, often on the road. When he did make it home, he often was thinking about the strike he was working on, or the negotiations he needed to wrap up, or the court hearing that required preparation. But there was a price to pay.

One night when he was home, he said to his oldest child, Jeff, "So, what's new these days in the fourth grade?" His son looked at him and said, "Dad, if you were here more, you would know that I'm in the fifth grade."

In hindsight, it's one of Chanin's few regrets that he did not find a better balance. He cannot get back those years when his children were growing up, but he now has five grandchildren, and he knows for sure what grade each one is in.[166]

Part II |

The Pursuit of Racial Diversity

"In the field of education, the doctrine of separate but equal has no place. Separate educational facilities are inherently unequal."
—*Chief Justice Earl Warren in the U.S. Supreme Court's opinion in* Brown v. Board of Education, *May 17, 1954*[1]

"Without Bob Chanin doing some convincing, we might not have desegregated NEA in Alabama. He could sell a refrigerator to an Eskimo."
—*Joe Reed, associate executive secretary, Alabama Education Association*[2]

Chapter 4

Bringing Black and White Together

In 1857, the year NEA was founded, the U.S. Supreme Court issued its infamous *Dred Scott* decision, which held that people of African descent, whether slave or free, were not citizens of the United States and had no legal rights. The black man was brought to America with "no rights which the white man was bound to respect," the Court said. "The Negro might justly and lawfully be reduced to slavery for his benefit. He was bought and sold and treated as an ordinary article of merchandise and traffic, whenever profit could be made by it."[3]

While Robert Campbell, a Jamaican teacher at the Philadelphia Institute for Colored Children, was a founding member of NEA and a few black educators attended the new education association's meetings, NEA tended to reflect the greater society of the era and was essentially an organization for white professionals. In 1904, teachers in schools for black children decided to form their own organization, which would eventually be known as the American Teachers Association (ATA). Like the schools themselves, ATA was separate from its white counterpart, NEA.[4]

At the time ATA was formed, all southern states had laws requiring that schools be segregated by race. Ninety percent of African Americans lived in those states.[5] The laws often went to the highest levels of specificity to ensure segregation. For example, a provision enacted in North Carolina in 1903 decreed that white schools were off limits to any child with African blood in his or her veins, "however remote the strain."[6] Although blacks were the majority in many parts of the South, they often were provided with no schooling at all. A study of the southern states for the 1903-04 school year found that less than six percent of high school students were African American.[7]

ATA was led by a series of distinguished black educators, including Mary McLeod Bethune, the daughter of former slaves and founder of what would become Bethune-Cookman University in Florida. In 1926, two years after Bethune became ATA's president, the organization formed a joint committee with NEA to pursue mutual concerns. But ATA leaders felt that the committee's activity resulted in little action to address the great inequality between the races. In 1927, the ATA president wrote to the president of NEA that "it is quite possible now to have Negro children sing at your national meetings, but it might cause consternation to call attention to their constitutional rights . . . ."[8]

In 1937, an ATA report found that, over the previous thirty years, the gap between educational opportunities for white children and black children had increased five-fold. It was "as if the white child were riding in an automobile, and the Negro on a mule," the report concluded.[9]

It was around this time that a young lawyer named Thurgood Marshall and other attorneys for the National Association for the Advancement of Colored People (NAACP) Legal Defense Fund began filing cases on behalf of teachers and students who were victims of racial discrimination. In 1936, the NAACP won a ruling from the Maryland Court of Appeals, the state's highest court, in *Murray v. Maryland* that the University of Maryland Law School violated the Fourteenth Amendment's Equal Protection Clause when it denied admission to Donald Murray, a minister's son and graduate of Amherst College, because he was African American. The Fourteenth Amendment, adopted after the Civil War, provides that no state shall deny to "any person within its jurisdiction the equal protection of the laws." That same year, the ATA affiliate in Maryland prompted the NAACP to file a lawsuit, *Gibbs v. Board of Education*, against the Montgomery County school board, charging that paying black teachers less than white teachers violated the Equal Protection Clause. Apparently convinced that it was going to lose the case, the school board agreed just before the decision would have been issued that it would equalize salaries over a two-year period. Over the next decade, the NAACP won nearly two dozen such cases nationwide, but progress was slow because lawsuits had to be filed school district by school district, and the pay gap persisted in most communities throughout the southern and border states.[10]

ATA was one of the NAACP's major funders, and it actively

encouraged black teachers to join the civil rights group.[11] This was in keeping with the special leadership role black teachers played in many African American communities, especially in the South. They were among the few residents who had college educations and the financial resources to support campaigns for equality.

With the start of World War II, blacks throughout American society began to intensify their insistence on equal rights. African Americans were playing an important role both in the military, where they served in segregated units, and in industries manufacturing weapons and other goods for the war effort, where they often were given the hardest and most hazardous jobs. Why, many of them asked, were they expected to defend democracy around the world while being denied equal opportunity at home? Responding to these increasing concerns, President Roosevelt issued an executive order in 1941 prohibiting discrimination in defense industries, and President Truman in 1948 issued an executive order ending segregation in the military itself.[12]

Reflecting this growing movement in the broader society, questions began to be raised within NEA about its commitment to equal justice. Some members of ATA were also members of NEA, and, together with liberal white allies, they were successful in winning passage of a resolution at NEA's 1943 Representative Assembly which provided that "in choosing the city for its conventions, the National Education Association shall see to it that only those cities shall be selected where it is possible to make provisions without discrimination for the housing, feeding, seating at the convention, and general welfare of all delegates and teachers, regardless of race, color, or creed."[13]

In 1947, delegates to the Representative Assembly adopted a resolution granting NEA-affiliate status to ATA's branches in 18 southern and border states. That meant that NEA would now have two state affiliates in each of those states—the existing white state affiliate and a separate black state affiliate that also remained affiliated with ATA. While ATA affiliates that were now also part of NEA were active in campaigns for equal salaries, funding for black schools, and voting rights for African Americans, they generally could not count on the support of the white NEA affiliate in the same state. At the national level, ATA and NEA were still separate organizations.[14]

Tension within NEA over racial issues continued for decades, as it did in the larger society. When NEA leaders picked the location for the Representative Assembly in 1950, they ignored the 1943 resolution requiring that the Assembly meet only in cities whose hotels and restaurants were integrated. Instead, they chose St. Louis, where blacks could not stay in white hotels. After much debate, delegates passed a new resolution that left more wiggle room, saying that future conventions should be held in cities "where it is possible to provide a maximum degree of equality for the housing, feeding, seating at the meetings, and for the general welfare of all members of the Association."[15]

When the NAACP brought *Brown v. Board of Education of Topeka* and its companion cases to the U.S. Supreme Court in the early 1950s, the AFT filed a friend-of-the-court brief, known by its Latin name as an *amicus curiae* brief, or *amicus* brief for short, on the side of the black schoolchildren seeking an end to segregated schools.[16] *Amicus* briefs are filed by groups or individuals that are not party to a case but have arguments and perspectives that might help the court in reaching its decision. In contrast to AFT, NEA did not file an *amicus* brief in the *Brown* case. Speculating on NEA's failure to file, Chanin noted that NEA did not have an active legal-advocacy program at that time and would not file its first *amicus* brief for several years. More significantly, as the aftermath of the *Brown* decision would make clear, the Association had not yet come to grips with the racial issues raised by the case.

On May 17, 1954, the High Court issued its landmark decision in *Brown*, declaring that racial segregation in the public schools—which was required by law in many southern and border states—was a violation of the Equal Protection Clause of the Fourteenth Amendment to the U.S. Constitution.[17]

When NEA's 1954 Representative Assembly met shortly after the *Brown* decision, it adopted a resolution that took no position in support of or opposition to the ruling, but simply stated that "the Association urges all citizens to approach this matter of integration in our public schools with the spirit of fair play and good will which has always been the outstanding characteristic of the American people."[18]

At each Representative Assembly from 1955 to 1960, delegates sought unsuccessfully to adopt resolutions endorsing the Supreme Court decision and school integration.[19]

The subject was raised again at the 1961 Representative Assembly at a time when AFT was stepping up its criticism of NEA for not taking a strong stand on integration. A delegate from the District of Columbia noted that passage of the proposed resolution backing *Brown* and integration would "remove the criticism that is so often levied against the NEA [by AFT] that it has never, in explicit terms, proclaimed its support of these decisions." An impatient delegate from New York complained that "this has gone on now for about seven years. It is about time that our people took a stand. . . . I believe that the weakness of the NEA in many large cities is similar to that in New York City where the teachers union has been able to say, 'We stand for the Supreme Court decision—the NEA does not.'"

Several speakers from white affiliates in the South spoke strongly against the resolution. A delegate from North Carolina warned the assembly that "there are many areas of the South where schools cannot be successfully integrated today. To force this issue will close the schools or reduce them to positions of poverty, which may be little better than no schools at all. There are millions of taxpayers who will not send their children to integrated schools; neither will they approve taxation which will support such schools."

After a lengthy debate that year, the RA for the first time adopted a resolution putting NEA on record in support of school integration and *Brown v. Board of Education*. Achieving integration, however, remained a difficult task.[20]

The Supreme Court had ordered school districts to integrate "with all deliberate speed," but in most places the edict was met with all deliberate resistance. As the *History of the American Teachers Association* recounts, southern legislatures "adopted resolutions aimed at nullifying the decrees of the highest court in the land. These acts of official defiance varied in the different states. Generally speaking, they included: amendments to state constitutions which denied that public education was a state obligation or an individual right; laws which gave local officials the authority for pupil assignment; censorship laws against books that seemed to favor racial equality or integration; laws declaring it illegal for teachers, students, or school officials to implement desegregation; abolishment of compulsory school attendance; passage of laws requiring loyalty oaths; laws against joining the NAACP; and provisions which permitted abolishment of state public schools."[21]

To ferret out educators who provided financial support to the NAACP, the Arkansas legislature passed a law in 1958 requiring teachers to report all organizations to which they had belonged or had donated money in the previous five years. The Arkansas Teachers Association, an ATA and NEA affiliate, was one of the plaintiffs in a lawsuit challenging this requirement. In a 1960 decision in *Shelton v. Tucker*, the U.S. Supreme Court ruled the Arkansas law unconstitutional. "The vigilant protection of constitutional freedoms is nowhere more vital than in the community of American schools," Justice Potter Stewart wrote for the majority. "The statute's comprehensive interference with associational freedom goes far beyond what might be justified in the exercise of the State's legitimate inquiry into the fitness and competency of its teachers."[22]

School boards also tried incentives to discourage black students from moving to white schools. According to the *History of the Alabama State Teachers Association*, "New construction projects [for black schools] after 1954 often involved gymnasiums, perhaps because school boards felt that this would most satisfy the black community because of the passion to participate in sports, particularly basketball. Some black schools suddenly were given their first indoor restrooms, libraries, and science labs."[23]

In many places in the South, public schools closed and private white schools suddenly appeared, sometimes in the same facilities, often with books and furniture they were given as "surplus."[24]

Another tactic was to establish a "freedom of choice" system in which black students could "voluntarily" decide—under heavy pressure—to stay right where they were. The school boards' hope was that black students would "choose" to remain in segregated schools, and that black teachers would then be wary of risking their jobs or personal safety by asking to integrate the faculty of a white school.[25]

It was difficult in those days for African Americans in the South to challenge segregation through the ballot box because most of them were denied the right to vote. To take one typical example, in Mississippi in 1960, blacks made up more than 40 percent of the population but only five percent of registered voters.[26] Some states charged a poll tax that few blacks could afford. Others required voters to pass a literacy test, and, since white officials judged the results, educated blacks failed even as illiterate whites passed. Black citizens who tried to register to vote might find a cross burned on their lawn by the Ku Klux Klan, lose their jobs, be evicted from their homes, or be beaten or even killed.[27]

With political avenues for change closed off, African Americans and their white allies from the North turned to direct action, including civil disobedience. On February 1, 1960, four black college students from North Carolina Agricultural & Technical College sat down at a Woolworth's lunch counter in Greensboro and refused to leave after being denied service because of their race.[28] The news media began to cover their peaceful sit-in, and soon the tactic spread to many other cities. One of those was Montgomery, Alabama, where Alabama State University students conducted a sit-in when denied service at the all-white snack bar in the county courthouse. One of those students was Joe Reed, who would later become a leader in both ATA and NEA.[29]

Meanwhile, brave black families, backed by federal court orders, were overcoming angry white mobs to integrate schools. In November 1960, six-year-old Ruby Bridges was taken by her mother to enroll at an all-white elementary school in New Orleans. White families responded by taking their children out of school, so Bridges spent the rest of the school year as the only student in her class. She was taught each day by a white teacher who had moved to Louisiana from Boston. Although Ruby's father lost his job, and the teacher was not rehired for the following year, their sacrifice established a precedent and, hence, paid off for others. By the next school year, some of the white students returned to the school, and other black families besides the Bridges sent their children.[30]

Confronted by a growing movement for integration, some school districts began to comply—but by laying off black teachers and principals, while keeping less senior white staff members. Many white administrators simply could not envision requiring white students to be educated by black teachers. Tens of thousands of black teachers lost their jobs. As Joe Reed later put it, "integration" often turned into "outegration" for black educators. This was especially devastating to black communities, because teaching was one of the only professions open to African Americans. At the time of *Brown v. Board of Education*, teaching was the career path for nearly half of black college graduates.[31]

To defend black teachers, ATA and its affiliates needed political support as well as financial resources for federal court challenges. In the early 1960s, ATA began talking with both NEA and AFT about a closer relationship that would provide the necessary assistance.

According to *All the People,* by historian Al-Tony Gilmore, R. G. Martin, then ATA's executive secretary, met with AFT officials in New York City to discuss the idea of a merger. When the meeting adjourned for the day, the white AFT officials went to dinner together, leaving Martin to eat separately with one of AFT's black officials. After eating his segregated meal, Martin never again pursued a merger with AFT, which continued to make overtures to ATA. It is possible that AFT's persistence helped motivate NEA to complete a merger with ATA.[32]

Delegates to the 1963 Representative Assembly adopted a resolution calling on the black and white state affiliates in the southern and border states to establish committees to facilitate an end to the system of racially segregated associations. The assembly also directed NEA to conduct merger discussions with ATA. The 1964 RA set July 1, 1966, as a deadline for the affiliates in each state to present their joint plan for merger.[33]

Merger discussions in the years 1963 to 1965 took place against a backdrop of the greatest civil rights activity the nation had ever seen. In the spring of 1963, the Southern Christian Leadership Conference, headed by the Rev. Dr. Martin Luther King, Jr., held nonviolent protests in Birmingham, Alabama, during which police chief Theophilus Eugene "Bull" Connor ordered attacks on demonstrators with fire hoses and dogs. In June, a gunman assassinated NAACP leader Medgar Evers at his home in Mississippi, as his children looked on. In August, hundreds of thousands gathered in front of the Lincoln Memorial in Washington for a March for Jobs and Freedom, at which Dr. King made his "I Have a Dream" speech. Less than a month later, four girls were killed by a bomb planted by Ku Klux Klansmen in a black church in Birmingham.[34]

In June 1963, spurred on by thousands of acts of civil disobedience throughout the South, President John F. Kennedy introduced into Congress a civil rights act that addressed many of the issues the protesters were raising. After Kennedy was assassinated in November, his successor, Lyndon B. Johnson, continued to press for the legislation. Johnson had been a longtime U.S. senator from Texas and majority leader in the Senate, where he was considered a master of deal-making and arm-twisting. Using his experience in dealing with his fellow white southerners who controlled key congressional committees, and the momentum built by continuing grassroots protests, Johnson persuaded Congress to pass the act, which he signed into law on July 2, 1964.

The Civil Rights Act of 1964 is one of the most far-reaching pieces of legislation ever enacted by Congress. Title IV of the statute authorizes the U.S. Department of Justice to go to federal court when public school districts or universities engage in unconstitutional discrimination. Title II bars discrimination in public accommodations such as hotels and restaurants. Although Title VII outlaws discrimination by employers based on race, religion, sex, or national origin, this protection was not extended to public school employees and other public workers until 1972.[35]

A few months after he signed the bill into law, Johnson persuaded Congress to pass other elements of his "Great Society" program that were aimed at addressing the needs of the poor, including many African Americans. With NEA's support, the Economic Opportunity Act established Head Start, a major preschool and child development program that today prepares more than a million low-income children per year to be more successful in school. The act also provides for job training and for work study grants for low-income college students.[36]

Also in 1964, black activists in the South, reinforced by thousands of black and white students from the North, conducted what they called Freedom Summer, going into communities across the region to encourage African Americans to register to vote. The campaign helped focus national attention on the practices that prevented most blacks from participating in the political process.[37]

When teachers who were active in voting rights protests or other aspects of the civil rights movement were targeted for firings or other discriminatory acts, NEA responded. The Association took up a major civil rights case, *Johnson v. Branch*, in 1964 on behalf of a black teacher from North Carolina. Willa Johnson, a high school English teacher with twelve years of experience and consistently high evaluations by her principal, was fired after she and her husband played a leadership role in voter registration drives and protests over discrimination against African Americans in the small town of Enfield, North Carolina. A federal district court upheld her firing, but the U.S. Court of Appeals for the Fourth Circuit found that her dismissal was motivated by her civil rights activity and was therefore illegal. NEA paid for her legal representation and provided a small stipend until the court ordered reinstatement to her job and awarded damages.[38]

Discrimination cases that stemmed from school integration also pushed NEA into action. The Association provided legal assistance in 1964 in *Franklin v. County School Board of Giles County* to seven African American teachers from Giles County, Virginia, who were fired when the school board decided to integrate the schools. The seven teachers had staffed the two all-black schools in the county, which were closed by the board after many African American students applied to attend the formerly all-white schools. Instead of allowing the black teachers to teach in the integrated schools, the superintendent sent each one a termination letter expressing thanks for his or her "years of service rendered the School Board . . . and the children of your race." The seven teachers—who had been the only African American teachers employed by the district—were replaced by eight newly hired white teachers.

The Fourth Circuit court rejected the superintendent's claim that the seven teachers were not retained because they were the least qualified of the 186 teachers employed by the district, ruling that they obviously had been fired because of their race. The court also entered an injunction ordering the board to re-employ the teachers for the next school year.[39]

In 1965, black teachers in Selma, Alabama, led a campaign to establish the right to vote. They called it "Fit to Teach—Fit to Vote."

NEA adopted a resolution in support of the effort and, together with ATA, sent leaders and staff to help.[40]

Local and state authorities resisted, and when on February 18, 1965, a black civil rights activist named Jimmie Lee Jackson was killed by a state trooper, teachers and other civil rights activists decided to hold a fifty-mile march from Selma to Montgomery, the state capital. Dr. King, along with a number of prominent black and white entertainers, came to take part and help generate publicity.

On March 7, 1965, more than 500 unarmed and peaceful marchers set out. They had gone only six blocks when as they reached the Edmund Pettus Bridge, they were tear-gassed and beaten with clubs and whips by local sheriffs and state troopers sent by Governor George Wallace, who had declared the march a threat to public safety.[41]

Images broadcast by the national news media forced the Johnson administration to act. Two days after the attack on the marchers, President Johnson vowed to pass legislation protecting all Americans' right to vote: "I am certain Americans everywhere join in deploring the brutality with which a number of Negro citizens of Alabama were treated when they sought to dramatize their deep and sincere interest in attaining the precious right to vote. The best legal talent in the federal government is engaged in preparing legislation which will secure that right for every American."[42]

The NAACP filed a lawsuit against Wallace in federal court seeking an order to protect the marchers, and the U.S. Department of Justice under Attorney General Robert F. Kennedy intervened in the suit in support of the NAACP's position. David Rubin, who would later become Chanin's deputy general counsel at NEA, wrote the Justice Department's brief and traveled to Alabama with Assistant Attorney General John Doar to try the case. U.S. District Judge Frank Johnson issued an injunction that ultimately allowed the Selma march to go forward and required law enforcement officials to provide the marchers with protection.[43]

Two weeks later, some 4,000 troops from the U.S. Army and National Guard provided protection for a renewed march, which swelled to 25,000 participants by the time it reached its destination. Celebrities such as Harry Belafonte, Lena Horne,

Sammy Davis Jr., Mahalia Jackson, Nina Simone, Dick Gregory, and Joan Baez participated in the march.[44]

James N. Williams, known as "Jimmy," a former middle school teacher from Georgia and the staff member in charge of NEA's Southeast Regional Office, was one of many whites—mostly from outside Alabama—who joined the march. He recalls that, as they approached the capitol in Montgomery, he decided to stop at the headquarters of NEA's white affiliate in the state to use the men's room. The staff had the outside doors locked, but let Williams in. He later learned, however, that once white Association officials realized why he was in Montgomery, one of them called NEA headquarters in Washington to demand that he be fired. He was defended by Allan West, who made clear that NEA fully supported the march.[45]

As marchers were being driven back to Selma when the protest was over, members of the KKK opened fire on one of the cars, killing Viola Liuzzo, a white woman who was the wife of a Teamsters union official in Detroit and who had come to join the march after seeing the earlier police violence on television.[46]

Responding to the Selma protests and years of voter registration efforts, President Johnson introduced the Voting Rights Act of 1965, which eventually passed Congress and was signed into law in August. It outlawed schemes that blocked African Americans from voting and gave the U.S. Department of Justice oversight over any changes in voting procedures in the southern states. As much as any other law, the act led to profound changes in the South as blacks were able for the first time since Reconstruction to elect African Americans to public office and force white politicians to take their needs into account.[47]

After the unfavorable media coverage that Governor Wallace received as a result of the attacks on the Selma marchers, he invited national reporters to tour the state with him to observe "racial harmony" for themselves. The tour ended with a news conference at a trade school built as a result of legislation Wallace had sponsored. Instead of serving as an opportunity to showcase how happy "our Negroes" are when not stirred up by "outside agitators," Wallace's press briefing was taken over by Joe Reed, then a 27-year-old teacher who worked at Alabama State University and had recently become executive secretary of the Alabama State Teachers Association, the black affiliate of ATA and NEA. Reed took advantage of the fact that Wallace had gathered the national media together to detail discrimination in the state and the brutality of the governor's response to the civil rights protests.[48]

A few months after the Selma protests, Chanin attended NEA's 1965 Representative Assembly in New York City. Reflecting the stature of NEA in both the education and civil rights fields, President Johnson accepted the Association's invitation to speak at the meeting. He voiced the concern he shared with NEA "about the problem of the dismissal of Negro teachers as we move forward with the desegregation of the schools of America." He said his administration would pay "special attention in reviewing the desegregation plans of school districts under [*Brown v. Board of Education*] to guard against any pattern of teacher dismissal based on race or national origin."[49]

Meeting with NEA and ATA leaders at the assembly, Don Wollett and others from Kaye Scholer helped develop details for a national merger between the two organizations that was to be completed the following year.[50] ATA insisted that NEA share its commitment to provide financial support for the NAACP Legal Defense Fund and litigation to protect black teachers. In response, NEA agreed to raise a million dollars for that purpose.[51]

With the NEA-ATA national merger ready to be formalized, the dual black and white affiliates in the states were facing a deadline, established by a resolution adopted by the Representative Assembly in 1964, to submit merger plans of their own by July 1966. As the deadline approached, however, many white and black state association leaders in some of the southern and border states resisted the merger requirement.

Leaders of many southern white associations opposed integration and feared a loss of white members if merger with the black associations occurred. At the same time, many leaders of southern black associations felt that the state mergers that had already taken place were nothing more than the absorption of the black affiliate into the white one rather than true mergers. They were afraid that blacks would not have access to any leadership role in merged state associations, since they would be in the minority. They also feared that merged affiliates would not continue to pursue legal cases defending black teachers and students. They observed, for example, that after the dual affiliates in West Virginia merged, blacks wanted the merged association to continue its annual contribution to the NAACP for legal defense work, but the merged association refused.[52]

Dr. Vernon McDaniel, executive secretary of the black association in Texas, expressed a fear shared by a number of his colleagues: "Unification, yes," he said. "A coalition of first and second class professionals, no."[53]

Before getting involved in the mergers that had not yet been completed, Chanin observed for himself that some of the early state consolidations appeared to have been mergers in name only. He visited what was supposed to be the already merged office of one of the state associations in the South. It was housed in the whites' building near the state capitol after the black association's building in a poor part of town had been sold. When he asked to see one of the white lawyers, the receptionist told him to turn right toward the white section of the building, and when he wanted to see one of the African American lawyers who had represented the black association, he was told to turn left toward the section for blacks. "They were still separate associations," Chanin recalled. "They just happened to be in the same building."[54]

NEA recognized the problems with these state "absorptions," and around the time that Chanin became general counsel in 1968, it sought to promote genuine mergers in the remaining states— Alabama, Arkansas, Georgia, Louisiana, Mississippi, and North Carolina. Deadlines for these mergers had been extended from one Representative Assembly to the next because the black and white affiliates were resistant and could not reach agreement on their own. Patience was running thin among the delegates from NEA affiliates around the country who wanted the Association to practice internally the integration policy that it supported for the schools.[55] The challenge was made even more delicate by the fact that NEA's merger with ATA was itself probably closer to an absorption. The merged organization, after all, was still called NEA, and the Association remained in its same headquarters in Washington.

With these states still at impasse, Allan West asked Kaye Scholer for help in bringing about equitable agreements. While the task did not involve labor law, it required some of the same skills in problem solving and negotiation that the firm had already demonstrated.[56]

Drawing on his experience with processes established for collective bargaining and dispute resolution with school districts, Chanin worked with Kaye Scholer partner Fred Bullen to develop a process for mediation between the black and white state associations. How would the mediation occur? Would the two sides exchange documents? Would there be deadlines for responses? When and how would they meet?[57]

Bullen, who was white, personally took part in on-site mediation in most of the states, working in each case with a black mediator. The mediators were men of considerable standing, including Sam Proctor, a dean at the University of Wisconsin, and Frank Williams, a former U.S. ambassador to Ghana and the head of the Urban Center at Columbia University.[58]

As the mediation moved forward, Chanin drafted memoranda that addressed the substantive issues surrounding the merger: How would a merged association be governed? How would the leadership and staff be chosen? What would happen to the buildings that each association owned?[59]

Before the merger negotiations began, some of the white and black state association leaders had never met each other, even though they all dealt with education issues in the same state. For that matter, some people who had taught in the same city for twenty years or more had never met because the schools and neighborhoods were separate. Some had never had lunch or dinner with a person of the other race.[60]

Chanin didn't know much about the South and was astounded by some of the stories he heard from Jimmy Williams, who told him that when merger negotiations were held in one black association's headquarters, some white leaders sprayed cleanser on the chairs before they sat down. Leaders from the two sides routinely would start meetings by bowing their heads and praying together, with repeated references to brotherly love and all being children of God, and immediately afterwards would show their bitter disdain for each other once they got down to business.[61]

With six states still not merged at the beginning of 1969, Chanin worked with West and the NEA Executive Committee to develop a process for bringing mergers to closure if mediation failed. Then, as today, the Executive Committee consisted of the Association's three executive officers and six other members elected by the Representative Assembly, and it made decisions between meetings of the larger Board of Directors or RA. Under the process the Executive Committee adopted at its February 1969 meeting, the state affiliates had several options. They could proceed on their own and submit to NEA for its approval a merger agreement that they had adopted without direct NEA involvement. If they chose to proceed on their own but were unable to reach complete agreement, they could ask NEA either to appoint a fact finder to make recommendations for resolving the remaining issues or to arrange for those issues to be submitted to binding arbitration by a neutral third party. A final option was simply to turn the matter over to NEA to propose a merger agreement that would then be voted on by the state affiliates.

The Executive Committee voted that any state affiliate that, despite all these options for assistance, had not reached a merger agreement by June 1969 would face appropriate action by NEA, including possible disaffiliation. Such consequences were unheard of in NEA, a confederation in which state affiliates had always played a powerful and generally independent role.[62]

Alabama was a prime example of a state in which Chanin was directly involved in helping the black and white affiliates reach an agreement. In 1969, the black association was led by Joe Reed, who had worked closely with Dr. King and had arranged for him to speak at the association's state assembly in 1967. The white association also had a dynamic young leader, named Paul Hubbert. Both were smart, and both wanted a merger to work. Neither was intimidated by the other, which was not the case in some other states.[63]

The black association had been the prime force in obtaining a federal district court order in *Lee v. Macon* that mandated full desegregation of the Alabama schools for the 1967-68 school year. Now the Association was following up on enforcement. In addition to other ruses, white school district officials were taking black principals—who, along with teachers, were members of the black education association—and assigning them to jobs with no authority or duties. Black educators refused, said Joe Reed, "to accept the thesis that just because a previously all-Negro school has been desegregated by students or staff, the Negro principal must be elevated to the assistant-to-the-assistant-to-the-vice-assistant in the superintendent's office and draw a fat salary with nothing to do, while a white person is assigned to do his job."[64]

Unless clear commitments were made before any merger, black leaders in Alabama questioned whether white association leaders would continue the legal work and provide financial resources to monitor compliance with *Lee v. Macon*. Chanin was asked to see if something could be worked out. He met with both associations and eventually developed a plan that was approved by both state associations and NEA. Under the plan, NEA itself would fund the legal work and be listed as plaintiff. That way, the white association leadership in the state would not have to explain to its members why a merged association was listed on lawsuits that many of them did not favor. In most cases, NEA would use and pay for the same civil rights lawyers the black association was already using.[65]

With that issue resolved, the Alabama merger was completed, and it quickly demonstrated how integration of the black and white affiliates benefited both teachers and students. It brought black and white teachers together in one organization with common goals, creating relationships that led to more acceptance of integration of the schools. Under the agreement, Hubbert became the executive secretary of the merged organization, and Reed, his deputy, with the presidency rotating between whites and blacks to ensure that the black minority would share a leadership role. Once united, Hubbert and Reed used their influence with both the white and black members of the legislature to make the merged organization much more effective on political issues than the separate affiliates ever had been. When Governor Wallace tried to raid the teachers' retirement fund in 1971, for example, the proposal was defeated by an overwhelming vote in the legislature.[66]

The merged association also demonstrated that it would defend all educators' rights, no matter their race. After the Greene County Board of Education became all-black following passage of the Voting Rights Act, it moved to fire a white superintendent a year before his contract expired. The merged association successfully sued on his behalf. Reed later recalled taking a lot of heat from black members in that county. "I journeyed to Greene County and met with the black teachers there and advised them that we would not back down, and that if an all-black board could fire a white superintendent without due process of law, then every white board could fire every black teacher in Alabama without due process."[67]

At the opposite end of the spectrum from Alabama were two states, Mississippi and Louisiana, in which there seemed to be little prospect for successful mergers. Chanin was assigned, along with Jimmy Williams, to work in both states. He soon recognized that bringing the two associations together involved more than approving a resolution or signing a document. It would involve overcoming legal problems, long-standing racial prejudices, social pressures, and personal agendas.

Chanin sat in on some of the meetings between the two associations in Mississippi and realized that little progress was being made. The blacks might be willing to merge, but the whites were not. The white leadership thought an integrated association would lose a significant number of white members, and that might be worse than being disaffiliated from NEA.[68]

When mediation failed, Dr. Fred Hipp, the veteran executive secretary of the NEA affiliate in New Jersey, was called in as a fact finder and seemed to break the log jam. Chanin helped him draft a report with merger recommendations that were acceptable to negotiators for both affiliates. It was then approved by a vote of the delegate assembly of the black association, but overwhelmingly rejected at the white assembly. After months of additional discussions between NEA and the white association failed, NEA expelled the white association on April 7, 1970. [69]

There was some precedent for this action. The year before, the black affiliate in North Carolina had briefly been suspended when it turned down a mediation proposal Hipp had prepared and the white association there had approved. But that dispute had been quickly resolved. The action against the white affiliate in Mississippi involved expulsion of the larger of the two organizations in the state, and there was no reason to think reconciliation would occur quickly. As it turned out, NEA's only affiliate in the state for the next six years was the black association. A few whites joined it, but for the most part white teachers stayed in their own unaffiliated association.[70]

Meanwhile, the issues in Louisiana also proved difficult to resolve. The leaders of the white association did not want to merge, and black association executive secretary J. K. Haynes wanted a merger even less. For starters, the white and black leaders personally disliked each other. Besides that, Haynes and the black association had a special status in the state. Haynes was a highly respected figure who was consulted by the governor and the legislature when they wanted the support of the black community. He believed that no matter what was written in a merger document, the independent voice of blacks would be lost. [71]

In April 1969, Dale Kennedy, the executive secretary of the NEA affiliate in Michigan, issued a fact-finder's report with recommendations, but neither Louisiana association accepted it. So, in a dramatic move, both were suspended by NEA.[72]

After further discussions between NEA and the two Louisiana associations, Chanin helped develop a modified merger plan and simultaneous votes by the delegate assemblies of each state association were scheduled for separate locations. Despite NEA's support for the compromise, delegates to the white assembly voted it down. Anticipating that this would happen, Jimmy Williams had concentrated on winning black association support for the proposed merger plan, using a Louisiana-style voter turnout operation. Working with those black leaders who disagreed with Haynes' opposition to merger, Williams arranged for buses to bring members from various points in the state to the meeting in Baton Rouge, with food and refreshments on board so members could socialize along the way.[73]

A two-thirds vote was required for approval, and with the news media eagerly awaiting the results, Williams called Chanin to report that the vote was 66 percent in favor.

"Exactly 66 percent, or a little more?" Chanin asked.

"A little more, like exactly 66.4," Williams said, which was slightly short of the required two-thirds.

Telling Williams to stall for time, and that he would get back to him as quickly as possible, Chanin called attorney Hugh Cannon, one of the nation's leading parliamentarians, for a professional opinion. The official parliamentarian at six Democratic National Conventions, and the author of one of the most commonly used textbooks on parliamentary procedure, Cannon had also served as parliamentarian at NEA's Representative Assemblies. Their conversation was brief and to the point:

> **Chanin:** We need two-thirds, and got 66.4 percent.
>
> **Cannon:** Normally, we round that figure to the closest whole number, which in this case would be 66 percent. That's less than the two-thirds requirement.
>
> **Chanin:** But the key threshold for approval here is 66.7, not 67. Wouldn't you say that 66.4 is closer to 66.7 than to 66? So shouldn't we round up to 66.7?
>
> **Cannon:** I've never heard that before. On the other hand, I don't see why you couldn't.
>
> **Chanin:** Can I take that as your official opinion?
>
> **Cannon:** I guess so.[74]

With Cannon's opinion in hand, Chanin called Williams back and advised him that the black association's approval of the proposed merger was official. Since the white association had turned down the proposal and was expelled, that left the black association as NEA's only Louisiana affiliate unless and until the white association changed its mind. J. K. Haynes, who still opposed merger, bitterly called the outcome "the second Louisiana Purchase."[75]

No longer constrained by the views of the now-expelled white associations in Mississippi and Louisiana, NEA responded in 1970 to requests from its black members to establish task forces to monitor school desegregation in those states. Williams coordinated the effort out of NEA's Southeast Regional Office, sending teams of staff from NEA and its northern affiliates to observe and document conditions in the schools. Sometimes they found classes in a supposedly integrated school where the teachers had arranged black students on one side of the room and white students on the other. Sometimes students of the two races were scheduled to take different recess or lunch periods. The NEA teams reported to Williams, and he held news conferences to announce the findings, exposing the continued segregation. To avoid physical danger, the NEA monitors used rented cars which they frequently exchanged for different ones so it would be harder to track them by license plate numbers.[76]

On a day when he was working in New Orleans, Williams arranged to have lunch with his parents, who were visiting from their home in Texas. As his parents entered the lobby of the French Quarter hotel, Williams introduced them to Haynes, with whom he had been meeting to discuss progress in the monitoring project.

"Dr. Haynes," Williams said, "I'd like you to meet my mother and father."

"Nice to meet you," Haynes said. "You must be very proud of your son for the work he's doing here."

"Well," said Williams' father, "I was at his sister's last night, and I saw him on TV. I turned to my wife and said, 'Somebody's going to shoot that little bastard.'"[77]

When the white association in Louisiana filed a lawsuit against NEA, challenging its expulsion, Chanin worked with Steve Pollak of Shea & Gardner to defend NEA. While the defense was time-consuming, the hearings and depositions provided continuing opportunities for contact between the white association's leaders and NEA officials. Based on these contacts, Chanin sensed that the Louisiana leaders were interested in resuming merger talks. They told him that they felt isolated and missed the national programs and support that NEA provided—not to mention the personal amenities such as the chance to socialize and play golf with leaders of other state associations at conferences.[78]

Adversarial feelings ebbed, and with assistance from Chanin, Williams, and other NEA leaders, the white association in Louisiana finally agreed to merge in 1977. Once it was clear that Louisiana was heading in that direction, the white association in Mississippi agreed to a merger in that state as well.[79]

One of the effects of the NEA-ATA merger was that NEA began for the first time to hire African Americans in professional and managerial positions. When, in 1974, one of those pioneers, NEA Director of Teacher Rights Sam Etheridge, compiled a report looking back on the eight years since the national merger, he found that the black-white mergers in the states had made significant progress. Most of the merged state associations now had more members than the separate organizations had had in total. The number of African Americans on NEA's Board of Directors had increased from six to nearly two dozen. Horace Tate of Georgia, who had originally voted against merger, had become the first black executive secretary of a merged state association. NEA held workshops in the South to promote black voter registration, publicized violations of the rights of black students, and worked with textbook publishers to encourage more accurate and inclusive treatment of blacks in their publications.[80]

The integration of NEA and ATA and their respective state affiliates contributed to a rapid transformation of NEA from an organization that had no high-ranking black staff or leadership before 1964 to one that by 2010 had had four African American presidents and one Hispanic. Braulio Alonso, the Hispanic, served for the 1967-68 school year. The black presidents were: Elizabeth Koontz, elected in 1968, three months after the assassination of Martin Luther King. Jr.; James Harris, president in 1974-75; Mary Hatwood Futrell, who led the association from 1983 to 1989, after service in the presidency was no longer limited to one year; and Reg Weaver, president from 2002 to 2008.[81]

NEA has not relied on good will or chance to ensure minority representation, but rather, has built guarantees into its structure. Under Chanin's guidance, it established requirements for minority representation in every aspect of the organization. The methods used to achieve that representation have changed over the years to accommodate legal requirements, particularly the Landrum-Griffin Act, the federal law addressing the governance of labor unions. In the early 1970s, the federal courts interpreted the 1959 law as barring racial qualifications for union offices unless the qualifications were objectively related to the duties of the office. Although NEA had to make adjustments to its ethnic-minority guarantees when it came under the Landrum-Griffin law in 1979, its goals have remained the same. Minorities should make up at least twenty percent of its Board of Directors, Executive Committee, and all other committees. Every state affiliate must have an approved plan for sending delegations to the Representative Assembly that reflect the proportion of ethnic minorities in the population of that particular state. Governing bodies of NEA affiliates should reflect the affiliates' ethnic minority membership. NEA is also committed, in Chanin's phrase, to "use all appropriate legal means" to ensure employment of ethnic minorities on its staff.[82]

NEA's guarantees of minority representation are highly unusual among large institutions in America. Even such a strong critic of NEA as Professor Myron Lieberman conceded in his book, *The Teacher Unions*, that "no other major organization in the United States has embraced racial quotas as explicitly and as pervasively as the NEA."[83]

Of course, not everyone has looked favorably on NEA's minority guarantees. When the Association adopted them, AFT President Al Shanker said that by taking race into account in order to ensure minority representation when choosing leaders, "the NEA has gone from one form of racism to another."[84]

Shanker certainly was not alone in this regard. Indeed, there were some within NEA itself who shared this view. Chanin was not among them, however. As he explained to the Board of Directors, "NEA and ATA merged because they believed that a single, racially diverse organization would be more effective than either organization acting alone, and would be better able to represent the interests of all of its members. But this will be so only if the policies, programs, and activities of the merged association reflect the background, experience, and world-view of its diverse membership. The ethnic-minority guarantees are designed to assure that this is the case. That is not 'racism' it is 'inclusion'."[85]

Chapter 5

Affirmative Action

As part of NEA's ongoing commitment to defend the rights of black teachers during school desegregation, Chanin and other NEA attorneys handled or supported a number of key court cases over the years. One was a 1979 U.S. Supreme Court case, *Givhan v. Western Line Consolidated School District*.[86]

The case involved a black teacher named Bessie Givhan who had been teaching English in a segregated black school in Mississippi for more than six years. In 1969, fifteen years after *Brown v. Board of Education*, a federal district court ordered the school system in which she taught to integrate its faculty and student body.[87]

Over the next two years, Givhan was assigned to two different integrated schools. During that time, she and other black teachers and students participated in a variety of protests over the way white administrators were implementing desegregation.[88]

At the end of the second year, Givhan's new principal, James Leach, who was white, recommended that her employment not be renewed for the following year. He wrote to the superintendent, saying, "Mrs. Givhan is a competent teacher; however, on many occasions she has taken an insulting and hostile attitude toward me and other administrators. She hampers my job greatly by making petty and unreasonable demands."[89] A trial court found that Givhan had made only two demands, and both concerned desegregation. She wanted blacks assigned to work alongside whites in the office, and she wanted the various job categories in the cafeteria to be integrated as well.[90]

Givhan testified that she told Leach that "whites were in all choice positions," including principal, secretary, head counselor, and cafeteria ticket taker. "When [students] see all white faces in the administration, it [isn't] good for the atmosphere of learning for the children," she testified.[91]

With financial assistance from NEA, Givhan challenged her nonrenewal in federal district court, claiming a violation of her right to free speech. The district court agreed, finding that "the school district's motivation in failing to renew Givhan's contract was almost entirely a desire to rid themselves of a vocal critic of the district's policies and practices which were capable of interpretation as embodying racial discrimination."[92]

The U.S. Court of Appeals for the Fifth Circuit reversed the lower court's decision, holding that Givhan's free speech right had not been violated because she raised her complaints about discriminatory practices in private meetings with the principal, and not in a public forum.[93] "Many, if not most, people would consider Givhan's expressions laudable," the appeals court said. But "if we held Givhan's expressions constitutionally protected, we would in effect force school principals to be ombudsmen, for damnable as well as laudable expressions."[94]

The U.S. Supreme Court agreed to review the case. David Rubin, NEA deputy general counsel, and Chanin prepared NEA's legal brief, and Rubin argued the case before the Court. If teachers and other employees are not protected by the First Amendment when they give their views to their boss, the Association's brief argued, they will refrain from free expression "that is of potentially great value in contributing to enlightened decision-making by public officials."[95]

The Supreme Court unanimously ruled in Givhan's favor. "The First Amendment forbids abridgment of the 'freedom of speech,'" said the unanimous opinion by then-Associate Justice William Rehnquist. "Neither the Amendment itself nor our decisions indicate that this freedom is lost to the public employee who arranges to communicate privately with his employer rather than to spread his views before the public."

But it was now January 1979, nearly eight years after she had been fired.[96] And it took another three years of litigation for her to win a total victory: reinstatement with back pay. The only job she had been able to find during that ten-year period was a part-time position as a community counselor for a church group. Because of the lawsuit, no school district had been willing to hire her. When reinstated by the court, she went back to teaching for six more years, and later became a Methodist minister.[97]

Like so many pioneers in the movement for social justice, Bessie Givhan paid a heavy personal price for standing up for principle. Today, her name is almost lost to history, although it is well-known to those lawyers and judges who still rely on the decision in her case as legal precedent. The decade-long struggle she undertook, however, helped establish vital rights for thousands of teachers and students who followed in her footsteps.[98]

As the civil rights movement evolved in the 1960s, occasional conflicts began to develop between its goals and certain core principles of the union movement. A major rift in the education field centered on Al Shanker, then the leader of the United Federation of Teachers, the AFT's affiliate in New York City.

Some black activists in the late 1960s argued that integration was not a sufficient goal and that what African American communities needed was "black power," including the ability to control their local schools and other public services. Parents in one of New York City's poorest areas, the Ocean Hill-Brownsville section of Brooklyn, were among those who sought community control of their schools. The high school dropout rate in their part of the city was more than 70 percent, and nearly 60 percent of those who remained in school were at least three years behind grade level in basic skills. In an effort to improve the situation, parents obtained support for a community control experiment from the Ford Foundation and from Mayor John Lindsay, a liberal Republican who hoped to maintain both black and labor support for his reelection campaign. One specific change community activists wanted was the hiring of more African American teachers who could serve as role models and instill pride in black heritage and culture. While about 70 percent of the students were black, the great majority of teachers were white and many were Jewish—the products of a hiring system that relied heavily on a standardized examination.[99]

Once a community school board was established, it replaced a number of white teachers with blacks in direct violation of the union contract, which provided that job security and assignments were to be based on seniority, not race. The city's board of education and school superintendent told the community board it had overreached its authority, but they did not actually step in to reverse the displacement of the white teachers. To force the central administration's hand, Shanker called a city-wide strike in the fall of 1968.[100]

"We are sympathetic to the community demands and the educational needs of minority students, but do not believe that educational improvements must be paid for at the expense of teachers," Shanker said.[101]

The dispute gripped New York for months, and most other unions stood with Shanker. If senior teachers could be displaced because a community board wanted to achieve greater racial representation, then the union contract could be violated at any time to achieve any social goal, regardless of how worthy, he argued.[102]

The dispute seriously strained the relationship between the African American and Jewish communities. Many Jews had been active supporters of the civil rights movement. Philip Hirschkop, who had worked on a number of civil rights cases for NEA, handled *Loving v. Virginia*, the landmark Supreme Court case in 1967 that overturned state laws that made it a crime to marry someone of another race.[103] William Kunstler, a noted constitutional lawyer, handled countless civil rights cases, including joining Hirschkop in representing Willa Johnson for NEA in 1964.[104] Jack Greenberg was assistant counsel of the NAACP Legal Defense Fund for a dozen years and became chief counsel in 1961, replacing Thurgood Marshall. In 1967, President Johnson would appoint Marshall the first African American to serve on the U.S. Supreme Court.[105]

During the Ocean Hill-Brownsville dispute, however, many blacks and Jews saw the situation from very different perspectives. For generations, Jews had been subjected to quotas or outright rejection when they applied for jobs or admission to colleges and graduate schools. New York City's examination system for teacher hiring, however, had allowed Jews to get jobs based on merit without quotas. Undermining that system and replacing Jewish teachers because of their race or ethnicity appeared to be a return to the exclusionary practices of the past.[106] Although Chanin and his wife were no longer living in New York City when the strike occurred, there was no question where their families and friends who still lived there stood on the issue.[107]

As the battle dragged on, UFT reprinted half a million copies of an anti-Semitic flier that it said had been found in teacher mailboxes at two schools. Union staff handed out the flier all over the city, with the predictable result of intensifying Jewish support for Shanker's position and polarizing the two sides even more.[108]

Eventually, the strike was settled, mainly in the union's favor. It solidified Shanker's stature as a union leader but left scars in black-Jewish relations that would take many years to heal. It also foreshadowed difficult issues that NEA would face in the following years, involving conflicts between civil rights goals and union principles.[109]

In the early 1970s, NEA's dual commitments to racial justice and unionism were put to another difficult test when affirmative action became the subject of a raging controversy in the country as a whole, particularly in public education.

In a graduation speech at Howard University in 1965, President Johnson had argued the need for affirmative action: "You do not wipe away the scars of centuries by saying: 'now, you are free to go where you want, do as you desire, and choose the leaders you please.' You do not take a man who for years has been hobbled by chains, liberate him, bring him to the starting line of a race, saying, 'You are free to compete with all the others,' and still justly believe you have been completely fair."

The prohibition against prospective race discrimination contained in Title VII of the Civil Rights Act of 1964 was not sufficient by itself, Johnson believed. Affirmative action was needed to overcome the effects of discrimination stemming from the past, he said. "[It] is the next and more profound stage of the battle for civil rights. We seek not just freedom but opportunity—not just legal equity but human ability—not just equality as a right and a theory, but equality as a fact and as a result."[110]

A few months after this speech, the president issued the first executive order requiring government contractors to take affirmative action to overcome the effects of past discrimination in hiring and employment.[111]

Some of the opposition to affirmative action was simply racist. Some was manipulated by politicians looking to exploit racial divisions. But some came from sincere people grappling with the difficult question of how to create the "equality as a fact and as a result" that Johnson talked about, while recognizing that it meant that some white workers would not get jobs or promotions for which they were qualified or had seniority rights under union collective-bargaining agreements.[112]

In the wake of President Johnson's executive order, affirmative-action policies took root in corporate America and in government agencies. As the economy boomed in the late 1960s, such policies were most often used in hiring, not for layoffs. The idea remained controversial, though, and slowly engendered a backlash among those—particularly white males—who perceived their employment opportunities as diminished by such policies.

In the summer of 1974, NEA's Representative Assembly, without a great deal of debate, adopted a resolution that endorsed affirmative action, declaring, "It may be necessary to give preference in hiring, retention, and promotion policies to certain racial groups or women or men to overcome past discrimination." By the end of that year, however, it became clear that some in the Association intended to overturn that decision at the 1975 RA. The U.S. economy was undergoing a recession, creating more opposition to any policy position that might decrease job opportunities for whites.[113]

As the largest organization representing people of all races who worked in the education field in every state, NEA's position on affirmative action was important both in the courts and in the political arena. The likely outcome of the RA vote in the summer of 1975 would be indicated months ahead of time at meetings of the leaders of state and local associations that composed NEA. The most important gathering was of the National Council of State Education Associations (NCSEA), scheduled three weeks before Christmas 1974 in Las Vegas. NCSEA then, as now, included the president and executive director of every NEA state affiliate, and the council's support greatly increased the chance of a resolution's passing.[114]

Because he was helping to develop NEA's positions on collective bargaining and affirmative action, Chanin was invited to give a presentation to NCSEA. The day before the meeting, he flew to Las Vegas with Irma Kramer, who, as special assistant for governance, was one of the few women in high-ranking positions at NEA at that time. Kramer had been a social studies teacher in New York City in the 1950s, before moving to the Washington area. When she had applied for a teaching position in the suburban school district in Montgomery County, Maryland, she had been told by school officials that, while she was clearly qualified, they were hoping to find a man for the job, who could coach football after school as well as teach during school hours. There were no laws against gender discrimination at the time, so Kramer had no recourse. Outraged by the experience, she left teaching, ultimately taking a job at NEA.[115]

As Chanin and Kramer sat on the plane, Chanin told her that he was struggling with exactly what position to take in his speech to NCSEA. If NEA took a strong position for affirmative action, it might become harder for many affiliates to recruit white members. In a period in which NEA was, for the first time, attempting to build close relationships with other major unions, could it afford to take a stand in opposition to many of those unions that were strongly defending the existing seniority system for promotions and layoffs? Should NEA look for some middle way or compromise, or perhaps let each state decide for itself? Could NEA say it supported affirmative action as a future goal, but to be achieved gradually and not overnight?[116]

Chanin and Kramer talked for hours, and by the time Chanin went to sleep that night, he knew what he was going to say the next day. As he always did before a speech, he wrote out notes on a yellow legal pad to organize his thoughts. He did not know how his remarks would be received in a room in which a full spectrum of opinions would be represented. Clearly, one person's speech alone would not determine the vote, but because of his stature in the organization and his expertise on the subject, his views were likely to have a significant impact on the discussion.[117]

Chanin began his remarks by admitting that "I find this a most troublesome issue and am forced to confess to some uncertainty." Then, he directly addressed a particular recent case NCSEA had asked him to talk about—*DeFunis v. Odegaard*—which, while it dealt specifically with preferential admissions programs for university students, involved principles that could be applied to affirmative action programs for employment as well.

Marco DeFunis, a white student, applied to the University of Washington Law School for the school year beginning in September 1971, but was rejected. To make its first cut in choosing 150 enrollees from more than 1,600 applicants, the school had a policy of using results on the Law School Admissions Test (LSAT) and college grades to calculate a "predicted first year average." As a general rule, no one was considered whose score on the predicted average was below a certain number. That rule, however, did not apply to minorities and military veterans. In practice that meant that 22 veterans and 36 minority-group members with lower predicted first year averages than that of DeFunis were admitted to the law school.

DeFunis filed a lawsuit in a state court, which ruled that the law school's affirmative action program for minorities in admissions violated the Equal Protection Clause of the Fourteenth Amendment. The court cited as precedent *Brown v. Board of Education*, which it interpreted as meaning that any use of race as a criterion was unconstitutional. As a result of the ruling, DeFunis was admitted to the school. Later, however, the Washington Supreme Court reversed the lower court decision. That did not affect DeFunis' own status, since he was already in school, but it did establish that such preferential admissions programs were constitutional. The U.S. Supreme Court heard arguments in DeFunis' case, but on April 23, 1974, the justices issued an unsigned opinion declaring his case moot because he would graduate from the law school before they could rule on the merits of his case.[118]

Stepping back from the particular facts of that case, Chanin discussed the core questions about affirmative action that are still relevant today as the country continues to wrestle with the issue.

He explained that the state supreme court made three findings. First, minorities are greatly underrepresented in colleges and universities, even though, like all other citizens, they pay taxes to support those institutions. Second, racially balanced student bodies enhance the educational experience for all students, minority and non-minority alike. Third, the shortage of minority lawyers contributes to the shortage of minority judges, lawmakers, and other elected officials, which undermines the rule of law.

Should affirmative action require a specific finding of discrimination by a particular school or employer? Chanin argued that the answer was no. "Given this country's history of race relations, what is needed is not a case-by-case adjudication but wholesale justice. Three hundred years of discrimination has taken its toll on our institutions, and it is the institutional structure itself which must be corrected."

Next, he refuted several arguments against preferential admissions programs:

> One of the objections is that these programs represent a departure from the practice of basing decisions as to student admissions on high school grades, scores on tests, etc. The difficulty with this objection is that it rests on the patently false assumption that such decisions traditionally derive from objective judgments regarding the academic ability of the applicants. In point of fact, the college and university admissions process is considerably more complex. There are, of course, easy cases at the top and bottom of the scale—applicants who would be acceptable to any institution simply on the basis of their paper records and others whose paper records indicate such little likelihood of academic success that they would just as readily be rejected. But for the broad middle range of applicants, personal interviews, letters of recommendation, extracurricular activities, community service, and a variety of other subjective criteria receive consideration and sometimes play a decisive role. Special concessions are made to applicants with unique talents, such as the ability to shoot baskets or kick a field goal. . . . Preferences are given to the children of trustees, wealthy alumni, public officials, and persons prominent in the arts, whose familial associations may bring the institution wealth and distinction, or at least a commencement speaker four years hence. Children of faculty members are often guaranteed admission. . . . The question is not whether the purity of the traditional admissions system should be defiled by allowing preferences, but whether race should be permitted as a

basis for dispensations of a kind long accorded for other reasons.

He noted that preferential admissions programs have also been criticized because they supposedly harm the interests of minority students themselves:

> It has been said, for example, that such programs stigmatize the minority students and brand them inferior. Others argue that the self-confidence of the minority students is undermined if they feel that they are in school because of race rather than ability. . . . I would suggest, however, that the proper comparison for purposes of stigma is not between attending college as the result of a preference and attending college without a preference, but between attending with a preference and not attending at all.

Then came the most difficult issue—affirmative action might mean that a qualified non-minority applicant would not be accepted:

> In point of fact, this objection is a difficult one to deal with. If a college or university implements a preferential admissions program it may well find itself using racial classifications to the detriment of innocent nonminorities. If, on the other hand, the institution does not accord some type of preference to minority applicants, it will be ignoring the unjustified status quo of such applicants and, in effect, closing its eyes to the consequences of a long history of racial discrimination.
>
> This is indeed a dilemma and it poses a hard choice. For myself, I make the choice by recognizing that one of this nation's highest priorities is the elimination of the adverse effects of past discrimination, and by invoking the principle of the 'lesser evil.' I believe that the lesser evil is to deny admission on racial grounds to some nonminorities for a few years rather than to continue indefinitely the current denial to minorities of an equal opportunity to higher education.

He noted that many people argue that affirmative action is not defensible because it is impossible to define who should benefit. Should the child of a black doctor or a chicano professor get preference over the son or daughter of a white construction worker?

This argument is not without its irony. For over three hundred years, society had no trouble determining who to discriminate against. Are we now to be precluded from providing redress because it may not be possible to identify the victimized class with appropriate legal precision?

In conclusion, Chanin acknowledged that affirmative action was not a perfect solution, only the best one available:

I do not like preferential admissions programs. A color blind society in which race plays no role in law or in practice ought to be our goal. But . . . we must provide equal educational opportunity for those who have historically been excluded from our campuses. I would much prefer to rely on reasonable, nondiscriminatory admissions policies to achieve this end. But the fact is that the use of such policies simply has not worked. . . .

Opponents of preferential admissions programs contend that we seek the same ends and differ only in regard to the means which we deem appropriate in order to achieve those ends. At first glance this may appear to be true, but it turns out upon closer analysis to be far too superficial a view of the situation. I think it is unrealistic to express support for the elimination of racial discrimination and then condemn the use of the only realistic means of achieving that end.[119]

After Chanin finished, NCSEA voted to support affirmative action at the upcoming Representative Assembly. No one could ever know for sure, of course, but Kramer said later that she thought the speech had helped to ensure the outcome. Chanin was invited to repeat his presentation to the delegate assemblies of many state affiliates. With NCSEA support, the 1975 RA rejected an amendment to weaken the 1974 resolution, and NEA emerged firmly committed to affirmative action.[120]

With the authorization provided by the Representative Assembly, NEA weighed in on virtually all of the key affirmative action cases that came before the U.S. Supreme Court during the next thirty years.[121]

The first was *Regents of University of California v. Bakke*, which was the subject of extensive media coverage and public debate. In order to increase the representation of "disadvantaged" students, the University of California Medical School at Davis established a firm quota system for admissions, reserving at least 16 percent of its slots for minorities. Allan Bakke, the white son of a milk delivery driver, sued when he was turned down for admission, even though his grades and scores were better than those of some minority applicants who were accepted.[122]

Having avoided taking up the question of affirmative action in *DeFunis*, the U.S. Supreme Court now had to make some hard decisions. When the *Bakke* case went to the High Court in 1977, the AFL-CIO did not file an *amicus* brief on either side because its affiliated unions could not agree on a position. Nor did the Leadership Conference on Civil Rights (LCCR), an influential lobbying coalition in Washington that included black, labor, and Jewish constituent organizations, take a position because of disagreement among its organizational members.[123]

AFT knew where it stood, however, filing an *amicus* brief against affirmative action and in favor of Bakke. "If this case is not resolved in favor of Bakke," Al Shanker wrote in his weekly paid advertising space in *The New York Times*, "we will have a permanent conflict in this society. The overwhelming majority, 85 percent, oppose giving preference on the basis of race."[124]

Despite the controversy, Chanin told NEA leaders that the Association could not sit the case out and needed to file an *amicus* brief on "the right side." NEA joined in a brief with other major organizations, including the UAW, AFSCME, the National Council of Churches, the YWCA, the National Organization for Women, and the American Coalition of Citizens with Disabilities. The brief argued that nonminorities had received racial preferences throughout American history and that affirmative action for minorities was a necessary remedy for that injustice.[125]

The *Bakke* case sharply divided the High Court. When the justices announced their decision on June 28, 1978, no opinion commanded a majority. Four justices—John Paul Stevens, Potter Stewart, William Rehnquist, and Chief Justice Warren Burger—sided with Allan Bakke and said that under Title VI of the Civil Rights Act of 1964, the university could not use race as a factor in admissions. Four other justices—William Brennan, Thurgood Marshall, Harry Blackmun, and Byron White—would have upheld the university's affirmative action program.

In the middle was Justice Lewis Powell, who had experience dealing with issues of race in education as a former member of the Richmond, Va., school board and the Virginia state board of education. Powell wrote a concurrence only for himself but which became the controlling opinion in the case by virtue of the middle ground it staked out between the two other blocs of justices. Powell said racial quotas were not permissible under Title VI or the Equal Protection Clause of the Fourteenth Amendment. He concluded that the specific admissions program in the case was invalid and that Bakke should be admitted to the medical school at UC-Davis.

But, Powell's opinion also established that affirmative action was valid not only as a remedy for discrimination but as a way to attain diversity in the student body in order to fulfill a school's educational mission. Because a great deal of learning occurs through interactions among students of different races, religions, sexes, backgrounds, experiences, and interests, a school has a substantial and compelling interest in selecting students who will contribute to a "robust exchange of ideas," Justice Powell said. He also found that diversity was in the national interest because it helped to ensure that future "leaders [are] trained through wide exposure to the ideas and mores of students as diverse as this nation of many peoples."[126]

The next Supreme Court case on affirmative action came in 1979, and this time it dealt with employment. In *United Steelworkers of America v. Weber*, the Court reviewed a voluntary agreement between Kaiser Aluminum and the Steelworkers' union. Both were under pressure from the federal government because, while nearly 40 percent of the local work force near the company's unionized chemical plant in Louisiana was black, African Americans held less than two percent of the skilled jobs such as electrician or mechanic. To remedy that imbalance, the agreement provided that half the workers accepted into a skilled trades training program would be black until the percentage of blacks in those jobs equaled the percentage in the local work force.[127]

Brian Weber, a white laboratory analyst at the plant, sued both the company and the union, claiming that allocating training opportunities based on race violated Title VII, the federal law prohibiting employment discrimination. He won in the federal district court and court of appeals, so the union and the company asked the Supreme Court to review the case, which it agreed to do. The union's case was argued by Michael Gottesman from the law firm that later became known as Bredhoff & Kaiser. In this case, the AFL-CIO filed an *amicus* brief in support of the union's position, not necessarily because it was committed to a position in favor of affirmative action per se, but because the integrity of a union contract was at stake. AFT President Al Shanker, who had strongly defended the sanctity of union contracts in the Ocean Hill-Brownsville dispute, took the opposite position in this case. He angrily demanded a meeting with the leaders of the AFL-CIO and the Steelworkers to ask that the AFL-CIO refrain from filing an *amicus* brief, but he could not change their minds, according to *Tough Liberal*, a biography of Shanker by Richard Kahlenberg.[128] NEA joined in a separate *amicus* brief with nine other unions, some of them AFL-CIO affiliates, in support of the validity, not just of the contract, but of affirmative action itself.[129]

Writing for a five-justice majority, Justice William Brennan said that it would be absurd to read Title VII, a law aimed at ending discrimination against African Americans, as a bar against reasonable affirmative action agreements that addressed such discrimination. The Supreme Court reversed the appeals court ruling, sustained the agreement, and established that voluntary affirmative action agreements were valid even where there was no finding by a court of past discrimination.[130]

Affirmative action in layoffs was the next—and most difficult—aspect of this issue to come before the U.S. Supreme Court. *Firefighters Local Union No. 1784 v. Stotts* stemmed from a court-approved consent decree reached after black firefighters in Memphis, Tennessee, sued the city over racial discrimination in hiring and promotions. The city agreed that 50 percent of new hires and 20 percent of those promoted would be African American, until the department's work force reached the same percentages as those in the population of Shelby County, which includes Memphis.[131]

When layoffs became necessary in May 1981, the city followed the last-hired, first-fired policy contained in the contract between the firefighters' union and the city. Because adherence to that layoff policy would have undone several years of progress in integrating the work force, a federal district court issued an injunction, ordering that black firefighters not be disproportionately laid off. The U.S. Court of Appeals for the Sixth Circuit affirmed the injunction.

The firefighters' union then asked the U.S. Supreme Court to review the case and to uphold the seniority provisions of its collective-bargaining agreement. The Leadership Conference on Civil Rights, of which NEA was a member, filed an *amicus* brief on the affirmative action side.

In June 1984, the U.S. Supreme Court overturned the lower courts, holding that because the consent decree dealt only with hiring and promotions and did not address the question of layoffs, the city was under no obligation to conduct layoffs in any other way than the seniority system contained in the collective-bargaining agreement.[132]

At the RA held in Minneapolis shortly after the decision came out, a delegate asked from the floor if Chanin would explain the Memphis firefighters' case to the assembly. In particular, the delegate wanted to know whether the ruling opened the door to court challenges to affirmative action provisions in collective-bargaining agreements negotiated by NEA affiliates. Because the question was not germane to the business before the delegates at that moment, NEA President Mary Futrell, who was chairing the assembly, said that she would call on Chanin to answer the delegate's question at an appropriate point before the RA ended.

That point was not reached until the last hour of the last session, just before delegates would be asked to approve the budget for the coming year. It was July 4, and the attendees were eager for adjournment after days of sitting through a lengthy agenda.

Normally, answers to delegates' questions were succinct, but Chanin never really observed that rule. He had a special relationship with the delegates, and many enjoyed hearing him speak so much that they made up questions to bring the general counsel to the podium. In fact, some were taken aback at the 2002 RA when Chanin could not answer a query from the floor. The question was put to then-President Bob Chase as to whether any federal laws would be broken if a United States citizen attended a medical school in Cuba, which was subject to various U.S. diplomatic and trade restrictions. "You got me," Chase told the delegate. "I'm not sure where general counsel is right now—here he comes."[133]

Chase stepped away from the microphone to repeat the question to Chanin, who whispered his reply to the president. "General counsel is unsure," a surprised Chase told the assembly. "He would have to check the laws on that. He does not—believe it or not . . . I want you to know what his answer was. You are going to love it, folks. His answer was, 'How the hell do I know?' I don't know how long it has been since I have been coming to these conventions, but someone finally stumped him!"[134]

Chanin was rarely stumped, however and in explaining the Memphis firefighters' case at the 1984 RA, he pointed out that the Supreme Court's decision was more than 22,000 words long, covering a series of complex legal issues. It was made more complicated because even members of the Court who agreed on the overall outcome issued separate opinions to explain their reasoning. Chanin wanted the delegates to understand the reasoning of the court and the ramifications for local associations' collective-bargaining agreements.[135]

He spoke for quite a while. When he completed his remarks, he received a very enthusiastic ovation, and some observers later suggested that the delegates may have been applauding not so much the brilliance of his explanation as the fact that he had finished. When Futrell called on the next speaker, NEA Vice President Keith Geiger, to present the NEA budget, Geiger began by saying, "I don't think the budget is going to take as long as the last speaker," which generated another spirited round of applause.[136]

When the RA was over, NEA leaders and staff made up a large contingent on a flight back to Washington. Giving his usual patter to welcome everyone on board, the pilot said over the public address system, "Our normal flight time today is two hours and twenty-five minutes—but it may take us three hours or more because we've asked Bob Chanin to explain the Memphis firefighters' case."

NEA leaders and staff burst into laughter, especially the staff person from the NEA Communications Department who had put the pilot up to it. The other passengers, on the other hand, had not the faintest idea what the pilot was talking about.

The issues at stake were serious, though, and they came before the Supreme Court again just two years later—this time in *Wygant v. Jackson Board of Education*, a case involving an NEA local affiliate, the Jackson Education Association (JEA) in Michigan.[137]

In an effort to address the effects of past discrimination, JEA and the school district in Jackson, a town about 80 miles west of Detroit, negotiated an affirmative action layoff provision guaranteeing that, "at no time will a greater percentage of minority personnel be laid off than the current percentage of minority personnel employed at the time of the layoff."

When a recession in 1981 made layoffs necessary, the school district complied with the contract and preserved the percentage of minorities in the teacher work force. More senior white teachers who had been laid off then challenged the layoff procedure on several grounds, including as an alleged violation of the Equal Protection Clause. The white teachers named both the school district and JEA as defendants. The federal district court rejected the white teachers' claim, as did the U.S. Court of Appeals for the Sixth Circuit. The U.S. Supreme Court then agreed to review the case.

The debate within NEA over whether it should file an *amicus* brief was heated and divisive. Some affiliates in the large industrial states argued strongly that NEA must put the principle of seniority ahead of the need for affirmative action.[138]

It would have been easy for NEA to quell the internal controversy by staying out of the case, since it was not a party. Chanin, however, urged NEA leaders to authorize him to file an *amicus* brief in support of affirmative action. JEA had already made the choice to negotiate affirmative action into its collective-bargaining agreement, and by supporting the local's position, NEA would be upholding two key principles that converged: the need for affirmative action, and the integrity of the union contract.[139]

NEA did decide to file a brief, which Chanin wrote on behalf of the

Association and a group of state affiliates. It was the only union to file in the case in favor of affirmative action.[140] AFT filed an *amicus* brief that took the opposite view, urging the Supreme Court to overturn the affirmative action provision of the agreement negotiated between the local association and the school district.[141]

NEA's brief argued that while the seniority principle provides an objective and equitable standard on which to base employment decisions, the validity of that principle is "not absolute," and must be balanced against other goals, including preserving progress made under affirmative action programs to address past discrimination and achieve a racially diverse faculty.

The brief pointed out that this case was different from *Weber* and some other cases in which equity for employees was the only issue. In school cases like this one, the interests of the students were also at stake. An integrated faculty enhanced the education of black and white students alike and created the opportunity for greater racial harmony and understanding among teachers and parents as well.

It made no sense, NEA's brief continued, for the Supreme Court to approve affirmative action programs in hiring and promotions but then reject them for layoff procedures designed to preserve gains already made. "Hiring and layoffs are opposite sides of the same coin," NEA pointed out.[142]

The Supreme Court did not agree. In May 1986, the Court ruled five to four, that the layoff procedure to which the local education association and school board had agreed was unconstitutional. Justice Lewis Powell wrote an opinion in favor of overturning the agreement that was joined by Chief Justice Warren Burger and Justice William Rehnquist. Justices Sandra Day O'Connor and Byron White, while agreeing with Justice Powell on the outcome, wrote their own opinions to give their reasoning.

"While hiring goals impose a diffuse burden, often foreclosing only one of several opportunities, layoffs impose the entire burden of achieving racial equality on particular individuals, often resulting in serious disruption of their lives," Justice Powell wrote in the majority opinion. "That burden is too intrusive. We therefore hold that, as a means of accomplishing purposes that otherwise may be legitimate, the Board's layoff plan is not sufficiently narrowly tailored. Other, less intrusive means of accomplishing similar purposes—such as the adoption of hiring goals—are available. For these reasons, the Board's selection of layoffs as the means to accomplish even a valid purpose cannot satisfy the demands of the Equal Protection Clause."[143]

When another potential landmark case involving layoffs of NEA members began to make its way through the federal courts, NEA and its civil rights allies played the unusual role of taking coordinated, strategic action to prevent the U.S. Supreme Court from making a decision that might set what they viewed as a devastatingly bad precedent.[144]

The case began in May 1989, when the school board in Piscataway, New Jersey, needed to lay off one of the ten teachers in the business education department of the district's lone high school. Under New Jersey law, teacher layoffs must be based on seniority, but the two most junior teachers in that department had begun their employment on the same day, eight years earlier. The board examined the two teachers' records, looking for grounds to break the tie. Both Debra Williams, who was black, and Sharon Taxman, who was white, had bachelor's degrees. In addition, Williams had a master's degree in business education. The school board decided to retain Williams and lay off Taxman. The board said that it was keeping Williams because, as the only African American teacher in the business education department, she contributed to the important educational goal of promoting racial diversity.[145]

The Equal Employment Opportunity Commission, under the administration of President George H.W. Bush, sued the school board, alleging a violation of Title VII. Taxman intervened as a plaintiff, and was represented by Stephen Klausner, an attorney who often did work for the New Jersey Education Association (NJEA), NEA's state affiliate. In 1993, a federal district court ruled in Taxman's favor and awarded her $144,000 in back pay and damages for some two years of work that she had missed. (By the time the decision was handed down, she had been recalled from layoff.)

In 1996, the U.S. Court of Appeals for the Third Circuit affirmed the district court decision, ruling that maintaining faculty diversity was not a legal justification for affirmative action. The school district asked the U.S. Supreme Court to review the case, and it agreed to do so.[146]

The likelihood that the Supreme Court would affirm the Third Circuit's decision and sharply limit the use of affirmative action set off alarm bells within NEA and the community of civil rights advocates. Such a ruling by the Supreme Court would apply in all federal courts, while the Third Circuit's decision applied only in the three states that circuit covered: New Jersey, Delaware, and Pennsylvania.[147]

As Chanin noted in a speech about the case a year later, there were several troubling facts that made the Piscataway case a less-than-ideal test of affirmative action. For one thing, race was not simply one factor in the school board's decision to lay off a white teacher; it was the dispositive factor. Secondly, the Piscataway school board had dug its affirmative action policy out of mothballs to apply in the case, and the school district was seeking to maintain racial diversity in a single high school academic department when the overall racial balance on its faculty was adequate. Finally, he noted, this case involved not a hiring or promotion decision but a layoff, and the white teacher lost her job solely on the basis of race.[148]

The first decision NEA had to make was whether to file an *amicus* brief, and, if so, on which side. NEA's state affiliate in New Jersey did not want NEA to intervene on the side of affirmative action. It did not want any ruling that possibly could be used to allow racial diversity to trump seniority in future situations.[149] The 1997 RA, however, reaffirmed the Association's commitment to affirmative action when it adopted the "NEA Policy Statement Regarding Use of Affirmative Action for Ethnic Minorities and Women in Educational Employment." In the policy statement, based on a committee report largely written by Chanin, NEA reaffirmed "its strong support for the use of affirmative action in educational employment," not only "to cure effects of past" discrimination, but also "to achieve or maintain ethnic or gender diversity in an educational employer's workforce."[150]

In response to the RA's action, NEA did file an *amicus* brief urging the Supreme Court to overturn the Third Circuit's "sweeping" and "categorical" ban on affirmative action in order to achieve or maintain a racially diverse faculty.[151]

In the fall of 1997, Chanin and Norman Chachkin of the NAACP

Legal Defense and Educational Fund took the lead in discussions among their groups, the National Urban League, and other organizations about raising money to help the school district, Taxman, and the U.S. Department of Justice settle the case before the Supreme Court could rule. The prospects for such a settlement were enhanced by the fact that President Bill Clinton's administration now controlled the Justice Department and was not eager to see an anti-affirmative action precedent established by the nation's highest court.[152]

With assistance from civil rights advocate Jesse Jackson and many others, a coalition of groups, including NEA, raised $300,000 that, together with Piscataway school district funds, made possible a $433,000 settlement covering Taxman's back pay, damages, and legal fees. The Supreme Court was notified that the case had been settled. The High Court granted the parties' request to withdraw the pending appeal, and a damaging precedent was avoided.[153]

"I think the settlement move by the coalition was somewhat unusual," U.S. Representative John Lewis (D-Georgia), a veteran civil rights leader, told reporters at the time. "But I think they were being realistic, knowing the conservative makeup of this Supreme Court."[154]

Conservative groups were upset that they were losing just such an opportunity to scale back affirmative action. "We believe [the settlement] indicates the desperation and weakness of pro-affirmative action groups," said William Mellor, the president of the Institute for Justice, a Washington organization that was also deeply involved in efforts to enact legislation supporting private school vouchers. "They know the law is against them. They sought to postpone the inevitable day of reckoning."[155]

The settlement of the case was also somewhat of a disappointment for Sharon Taxman's lawyer, Stephen Klausner. Although he and his client won compensation, Klausner lost what would have been his first opportunity to argue before the U.S. Supreme Court. Because the case had been set for oral argument, Klausner had bought an expensive new suit to wear for the big day. As a consolation after the settlement, Chanin offered Klausner the chance to wear his new suit and make his argument before a moot court at a meeting of NOLEA. Klausner went head-to-head with the lawyer for the Piscataway school district, David

Rubin. (Not the same David Rubin who had been Chanin's deputy general counsel at NEA.) The arguments were heard by a distinguished panel of judges made up of Abner Mikva, a former member of the U.S. Court of Appeals for the District of Columbia Circuit and later a White House counsel to President Clinton; Ruth McGregor, a justice on the Arizona Supreme Court; and Robert Durham, a member of the Oregon Supreme Court. The stakes were much lower than they would have been had the venue been the U.S. Supreme Court, and Chanin recalled later that, although the moot court critiqued the attorneys' presentations, it rendered no decision on the deeply divisive affirmative action dispute.

The Supreme Court continued, meanwhile, to refine and narrow the remedies that might be used to address racial discrimination, ruling in two closely related student admissions cases in which Chanin filed *amicus* briefs on behalf of NEA and 39 state affiliates. In its decision in *Gratz v. Bollinger*, issued in June 2003, the Court rejected an affirmative action program for undergraduate admissions at the University of Michigan because the program automatically awarded points in the selection process to every minority applicant. On the same day, in *Grutter v. Bollinger*, the Court upheld an affirmative action program for admissions at the University of Michigan Law School because it required individual assessments of applicants on many factors, only one of which was their ability to contribute to the diversity of the learning environment.[156]

While NEA and other supporters of affirmative action saw the *Grutter* decision as a major victory for the basic concept of affirmative action in education, the ruling in *Gratz* had troubling implications for the future. On the surface, the principle that affirmative action programs should consider people as individuals and not solely as part of a larger group sounded reasonable. And, indeed, individualized assessments might work in the context of law school admissions where the number of applicants is not huge and each application has to be carefully reviewed. But such assessments may not be feasible to achieve diversity in large institutions such as school districts in big cities.[157]

Moreover, as Chanin noted in remarks delivered within weeks of the *Grutter* and *Gratz* decisions, questions remained about whether a racially diverse student body constitutes a compelling state interest only in higher education, or also in elementary and secondary education, and "whether school districts can use race in setting school attendance zones, in student admissions to magnet schools and other special programs, and in student assignments and transfers."[158]

Those questions would come before the U.S. Supreme Court just three years later when legal challenges to voluntary, race-conscious student assignment plans adopted by the Seattle School District in Washington and the Jefferson County school district in Kentucky, reached the High Court. Both districts were concerned that their schools had become highly segregated. It is an unfortunate fact that if the makeup of the student body at a school is determined solely by neighborhood demographics, then schools will be segregated by race because most neighborhoods are.[159]

To avoid such racial segregation, both districts voluntarily developed student assignment plans aimed at increasing racial diversity. The Seattle policy allowed students to attend the school of their choice, but used race as one of several tiebreakers for popular schools if it would help bring the school closer to the district's average racial composition. A similar program at issue in the Jefferson County case was designed to keep the black student enrollment between 15 and 50 percent of the total enrollment at most of the county's schools.[160]

The two programs were challenged by white parents, but were upheld in 2005 by the U.S. Courts of Appeals for the Sixth Circuit for the Jefferson County plan, and the Ninth Circuit for the Seattle plan. When the U.S. Supreme Court agreed to review those decisions, NEA filed a lengthy *amicus* brief written by Chanin and others supporting the school districts' race-conscious assignment plans. A host of other organizations also signed on to NEA's *amicus* brief, including the AFL-CIO, AFT, and 43 of NEA's state affiliates.[161]

The NEA brief cited a substantial body of empirical research demonstrating that "students who learn to interact with students of other races in school are far more likely to function effectively in a racially diverse environment and to promote cross-racial understanding in later life than are students who do not have such interactions. . . . The impact of encountering and dealing with racial diversity as part of their education is positively linked to growth in cognitive and academic skills of both racial minority and white students. These educational benefits are realized not only while children are in school, but in their subsequent lives as well."[162]

In June 2007, the Supreme Court issued a consolidated, five-to-four decision covering the two cases, *Parents Involved in Community Schools v. Seattle School District No. 1* and *Meredith v. Jefferson County Public Schools*. The majority stated that both voluntary school desegregation plans violated the Equal Protection Clause of the Fourteenth Amendment. Chief Justice John Roberts, who had been appointed by President George W. Bush in 2005 upon the death of Chief Justice William Rehnquist, wrote the main, plurality opinion and was joined by Justices Samuel Alito, who had replaced Justice Sandra Day O'Connor in 2006, Justice Antonin Scalia, and Justice Clarence Thomas. Justice Anthony Kennedy wrote a concurring opinion, disagreeing with some of Roberts' reasoning but providing the fifth and deciding vote for the Roberts outcome. Justices Stephen Breyer, Ruth Bader Ginsburg, David Souter, and John Paul Stevens were in the minority, voting to uphold the race-conscious programs.[163]

"To invalidate the plans under review is to threaten the promise of *Brown*," Justice Breyer said in a reference to the court's 1954 ruling in *Brown v. Board of Education*. "This is a decision that the court and the nation will come to regret."[164]

In Chief Justice Roberts's view, the beneficial impact of the school districts' diversity programs was not relevant because it was a violation of the federal Constitution to use race as a factor in deciding which school a student will attend. He concluded that the school systems' evidence that only a small number of students were affected was a further reason not to allow the race-conscious plans. "The minimal impact of the districts' racial classifications on school enrollment casts doubt on the necessity of using such classifications," Roberts said.[165]

Most legal scholars viewed Justice Kennedy's concurrence as the controlling opinion in the case, since it was at the center between the court's conservative and liberal blocs and provided the fifth vote for the outcome of the case.

Kennedy did not wholly cast his vote with either bloc. He said that achieving a broadly defined diverse student population and avoiding racial isolation could be constitutionally valid goals for a voluntary student assignment plan if the plan were narrowly tailored. And he emphasized that the Court's decision "should not prevent school districts from continuing the important work of bringing together students of different racial, ethnic, and economic backgrounds." To be lawful, he said, such a plan must "address the problem in a general way and without treating each student in a different fashion solely on the basis of a systematic, individual typing by race." He gave as examples of approaches that might be constitutional: "strategic site selection of new schools, drawing attendance zones with general recognition of the demographics of neighborhoods, allocating resources for special programs, recruiting students and faculty in a targeted fashion, and tracking enrollments, performance, and other statistics by race. These mechanisms are race conscious but do not lead to different treatment based on a classification that tells each student he or she is to be defined by race."[166]

After the *Seattle/Jefferson County* decision was issued, Chanin prepared a memorandum for NEA leaders pointing out that Justice Kennedy's controlling opinion indicated alternative measures that school districts could adopt lawfully to promote student diversity in schools. He worked with other organizations to devise plans that could be used to achieve diverse student bodies and would pass muster in the federal courts. Subsequently, there have been strong indications that such efforts can succeed. Two courts in 2009 upheld student assignment plans that use proxies for race to maintain integrated schools. In August 2009, the federal district court in the ongoing Jefferson County lawsuit approved the school district's student assignment plan that was revised after the Supreme Court's ruling, rejecting a lawsuit by two disgruntled families. The revised plan uses economic status to promote student diversity by requiring that between 15 and 50 percent of a school's enrollment come from a neighborhood where the average household income is below $41,000. In March 2009, a California state appeals court upheld a school diversity plan adopted by the Berkeley Unified School District that uses the demographics of a student's residential neighborhood to make student assignment decisions. The demographic factors that the court said could lawfully be considered include the average household income in the neighborhood, the average education level of adults residing in the neighborhood, and the racial composition of the neighborhood as a whole.[167]

As these rulings make clear, the *Seattle/Jefferson County* decision does not prevent school districts from taking effective measures to achieve and maintain fully integrated schools. And, indeed, NEA remains committed to the principles that students should be exposed to different people, cultures, and ideas and that learning in a racially diverse setting strengthens student performance and promotes positive social interaction among people of different backgrounds.[168]

As a result of the broad civil rights movement of which NEA has been a vital part, a great deal has changed in America since Chanin first became involved in equal justice issues more than 40 years ago. His daughter, Lisa, and her African American husband, Lee, have three biracial children. His son, Jeff, and Jeff's wife, Susan, have two children adopted from China. The world that those grandchildren are growing up in is far different from the one Chanin knew as a boy in New York. Although there are more opportunities, more tolerance, and more value given to diversity, there is still much more needed to address racial injustice and discrimination. Every time he has gone to the U.S. Supreme Court building in Washington, he has passed under the motto etched in stone over its entrance: "Equal Justice Under Law." And each visit has been a reminder to him that while America has made great progress toward racial equality, it still has a long way to go to fully achieve that lofty goal.

Bob with his older brother, Irv, on Thanksgiving Day, 1950.

Bob's parents, Frank and Irene Chanin (1955).

Rhoda Paley and Bob at Bob's Brooklyn
College graduation (1956). They married the
following June.

William Carr, NEA Executive Secretary from 1952 to 1967, embodied NEA's "old guard." A prestigious leader of the education establishment, Carr believed in "professionalism not unionism."

Sam Lambert addressing the NEA staff on his first day as Executive Secretary (August 1, 1967). While conflicted over the direction of the Association, he presided over some of the most significant changes in NEA's history during his five-year tenure.

Allan West, a quiet yet driving force behind NEA's transformation, became the Association's Interim Executive Secretary in 1972, serving until 1973.

The NEA staff leadership in 1972. Top Row (left to right) Glen Robinson, Sam Ethridge, Stan McFarland, Bob Chanin, Gary Watts, Margaret Stevenson, John Sullivan, Richard Carpenter, John Lumley, Lyle Ashby. Bottom Row (left to right)Tom McLernon, Laurence Derthick, Sam Lambert, Allan West, James Becker

Don Wollett, Chanin's mentor at the Kaye Scholer law firm and his coauthor of *The Law and Practice of Teacher Negotiations*. The most comprehensive guide to collective bargaining in the education sector, the book was hailed as the essential resource by some. To others, it was "the mein kampf of teacher unionism."

The New Breed: Terry Herndon, NEA Executive Director from 1973 to 1983, brought an aggressive commitment to organizing, collective bargaining, and political action.

Credit: Published with permission of the NEA Archives

In the trenches: Chanin and New Jersey Education Association field director Jack Bertolino appearing before the New Jersey Public Employment Relations Board (1972).

Stratford Teachers Contract Signed

Credit: Connecticut Post

Chanin negotiated the first teacher collective-bargaining agreement in Stratford, Connecticut, in 1964. Stratford was a "lighthouse district" in the quest for collective bargaining, and the agreement became a model for other locals to follow.

Chanin helped draft and lobby for the enactment of state teacher bargaining laws in Connecticut, Hawaii, Illinois, Maryland, Massachusetts, Minnesota, New Jersey, New York, Pennsylvania, Rhode Island and Vermont. The laws became the models for other states across the country.

The recognized expert on public employee collective bargaining, Chanin crisscrossed the country advocating for education employee bargaining rights. Pictured: Chanin addressing the 1970 National Conference of State Legislative Leaders in Honolulu, Hawaii.

The 1968 campaign for collective bargaining in Manchester, New Hampshire, brought an all-out response from the vehemently anti-labor *Manchester Union Leader*, which repeatedly portrayed Chanin as an outside "invader" and a threat to the community. Rather than hurting Chanin, these attacks solidified his role and support for workers' rights.

Another cartoon from the *Manchester Union Leader*.

Despite its long history of staunch independence from the rest of organized labor, NEA embarked on a new path of collaboration with other unions in 1973 with the formation of the Coalition of American Public Employees (CAPE). Pictured: CAPE press conference advocating a national public employee collective-bargaining law (from left to right: International Association of Fire Fighters President William McClennan; NEA Interim Executive Secretary Allan West; American Federation of State, County and Municipal Employees President Jerry Wurf; NEA President Catherine Barrett, and AFSCME Secretary-Treasurer William Lucy. (March 8, 1973).

Albert Shanker, president of the American Federation of Teachers from 1974 until his death in 1997. NEA and the AFT have had a complex relationship over the past 50 years: fierce competitors at times; strong allies at others.

Bringing black and white together. American Teachers Association President R.J. Martin and NEA President Richard D. Batchelder (seated) seal the merger between the two organizations in 1966. With them (standing left to right) are ATA Executive Secretary Joseph T. Brooks, NEA Executive Secretary William Carr, and ATA President-elect Hudson L. Barksdale. "Outstretched hands must extend on all sides if this unity is to become a reality," NEA told its members.

Forty years of unity were recognized when the Alabama Education Association's Paul Hubbert and Joe Reed received NEA's H. Councill Trenholm Memorial Award for their work in expanding educational opportunities and enhancing civil rights. Hubbert and Reed forged the merger of the black and white Alabama associations in 1969 and have led the affiliate ever since.

NEA entered U.S. presidential politics for the first time when it endorsed Jimmy Carter in 1976. NEA's director of government relations Stan McFarland, Bob Chanin, Irma Kramer, and Jimmy Williams at the White House in 1978.

Bob Chanin and NEA Executive Director Don Cameron drink champagne on the morning of "the Great Race." In exchange for pledges to NEA's political action committee, the pair had agreed to run in a race during the 1984 Representative Assembly in Minneapolis. But they arranged for surrogates to take their places in the race, and Chanin and Cameron watched from the sidelines in their white tie and tails.

In a major National Press Club speech in February 1997, NEA President Robert Chase called for NEA to reinvent itself and embark on a "new unionism." The speech set off a nationwide debate on the relationship between collective bargaining, employee rights, and education reform.

Bob Chanin arguing the private school voucher case before the Wisconsin Supreme Court on March 4, 1998. Although he usually advanced legal arguments over policy ones, this day Chanin made an exception to respond to what he considered voucher proponents' portrayal of him and NEA as "the bad guys."

Bob Chanin outside the Wisconsin Supreme Court with Clint Bolick, his frequent adversary in legal battles over private school vouchers. Bolick has described Chanin as "the quintessential obnoxious labor lawyer," but also as "a masterful orator" and one who "represents his clients with zeal."

Bob Chanin speaks to reporters outside the U.S. Supreme Court after arguing against the constitutionality of the Cleveland voucher program (February 20, 2002). It was the last of Chanin's five oral arguments before the high court.

AFL-CIO President John Sweeney (left) and NEA President Reg Weaver sign the NEA/AFL-CIO Labor Solidarity Partnership Agreement in February 2007. By 2010, more than 30,000 NEA members were also members of the AFL-CIO.

Bob Chanin gives his farewell address to the 2009 NEA Representative Assembly in San Diego. Chanin told delegates that NEA and its affiliates had been targeted for criticism because "they are the most effective unions in the United States."

The general counsel and NEA Vice President Lily Eskelsen show T-shirts for the "Bob Chanin Caucus" at the 2009 Representative Assembly. The shirts were first presented at the 2008 RA by the New Jersey delegation. "Show Us Your Amicus Briefs" playfully refers to the many "friend-of-the-court" briefs filed by Chanin in cases with stakes for NEA.

Bob Chanin and NEA President Dennis Van Roekel at the 2009 Representative Assembly. "When all is said and done, NEA and its affiliates must never lose sight of the fact that they are unions—and what unions do first and foremost is represent their members," Chanin said in his farewell speech.

Bob and Rhoda Chanin gathered with their children and grandchildren when the main auditorium at NEA's Washington headquarters was named for Bob on December 12, 2009, soon before he retired after 41 years as general counsel.

The Chanin grandchildren: (from left) Margo, Cara, Frankie, Max, and Jayne.

THE
AMERICAN LAWYER

May 2000

Blackboard Jungle

Barnstorming with
the school voucher
litigation road show

By Alison Frankel

The Phony Case
Against Al Gore

By Roger Parloff

Robert Chanin, for
the teachers union

PLUS

• Headnotes: Stop Hiring
First-Year Associates!

• Net Clients from Hell

• How Dow Jones
Averted Disaster

• The Real *Roe* Story

Bob Chanin on cover of *The American Lawyer* magazine, May 2000.

Part III |

Give Me Liberty

"I have never brought my private life into the classroom—my sexuality or any other part of my private life into the classroom—or discussed sexuality with any of my students . . . But the fact is that I'm gay, just like the fact is that other teachers are straight or heterosexual . . . I have every right to be what I am. I have every right to be a teacher. And I plan on doing both."
—*Joe Acanfora on "60 Minutes," February 25, 1973*[1]

"Irremedial and immoral conduct outside the state of lawful matrimony in a manner which has been open and notorious . . . [makes you] not qualified to teach, and your dismissal is in the best interests of the school."
—*Hawthorn, Illinois School District dismissal notice to Jeanne Eckmann, unwed teacher who refused to have an abortion or put her child up for adoption when she became pregnant, January 18, 1982*[2]

"What does NEA profess to stand for and what is it willing to do to defend its principles? Phrased otherwise, how large a gap is tolerable between what we say and what we do— between our words and our deeds?"
—*Bob Chanin, speaking to NEA's Oklahoma state affiliate, December 15, 1984*[3]

Chapter 6

Out of the Closet and Into the Classroom

In late August 1972, a recent college graduate named Joe Acanfora started his first teaching job at a junior high school in Montgomery County, Maryland, the suburb of Washington where Bob Chanin and his family lived. The first month went smoothly for Acanfora, who was well liked by the students in his science classes and by the other members of the faculty.

Then, on September 25, he received a letter from the deputy superintendent of schools, saying that he was being removed immediately from his classroom duties. His transgression was not that his teaching was ineffective or that he was breaking any school rules, but rather, that the school district had just learned that he was gay.[4]

In the social and political atmosphere of America in 1972 there was little acceptance of people who acknowledged themselves as gay. There had never been an openly gay elected public official at any level of government—no school board member, no mayor, no governor, no U.S. senator. Harvey Milk, one of the first openly gay elected public officials, would not win election to the San Francisco Board of Supervisors until 1977.[5] One of the first members of Congress to come out of the closet, Representative Barney Frank of Massachusetts, would not do so until 1987. In fact, being gay was still officially considered a mental illness by the American Psychiatric Association, which did not end the classification until 1973.[6] Official policy of the federal government said that gay men and lesbians could not serve in the military at all. No state had a law outlawing discrimination against gay men and lesbians or permitting civil unions, let alone same-sex marriages. There was virtually no court precedent at the federal or state level establishing that a teacher could not be fired for homosexuality.[7]

When Acanfora received the letter, he knew that the odds would be against him if he challenged the school district's action, but he was determined to fulfill his dream of being a science teacher. He had been interested in science from the time he was a young boy in New Jersey and would take his parents outside when thunderstorms were brewing to explain the weather patterns involved in such storms. Valedictorian of his high school class, Acanfora was admitted to Pennsylvania State University, where he planned to study meteorology. Part way through college, however, he decided that becoming a school teacher would be a better use of his interest in science, and he became an education major. He also came out of the closet and joined a campus organization for gay rights.[8]

In the winter of 1972, during his final semester at Penn State, Acanfora started a ten-week assignment at a nearby junior high school, teaching seventh and ninth grade general science and biology. While he was doing his student teaching, the gay rights organization to which he belonged filed a lawsuit challenging the university's refusal to provide the group the same official recognition and campus privileges accorded to other student organizations. The case generated news coverage which mentioned that Acanfora was one of the four plaintiffs. Hence, when the local school district learned from the media that he was gay, it suspended him from his student teaching. Because his suspension would prevent him from becoming a teacher, Acanfora challenged the action in state court. Almost immediately, the court issued an order reinstating him as a student teacher.[9]

After successfully completing his final semester, Acanfora applied for a teaching certificate from the state of Pennsylvania. The dean of the Penn State College of Education refused to sign what was normally a routine form required by the state to confirm that he was of "good moral character." Instead, the college convened a council of six Penn State deans to consider that question. When they met with Acanfora, the dean asked him such questions as, "What homosexual acts do you prefer to engage in or are you willing to engage in?" Following this interrogation, which had no bearing on his ability to teach, the deans deadlocked three to three, leaving to the state secretary of education, John C. Pittenger, the issue of his moral fitness to receive a teaching certificate.[10]

With his Pennsylvania teaching certificate pending, Acanfora was hired by the Montgomery County school district to teach eighth grade earth science, beginning on August 29, 1972. His teaching career got off to a good start, but that would last only a few weeks. On September 21, he received calls from reporters with what should have been good news. Pittenger had scheduled a news conference for the next day to announce that he had decided to give Acanfora his teaching certificate. Realizing that news from that announcement would filter back to his new employer, Acanfora immediately informed his assistant principal. The next day, Pittenger held his news conference, and coverage appeared in the Saturday editions of *The Washington Evening Star* and *The New York Times*.[11]

On September 25, the deputy superintendent notified the Montgomery County school board that Acanfora would be reassigned to a position that would not require "contact with youngsters." The following day, the young teacher was taken out of the classroom and moved to the central office, where he was given busy work such as proofreading. The school district was so concerned that he not have any contact with children that he was warned not to pick up his paychecks at his old school until after school hours, when no students would be present.[12]

No allegation was ever made that Acanfora's performance as a teacher was unsatisfactory or that he had engaged in any inappropriate behavior at school. To the contrary, a majority of teachers at his school signed a petition asking that he be reinstated, saying he was a "highly competent teacher" and that his removal was "unfair, unjust, and unwarranted." The first colleague to sign the petition was his department head. More than fifty of his students signed a petition of support as well.[13]

As a member of the local NEA affiliate that represented the Montgomery County teachers, Acanfora brought the situation to the attention of his union and asked what could be done. The local affiliate, in turn, asked Chanin for advice and assistance.

Chanin immediately recognized that this was an important civil rights case that NEA should pursue, but he also realized that coming to Acanfora's defense would require breaking new ground. NEA had never taken an official position on the rights of gay teachers, and the case would raise new constitutional issues that had never been addressed by the courts.[14]

Chanin and his deputy general counsel, David Rubin, developed a legal theory that the removal from the classroom violated both the freedom of association protections of the First Amendment and the rights to due process and equal protection guaranteed by the Fourteenth Amendment.[15]

The next step was to convince the leaders of NEA and its Maryland state affiliate that NEA should provide Acanfora with legal counsel. Some of those leaders had misgivings, knowing that such action could cause controversy within the organization in the more conservative parts of the state and the country as a whole. To give one indication of the political environment in the state at that time, voters in Maryland's Democratic presidential primary just four months earlier had provided a substantial victory to George Wallace, the Alabama governor who openly appealed to bigotry in his campaigns and who finished ahead of liberals Hubert Humphrey and the eventual nominee, George McGovern. The subject of gays in the classroom was highly sensitive because of fears that homosexual teachers would prey upon students or "recruit" them to be gay. Nonetheless, Chanin was able to get authorization to pursue litigation on Acanfora's behalf.[16]

Chanin also made sure that Acanfora knew what he was getting himself into. The case would draw a great deal of media attention, it might take years to resolve in the courts, and the prospects for success were uncertain at best. Despite the risks and consequences, Acanfora was determined to proceed with the case.[17]

Then, Chanin had to find outside counsel to help. The litigation would be quite time consuming, and NEA's small in-house legal staff consisted only of Chanin, Rubin, and three staff attorneys, who were working at capacity. Kaye Scholer had been doing most of the legal work that NEA farmed out, but in this case a local firm with lawyers on the ground was preferable.[18]

Around this time, Chanin was taking the bus to work one day when he ran into Michael Gottesman, a classmate from Yale Law School whom he had not seen in years. They struck up a conversation, and Gottesman told Chanin that he was working with the firm that would later become known as Bredhoff & Kaiser and that it specialized in labor and constitutional law. Chanin asked Gottesman if he would be interested in working on the Acanfora case. As a result of their conversation the firm was retained and Gottesman and another of its attorneys, George Cohen, worked with the NEA Office of General Counsel on Acanfora's behalf. On November 7, 1972, a complaint against the school district was filed in U.S. district court.[19]

Because the case involved a new social and legal frontier, it attracted major attention in the national media as well as local coverage in the Washington area. Acanfora's parents appeared with him on national public television—not an everyday occurrence in a country in which millions of gays and lesbians chose not to come out to their parents. Discussing on camera how it felt to learn that his son was gay, Acanfora's father, a truck driver and ex-Marine, said simply, "I loved him then, I love him now."[20] On the CBS News program "60 Minutes," one of Acanfora's many student supporters spoke out on his behalf. "He didn't do anything, and he was really a good teacher," the student said. "I don't understand why they took him out." Acanfora pointed out to viewers that he had never discussed his sexuality with any student or teacher and that most had found out only because of the school district's own action in removing him from the classroom. "I have every right to be what I am," he said. "I [also] have every right to be a teacher. And I plan on doing both."[21] In a subsequent newspaper interview, his mother, Lee, said that Joe's courage had inspired her to publicly stand by his side. "When Joe came out of the closet," she said, "I came out of the kitchen."[22]

On April 12, 1973, Acanfora's civil case went to trial before a federal district court in Baltimore. For strategic reasons, Chanin and the outside counsel chose not to exercise the plaintiff's right to request a trial by jury. They believed they had a better chance of persuading a judge on the constitutional issues, and that members of a jury, some of whom might have children in the Montgomery County schools, were likely to be prejudiced against a gay teacher.[23]

By the time of the trial, school system officials had recognized that they might be on shaky legal ground and so they added a new legal defense. For the first time, they claimed that Acanfora was removed from his classroom not just for being a homosexual, but because his students had become aware of his sexual identity through media coverage and interviews he granted regarding his teacher certification, and that this knowledge might lead to disruption at school.[24]

Laying the groundwork for an additional fallback defense, the school district's attorney questioned Acanfora during the trial about the fact that on his employment application he had not listed his involvement in the gay-rights group in a section that asked about an applicant's extracurricular activities in college.

In submitting the employment application, Acanfora had signed a statement that "the information I submitted on this application is accurate to the best of my knowledge. . . . I understand the falsification of any information submitted on this application shall be cause for dismissal from service." Hadn't he violated that pledge, the school district attorney asked, by omitting mention of his participation in the gay-rights group?

No, said Acanfora, he had not falsified any information submitted on the application. "As far as I am concerned," he testified, "everything that is on this application is accurate."

His omission of the gay-rights group affiliation, he testified, "was based primarily on the experience I had just had with the [Pennsylvania] school district. I realized I had just completed four years of training to become a teacher and was judged perfectly qualified; and I realized had I put down the Homophiles of Penn State as an organization or as an extracurricular activity that I would not be given a chance to even go through the normal application process for a teaching job; that I would not be considered on an equal par with all other applicants and, in fact, would guarantee that I would not receive any sort of teaching job. So, I decided not to put it down so that I might be able to be judged on an equal par with everyone else."[25]

In an attempt to buttress its central claim that Acanfora's presence as a teacher in a junior high school classroom would be harmful to students, the school district brought in two highly credentialed expert witnesses, one a pediatrician and child psychiatrist, Dr. Reginald Lourie, who was a professor at the George Washington University Medical School, and the other a pediatrician named Dr. Felix Heald, who was a professor at the University of Maryland Medical School.

Both doctors testified that having a class with a known homosexual teacher would be a hazard to certain boys of junior high school age who were not sure of their sexual identity. This testimony collapsed, however, under questioning from Acanfora's lawyers.

Would it pose a risk just to boys in junior high school, or boys of any age? Both doctors said no risk would be posed to elementary school boys. Dr. Lourie said there would be no hazard in high school either, while Dr. Heald said he was "less certain" about that because some high school boys might still be going through adolescence.

Were all junior high boys at risk? No, said the doctors, just those who are "on the fence" about their sexual identity. Lourie said preventing exposure to known homosexuals was comparable to inoculation programs in which the whole community has to be protected even though only a handful of individuals might be at risk.

Pressed by Acanfora's lawyers for proof from research or their own practical experience and observations, both doctors admitted they could cite no evidence or instance of a junior high school student suffering psychological problems because he knew a teacher was gay.

"I am not saying this is true in the area we are discussing," Dr. Heald conceded under questioning. "I am only raising the issue that the possibility exists and remains so as long as we don't have good information about it. . . . I am suggesting the possibility that it may, in some way, influence them."

Weren't there documented cases of severe anxiety among female students who developed crushes on heterosexual male teachers, even leading in some cases to suicide? Both doctors agreed that there were. Yet, the school district had no policy of removing straight male teachers from all professional contact with female junior high school students.[26]

Acanfora's lawyers called three expert witnesses—all respected professors and practitioners in the field of pediatric psychiatry. They testified for hours about extensive research showing that being taught by a gay teacher was no more likely to be disturbing to a junior high school student uncertain about his sexual identity than being taught by any other teacher. In fact, knowing a capable and effective gay teacher actually might reduce anxieties for gay-leaning students by making them more accepting of their own feelings and more willing to talk with parents and counselors.[27]

On May 31, 1973, U.S. District Judge Joseph Young ruled that Acanfora had been unconstitutionally denied the opportunity to teach not because of his job performance, but because he was gay. In ground-breaking language, the court said that under the due process protections of the Fourteenth Amendment and freedom of association under the First Amendment, "mere knowledge that a teacher is homosexual is not sufficient to justify transfer or dismissal." Judge Young cited the decision that had just been issued that January by the U.S. Supreme Court in *Roe v. Wade*, protecting a woman's right of privacy under the due-process clause of the Fourteenth Amendment, including the right to choose whether to have an abortion. The right of privacy recognized by the high court in *Roe* was not only helpful in this case, but, in the years that followed, would have a huge effect on a wide range of women's rights cases involving NEA members.

"The time has come today," Judge Young said, "for private, consenting, adult homosexuality to enter the sphere of constitutionally protectable interests. . . . Intolerance of the unconventional halts the growth of liberty."[28]

Joe Acanfora and his family should have been able to celebrate the pioneering decision, but the court threw him a devastating curve. Judge Young refused to order Acanfora's reinstatement to the classroom, agreeing with the school district that the teacher's media interviews after his unlawful removal from the classroom "sparked controversy" that might disrupt the school. The court recognized that Acanfora's "controversial" public statements voiced "his opinion of the injustice and discrimination practiced against homosexuals in this country," but found nonetheless that his interviews "were likely to incite or produce imminent effects deleterious to the educational process."[29]

Acanfora appealed to the U.S. Court of Appeals for the Fourth Circuit, arguing that a school district's refusal to reinstate a teacher because of his statements to the news media violated the First Amendment. The appeals court agreed on that point. The media "considered homosexuality in general, and Acanfora's plight in particular, to be a matter of public interest about which reasonable people could differ, and Acanfora responded to their inquiries in a rational manner," the appeals court found. "There is no evidence that the interviews disrupted the school, substantially impaired his capacity as a teacher, or gave the school officials reasonable grounds to forecast that these results would flow from what he said." The appellate judges also upheld Judge Young's finding that a teacher could not be taken out of the classroom just for being gay. Acanfora was two for two on those core issues.

To Acanfora's huge disappointment, however, the appeals court found merit in the school district's fallback claim that failing to list the gay-rights group on his employment application as a collegiate extracurricular activity violated his signed pledge that "the information I submitted on this application is accurate to the best of my knowledge." Even though Acanfora had been removed unconstitutionally for being gay and then denied reinstatement in violation of the First Amendment, the court ruled that he was not entitled to get his teaching job back.[30]

Acanfora filed an appeal seeking Supreme Court review, but the justices declined to take the case, letting the appeals court ruling stand without comment.

Like the pioneering black plaintiffs NEA had supported in other civil rights cases, Joe Acanfora had established a constitutional principle that would lead to slow, gradual progress for millions of Americans: a teacher, or indeed any public employee, could not be fired because he or she was a homosexual. National media coverage of the case helped build public awareness of the gay rights issue. The case also set NEA on a path of defending the rights of gay teachers that has continued to this day, and sent a strong signal to school boards that they could face lengthy and costly litigation if they discriminated against gay employees. It was an issue for which not everyone in the Association had shown the same enthusiasm, Chanin recalled, but it was one which NEA could not duck. It had to be a leader, he believed.[31]

Yet, Acanfora himself would not be able to enjoy the benefits of his pioneering legal stand. Given the climate of the times, he did not believe he could resume his teaching career somewhere else. He eventually moved to the west coast, where he was employed in a non-teaching job in a technology office at the University of California. To this day, he continues to be active in gay-rights organizations.[32]

In the years that followed, right-wing groups targeted gay teachers in their offensive against what they saw as the cultural liberalization that had begun in America in the 1960s. The "culture war" they mounted also concerned such issues as abortion, affirmative action, and prayer in the public schools, but some of the earliest and strongest attacks were reserved for the supposed threat posed by having gay teachers in the classroom.[33]

In 1977, a national celebrity spokesperson emerged for their cause. Anita Bryant was a former Miss Oklahoma and Miss America runner-up. A mildly successful recording artist, she sang the national anthem at a Super Bowl, as well as the "Battle Hymn of the Republic" at President Lyndon Johnson's funeral. She later was hired by the Florida orange juice industry to appear in national television commercials pitching their products.[34]

But Bryant became a true household name when she emerged as the national spokeswoman for the opponents of gay rights. In 1977, Dade County, Florida, which includes Miami, passed an ordinance prohibiting discrimination against gays and lesbians in housing, employment, and public accommodations. Abetted by the Reverend Jerry Falwell and other right-wing leaders, Bryant helped to persuade Dade County voters to overturn the gay rights ordinance through a popular referendum. Her well-financed "Save Our Children" campaign moved on to bring about the repeal of similar ordinances in St. Paul, Minnesota; Wichita, Kansas; and Eugene, Oregon.[35]

Emboldened by that success, right-wing activists targeted gay public school teachers in California, the nation's most populous state. John Briggs, a Republican leader in the state senate who had aspirations for higher office, sponsored an initiative called Proposition 6 on the November 1978 ballot. This proposition would require the dismissal of any school employee who was found to be "advocating, soliciting, imposing, encouraging, or promoting private or public homosexual activity directed at, or likely to come to the attention of, schoolchildren and/or other employees."[36]

Early polls showed that Proposition 6 would win easily as voters were inundated with dire warnings about the dangers of gay teachers "recruiting children" to a "homosexual lifestyle" or even to become their sexual partners.[37] William Bennett, a college professor who later would be appointed U.S. secretary of education by President Ronald Reagan, wrote a widely quoted article titled "The Homosexual Teacher," which argued that "overt" gays and lesbians should not be allowed to work in the public schools.[38]

Although Prop 6's backers did not lack for resources, voter opinion began to turn as Election Day approached. NEA and its affiliate, the California Teachers Association, spoke out against the proposition. Harvey Milk, by then a member of the San Francisco Board of Supervisors, traveled throughout the state, debating Briggs wherever he could. He also urged the state's gays and lesbians, the vast majority of whom were still in the closet, to come out to their families, friends, and co-workers, believing that voters would be more likely to oppose Prop 6 if they saw it as an attack on people they knew and cared about.[39]

Opponents of Prop 6 found an important ally in Reagan, then the governor of California. A former actor, Reagan had gay friends in Hollywood, and he denounced the measure. "Homosexuality is not a contagious disease like the measles," he noted. "Prevailing scientific opinion is that an individual's sexuality is determined at a very early age and that a child's teachers do not really influence this."[40]

When the votes were counted, defenders of gay rights won an amazing comeback victory as Prop 6 was defeated by a two-to-one margin.[41]

Having lost in California, the right wing tried to rebuild momentum in a friendlier political environment—Anita Bryant's home state of Oklahoma. In 1978, the legislature enacted a law that used much of the same wording as California's Prop 6, and would, according to the state's attorney general, "remove 'gay rights' activists from teaching."[42]

The Oklahoma law had two sections, one dealing with teachers' conduct and the other with their speech. The first section provided that no teacher, student teacher, or teacher's aide could engage in "public homosexual activity." The second section provided that they could not engage in "advocating, encouraging, or promoting public or private homosexual activity in a manner that creates a substantial risk that such conduct will come to the attention of school children or school employees."[43]

The National Gay Task Force filed suit in federal district court, challenging both sections under the First Amendment, but the court upheld the law. The case then went to the U.S. Court of Appeals for the Tenth Circuit, which also upheld the first section barring teachers' public homosexual activity. But the appeals court reversed the lower court decision regarding the second section, ruling that the prohibition against "advocating, encouraging or promoting" homosexual activity violated the First Amendment. The court emphasized that the statute would prohibit a broad category of protected speech and would bar, for example, a teacher from going before the legislature or appearing on television to urge the repeal of Oklahoma's anti-sodomy statute. "Such statements, which are aimed at legal and social change, are at the core of First Amendment protections," the Tenth Circuit court said.[44]

The National Gay Task Force decided not to ask the U.S. Supreme Court to review the case. The appeals court ruling upholding the prohibition on teachers' public homosexual activity applied only to such laws that might be passed in the six states covered by the Tenth Circuit (Colorado, Kansas, Oklahoma, New Mexico, Utah, and Wyoming), while an affirmation of that ruling by the Supreme Court would establish a national precedent.[45]

The Oklahoma City Board of Education, however, filed its own appeal with the High Court, asking the justices to reinstate the section of the law that prohibited teachers from speaking out in favor of gay rights. The Supreme Court granted the petition for review in the fall of 1984.[46]

Chanin recommended to the NEA Executive Committee that NEA file an *amicus* brief supporting the appeals court decision on teachers' free speech rights. Although NEA already had taken a stand by supporting Joe Acanfora and had since adopted policies supporting the rights of gay teachers, this was a particularly high-profile case, and some members of the Executive Committee were concerned that right-wing groups would use NEA's involvement to drive a wedge between the Association and its more conservative members. By this time, NEA had begun to be castigated as the poster child for gay rights in right-wing fundraising campaigns that accused the Association of attempting to impose its liberal social agenda on the nation's schoolchildren. Members of the Executive Committee, however, ultimately recognized the importance of the free speech issues that were involved, and their vote to file a brief against the Oklahoma City board was unanimous.[47]

Not unexpectedly, however, the Oklahoma Education Association (OEA) reacted negatively to NEA's decision to step into the case, and there was even talk that OEA might disaffiliate. NEA needed to send a high-level spokesperson to meet with the OEA Board of Directors. Chanin was the obvious choice. He possessed gravitas and was well respected by the state affiliates. He also had a command of the legal issues, and, while most NEA leaders and senior staff supported the Executive Committee's action, some were not comfortable talking publicly in favor of gay rights. Chanin had become the Association's point person on the issue.[48]

Chanin flew to Oklahoma City on December 14, 1984, to meet the next day with the OEA Board. He had dinner that evening with Nancy Jewell, the member of the NEA Board of Directors from Oklahoma who also sat on the OEA Board, and a few other members of the OEA Board. They were supportive, but cautioned that many other members were not, given the strong church influence in that region. Chanin told them that he was going to explain to the board that the case was not just about gay rights but involved the free speech rights of all teachers.

Perhaps out of confidence in his powers of persuasion, or more likely to engage Jewell in the presentation, Chanin told her, "I'll make you a bet. Not only will the Board approve of the fact that NEA is filing a brief, but when I'm done they will vote to make OEA a co-signer on the brief as well." Although she was a fan of Chanin's, Jewell knew her colleagues and took the bet.[49]

During his presentation to the OEA Board the next day, the palpable tension in the room increased when Chanin advised the members at the outset that NEA's decision to file a brief was not subject to their veto. He was there only to explain NEA's reasons for filing, and if possible, to gain their support for the course NEA had decided to take.[50]

He went on to explain forcefully that this case would set a precedent for *all teachers*, not just gay and lesbian teachers, and would have an effect in *every state*, not just Oklahoma. At issue were every educator's First Amendment free-expression rights.

The Oklahoma law, Chanin warned, prohibited statements made by teachers and aides "anywhere at any time," not just in the classroom. The Oklahoma attorney general had argued in the state's brief that "a state should be permitted to require that a public school teacher remain neutral with regard to public advocacy of issues which are controversial and which may promote strife within a school system."

Chanin explained the ramifications if the state's position were upheld:

> The inevitable consequence of this position is that no education employee could publicly address any issue of public concern without fear of discharge. If the Supreme Court accepts this position, it would give the green light to Arkansas to pass a statute prohibiting education employees from speaking in support of affirmative action; to Utah to pass a statute prohibiting education employees from speaking in support of legalized abortion; to Virginia to pass a statute prohibiting education employees from speaking in support of collective bargaining and teacher strikes; and to every other conservative legislature to pass a statute to prohibit education employees from making any statement that is contrary to what that particular state considers morally, socially, or politically acceptable. That, in short, is what this case is about.

NEA's participation in the case would send an important signal, Chanin added:

> The conservative wing of the Supreme Court has for several years been attempting to cut back on the constitutional rights of public employees. Because we are dealing here with speech about a generally unpopular topic, this is an appealing case in which to move that agenda. It surely would not go unnoticed if the largest public employee union in the nation did not appear to care enough even to file a brief. . . .
>
> The impact on NEA's relationship with the civil rights community is also a consideration. Because this is a public school case, the civil rights community looks to us for

leadership, and it is largely because we became involved that certain other groups were willing to take a stand in opposition to the Oklahoma statute.

Knowing the mixed feelings of many in the room, Chanin conceded that some state affiliates were saying that it was not a good time to be perceived as "pro-gay" when NEA was already under attack from the Right. Some feared this might make it more difficult to attract new members. Perhaps that was the reason, Chanin suggested, that the AFL-CIO and the AFT had decided not to speak out or file *amicus* briefs. But in the final analysis, he argued, NEA was subject to attack by the Right, not because of filing a brief in this particular case, but because of its core organizational principles.

The decision to file a brief, Chanin said in conclusion, was a matter of "organizational integrity":

> What does NEA profess to stand for and what is it willing to do to defend its principles? Phrased otherwise, how large a gap is tolerable between what we say and what we do—between our words and our deeds? . . .
>
> For more than a decade, NEA has had a firm policy in support of the First Amendment right of educational employees to speak on matters of public concern, and we have defended that right in literally hundreds of cases. NEA has been vigorous and vocal in this regard, and never has been reluctant to criticize other organizations that have been viewed as 'less committed.' Admittedly, this may not be the most popular case in which to stand up for our policy, but NEA would be substantially less of an organization if its elected leaders chose to selectively implement the policies of the NEA Representative Assembly by entering those cases that are popular and staying out of those cases that are unpopular.[51]

As Chanin said his final "thank you," the members of the OEA Board rose in unison and responded to his message with a standing ovation. He lost his fanciful bet with Nancy Jewell: The state affiliate did not agree to sign on to NEA's brief, but the board voted unanimously to support NEA's decision to file an *amicus* brief in its own name.[52]

The brief for NEA (and the American Jewish Congress) filed by

Chanin and other lawyers from Bredhoff & Kaiser made many of the
arguments Chanin had presented to the OEA board. "Because the terms
'advocate, encourage, or promote' are so broad, there is no speech on
the subject of homosexuality—other than speech unremittingly hostile
to homosexuals and homosexual rights—that can be considered safely
beyond the reach of the Oklahoma law," the brief said. "A teacher who
sought legal counsel as to what speech is permissible under the statute
would have to be told by any lawyer concerned about protecting that
teacher's interests that it is impossible to know how far the statute
extends; that virtually any speech on the subject of homosexuality or
the rights of homosexuals could be deemed to 'encourage' or 'promote'
homosexual activity and thereby trigger the law; and that the only
prudent course is to avoid speaking on such subjects altogether."[53]

On January 14, 1985, the High Court heard arguments in the case,
with Justice Lewis Powell, who was undergoing treatment for prostate
cancer, absent from the bench. Dennis Arrow argued for the Oklahoma
City school board, and Laurence Tribe, a noted Harvard Law School
professor and constitutional scholar, argued for the National Gay Task
Force.

"We would submit . . . that the statute does clearly target the
aforementioned goals of producing effective public education, making
sure that student morality is not corrupted, ensuring that the students
are protected in their psychological as well as physical well-being and
that the obligations of citizenship, which include the obligation to obey
the law, . . . [are] in fact preserved in the statute," Arrow told the
Court.[54]

Liberal justice William Brennan asked Arrow, "Suppose a teacher
sat down at lunch with a number of other teachers and said, 'I wish
they'd leave these homosexuals alone, they are not hurting anyone
except themselves,' and that was heard by everybody in the room,
students and everybody else. . . . Would that violate the statute?"
Arrow said no, that would be one form of calling for the law to be
repealed, and that would be "core political speech" protected by the
First Amendment.

Tribe, making what two authors subsequently called the first
Supreme Court argument to frame a gay-rights case as a civil rights

issue,[55] stressed the free speech rights of teachers.

"This law in effect tells teachers, you had better shut up about this subject, or if you talk about it, you had better be totally hostile to homosexuals," Tribe said. "And the real question is whether it is consistent with the traditions of free speech and open inquiry for [that] lesson to be given."[56]

Chief Justice Warren Burger pressed Tribe about whether state legislatures, in considering such laws, are entitled to take into account that teachers "are role models for the pupils?" Tribe replied: "Certainly [that] can be taken into account, but when President Reagan editorialized against this very [type of] law in California, about six years ago, his answer to the role model point was, first of all, as a matter of common sense, there is no reason to believe that homosexuality is something like a contagious disease. He quoted a woman who said that 'if teachers had all that much power as role models, I would have been a nun many years ago.'"[57]

On March 26, 1985, the Supreme Court issued its decision in *Board of Education of Oklahoma City v. National Gay Task Force*. Without Justice Powell's participation, the court was deadlocked, with four justices voting on each side. Under the Supreme Court's practice, a tie means that the lower court's decision is affirmed without an opinion. Such a disposition also means that the Supreme Court's action has no precedential value for lower courts across the country. But the tie did mean an affirmation of the Tenth Circuit's decision striking down the Oklahoma law's restrictions on teachers' free speech.[58]

The stakes had been high. If the Supreme Court had upheld the Oklahoma provisions, similar measures would have been introduced in dozens of state legislatures. After the victory for NEA and its allies, no other state attempted to adopt such a broad attack on the rights of gay teachers.[59]

At the same time the High Court was considering the Oklahoma City case during its 1985-86 term, another appeal involving the rights of gay teachers showed up at its doors. Marjorie Rowland was a 34-year-old high school guidance counselor in 1974 when she confided to a school secretary in the Mad River Local School District in Ohio that she was bisexual and had fallen in love with a woman. She also told her assistant principal and several friends who were fellow teachers about her bisexuality. Her principal learned about her sexual orientation within days, and he demanded that she resign. She refused, and refused again in later meetings with the superintendent. She was suspended with pay, and given a make-work job that involved no contact with students. The school board refused to renew her one-year contract.[60]

Aided by the Ohio Education Association, Rowland sued the district, alleging violations of her First Amendment right to free speech and her Fourteenth Amendment right to equal protection of the law. Her case eventually went before a federal district court, and the jury found that she was suspended and not rehired solely because she had discussed her bisexuality with her fellow school employees. It also found that her disclosures did not interfere with the performance of her duties or the operations of the school. The district court awarded her damages on both the First and Fourteenth Amendment claims.

The Mad River school district appealed to the U.S. Court of Appeals for the Sixth Circuit. At this stage, Rowland was represented by NEA, with Michael Simpson of the general counsel's office arguing her cause. A panel of the Sixth Circuit ruled two to one to reverse Rowland's victory, with the majority ruling that the counselor's speech about her sexuality was not protected by the First Amendment because it was not about "a matter of public concern." The court also reversed her Equal Protection claim. The dissenting judge accused his colleagues of viewing Rowland as a "sick" individual whose "homosexual status" justified her dismissal by the school district. "The Constitution protects all citizens of the United States; no language therein excludes the homosexual minority."[61]

Rowland appealed to the Supreme Court, and like the appeals of several gay teachers before her, including Joe Acanfora's, hers would be denied. But in this case, for the first time, there would be a public written dissent by two justices. As Joyce Murdoch and Deb Price describe in their 2001 book, *Courting Justice: Gay Men and Lesbians v. The Supreme Court*, the dissent from denial of certiorari by Justice William Brennan, joined by Justice Thurgood Marshall, was "a stirring and historic plea for the U.S. Supreme Court to begin treating gay

Americans and their constitutional rights respectfully."[62]

"This case starkly presents issues of individual constitutional rights that have, as the dissent below noted, 'swirled nationwide for many years,'" Brennan wrote in the April 22, 1985, dissent. "Petitioner did not lose her job because she disrupted the school environment or failed to perform her job. She was discharged merely because she is bisexual and revealed this fact to acquaintances at her workplace."[63]

Noting that the Supreme Court had held that speech about racial discrimination was "inherently of public concern," Brennan wrote, "I think it is impossible not to note that a similar public debate is currently ongoing regarding the rights of homosexuals." And while he couched his dissent in terms suggesting that the court should take up Rowland's case, Brennan left little doubt how he would likely have ruled had the court done so.

"The Equal Protection Clause protects against arbitrary and irrational classifications, and against invidious discrimination stemming from prejudice and hostility," Brennan stated. "Under this rubric, discrimination against homosexuals or bisexuals based solely on their sexual preference raises significant constitutional questions under both prongs of our settled equal protection analysis." And he essentially invited further legal challenges from gay and lesbian Americans. Rowland's case "raises serious and unsettled constitutional questions relating to this issue of national importance, an issue that cannot any longer be ignored," he wrote.

Despite Brennan's plaintive dissent in the *Rowland* case, it would be ten years before NEA had another opportunity to advocate for gay rights before the Supreme Court. In 1996, the Court agreed to review *Romer v. Evans*. NEA's *amicus* brief urged the Court to overturn an amendment (Amendment 2) to the Colorado Constitution, passed by popular vote in 1992, that prohibited state and local governments— including school districts—from barring discrimination against gay, lesbian, and bisexual people. In this case, NEA's brief focused less on the amendment's potential impact on gay teachers or other school employees than it did on the role of public schools in addressing the needs of gay and lesbian students.

"Not only does Amendment 2 undermine the ability of the public schools to meet the needs of gay and lesbian students, but it impacts more broadly on the educational mission of the public schools," said the brief written by Chanin and John West of Bredhoff & Kaiser on behalf of NEA and several other groups. "In raising discrimination against those perceived as different to the level of high constitutional principle, Amendment 2 calls into question one of the most important values the public schools attempt to teach their students—tolerance and respect for those who are different."[64]

The Court ruled six to three that the Colorado amendment violated the Equal Protection Clause of the Fourteenth Amendment because it was designed to single out and deny rights to a politically unpopular group. "We must conclude that Amendment 2 classifies homosexuals not to further a proper legislative end but to make them unequal to everyone else," said the majority opinion by Justice Anthony Kennedy. "This Colorado cannot do. A state cannot so deem a class of persons a stranger to its law."[65]

This legal principle has been used by NEA in a number of lower court cases, including one involving NEA member Wendy Weaver from the small town of Salem, Utah. Weaver taught psychology and physical education, with favorable evaluations for nineteen years. In addition, she coached the girls' volleyball team to four state championships. Before the start of the 1997-98 school year, a female student who was thinking about joining the team asked Weaver if she was a lesbian. Weaver answered honestly that she was. The student decided not to join the team, and she and her parents met with school district officials to express their concern. The school board responded quickly and took away Weaver's coaching responsibility, despite her years of success in working with student athletes and her unblemished record.

NEA filed a lawsuit on Weaver's behalf, alleging that her removal violated the Equal Protection Clause. The Utah Education Association, NEA's affiliate in one of the most conservative states in the country, supported the litigation. In an important ruling, the federal district court agreed and ordered her reinstatement as coach.[66] But Salem, Utah, was not as tolerant as a major urban center, and, despite her legal victory, Weaver paid a personal price. "It's been hard," she told a reporter. "All the publicity. The charges of immorality. We were worried about the impact of going public."[67]

Despite NEA's steadfast support for gay rights, beginning with the Acanfora case, the issue caused controversy within the Association's ranks. At the 1995 Representative Assembly, gay-rights supporters introduced a resolution that was modeled after existing NEA policy encouraging the schools to celebrate and teach about black history. The resolution expressed NEA support for school programs that provide "accurate portrayal of roles and contributions of gay, lesbian, and bisexual people throughout history, with acknowledgment of their sexual orientation," and support for "the celebration of a Lesbian and Gay History Month as a means of acknowledging the contributions of lesbians, gays, and bisexuals throughout history."[68]

After the resolution passed, right-wing groups responded immediately and vehemently, using it as the centerpiece for a new round of fund-raising appeals to their followers. "Will you please help me stop the National Education Association (NEA) from teaching your grandchildren that Jesus Christ was a homosexual?" blared one fundraising letter aimed at senior citizens in one group, the American Christian Cause. "They actually want to teach your grandchildren that Jesus Christ and George Washington were both homosexuals! The NEA must learn that they have finally pushed you too far."[69]

Concerned Women of America (CWA), a group devoted to attacking feminism as well as gay rights, urged potential donors to give generously because "if we remain silent, the NEA may conclude that most Americans don't care if their sons and daughters are taught the 'virtues' of the gay and lesbian lifestyle." CWA promised that, in return for donors' dollars, it would "continue to oppose all of the NEA's attempts to force 'tolerance' of homosexuality on public schoolchildren."[70]

Gay-rights issues grew in prominence in the late 1990s and into the new century, and by the time preparations were being made for the 2001 Representative Assembly, tension within NEA over this issue had increased to the point that it was clear that amendments were going to be introduced by both sides—those who wanted an even more explicit and aggressive endeavor to promote educational programs on issues related to sexual orientation, and those who wanted to weaken NEA's commitment to gay rights. Chanin recognized the risks of an unstructured debate on such a controversial and emotional issue before a large contingent of reporters. Chase agreed it would be preferable for a serious discussion of the issues to first take place in a committee setting.[71] Toward that end, Chase told the delegates that he would, immediately after the RA, appoint an NEA Task Force on Sexual Orientation to develop recommendations for the Association's policies and programs to be considered by the 2002 Representative Assembly. He carefully chose nineteen members for the Task Force who represented as wide a range as possible in terms of region and point of view. Chase made it clear to Chanin, who served as advisor to the Task Force, that he wanted a report that everyone could accept, even if it was not exactly what each of them might have written. After working together for more than six months, in January 2002, the Task Force unanimously adopted a report that had been largely drafted by Chanin.[72]

Using the short-hand term "GLBT" to refer to gays, lesbians, bisexuals, and transgendered people, the report acknowledged that this topic "is to be sure a controversial area—with religious implications for some people—and the Task Force recognizes that there are NEA affiliates and members who would prefer that NEA keep a low profile regarding GLBT issues. Because NEA is committed by its Mission Statement to 'advocate human, civil, and economic rights for all,' and because NEA is the nation's preeminent voice for public education, keeping a low profile simply is not an option."[73]

The report cited studies showing that, for many GLBT students, harassment at school was a nearly daily reality. Regarding education employees, it went on to state that "because many GLBT education employees are vulnerable to adverse employment action if they reveal their sexual orientation/gender identification, victims of such discrimination are caught in a Catch-22 situation. Challenging a discriminatory employment action serves to draw attention to the victim's sexual orientation/gender identification, and thus increases the risk of further discrimination. Consequently, the cases that do arise are surely only the tip of the iceberg."[74]

The heart of the report was a proposed NEA action plan to provide support and assistance to GLBT members. The action plan, which was adopted by the 2002 Representative Assembly, directed NEA to seek a federal law prohibiting employment discrimination on the basis of sexual orientation, just as Title VII bans such discrimination on the basis of race, gender, religion, and national origin. The plan also committed NEA to help state affiliates secure counterpart state laws, given that fewer than half of the states prohibited employment discrimination on the basis of sexual orientation. In addition, NEA committed to help local affiliates negotiate contract provisions or school district policies barring such discrimination—the most direct and immediate way to protect GLBT members.[75]

Additional steps were taken when the RA revisited the subject in 2009. The Assembly was held in July in California, about eight months after voters narrowly approved Proposition 8, an amendment to the California Constitution that prohibits gay marriage in the state. The NEA action plan with regard to same-sex couples, again largely drafted by Chanin with an aim toward achieving broad consensus based on the Association's core principles, directs NEA to "support its affiliates in seeking to enact state legislation that guarantees to same-sex couples the right to enter into a legally recognized relationship pursuant to which they have the same rights and benefits as similarly-situated heterosexual couples." It also directs NEA to support efforts to repeal the federal Defense of Marriage Act of 1996, which denies federal recognition and benefits to same-sex couples. To reflect the range of views among NEA delegates, the action plan took no position on whether a legally recognized relationship that guarantees equal rights and benefits should be called "marriage," "civil union," "domestic partnership," or some other term appropriate to the state. It also provides that "NEA recognizes that the term 'marriage' has religious connotations and that same-sex marriages may not be compatible with the beliefs, values, and/or practices of certain religions. Because of its support for the separation of church and state and the right to religious freedom guaranteed by the First Amendment to the United States Constitution, NEA supports the right of religious institutions to refuse to perform or recognize same-sex marriages."[76]

Even this carefully worded compromise position was immediately attacked by right-wing groups such as the Eagle Forum, headed by long-time NEA critic Phyllis Schlafly. She wrote that "the long list of policy resolutions approved by the nation's most powerful teachers union included many references to 'sexual orientation,' 'gender identification,' and 'diversity.' Since the NEA is the largest and most powerful teachers union, it is reasonable to assume that these attitudes will follow the teachers into the classroom."[77]

As a result of nearly four decades of work by NEA and many others, some of the gay rights goals adopted by the Representative Assemblies have been achieved, while others have not. Some states both prohibit employment discrimination and provide legal recognition of domestic partnerships or civil unions, and a few have recognized gay marriage. Without a doubt, the nation has come a long way from a time when states and school districts refused to hire or sought to dismiss gay and lesbian teachers.

In 2003, the Supreme Court ruled six to three to strike down a Texas law that criminalized intimate sexual contact between two persons of the same sex. The decision in *Lawrence v. Texas* overruled the High Court's 1986 decision in *Bowers v. Hardwick*,[78] which had narrowly upheld Georgia's law against homosexual sodomy (with Justice Lewis Powell, who did not participate in the Oklahoma City teachers' case, casting the decisive fifth vote).

Although *Lawrence* dealt with conduct in the bedroom, not with the rights of teachers, the majority's reversal of *Bowers* sent Justice Antonin Scalia into a fury. "It is clear" from this decision, Scalia said in a dissent joined by Chief Justice William Rehnquist and Justice Clarence Thomas, "that the Court has taken sides in the culture war. . . . Many Americans do not want persons who openly engage in homosexual conduct as partners in their business, as scoutmasters for their children, as teachers in their children's schools, or as boarders in their home. They view this as protecting themselves and their families from a lifestyle that they believe to be immoral and destructive."[79]

Justice Anthony Kennedy, in the majority opinion in *Lawrence*, did not specifically respond to Scalia's "culture war" comment or address the ruling's potential effects on education. But he offered a lofty conception of liberty and constitutional rights for gay and lesbian Americans. "Liberty protects the person from unwarranted government intrusions into a dwelling or other private places," Justice Kennedy wrote. "In our tradition the State is not omnipresent in the home. And there are other spheres of our lives and existence, outside the home, where the State should not be a dominant presence. Freedom extends beyond spatial bounds. Liberty presumes an autonomy of self that includes freedom of thought, belief, expression, and certain intimate conduct. . . . [T]imes can blind us to certain truths and later generations can see that laws once thought necessary and proper in fact serve only to oppress. As the Constitution endures, persons in every generation can invoke its principles in their own search for greater freedom."[80]

Chapter 7

Gender and Other Civil Rights Battles

As one of the nation's largest organizations with a predominantly female membership, NEA has long been a strong defender of women's rights. Although the Association did not initially grant women full membership at its founding in 1857, they could be elected honorary members, but without the right to speak at Association meetings. Their views could be presented in written essays, which were read aloud to attendees by men. In 1866, the Association's constitution was changed to reflect that membership would be open "to persons" instead of "to gentlemen," and, in 1869, the organization elected its first female officer—a vice president. By the early 20th Century, NEA would find itself advocating for women's suffrage, for equal pay among male and female teachers, and for equity for women teachers who sometimes faced discriminatory treatment because they were married. In the 1970s, NEA backed the Equal Rights Amendment by refusing to hold its Representative Assemblies in any state that had not ratified the amendment and by assigning staff to work in the unsuccessful drive for ratification.[81]

NEA has also long stood for a woman's right to reproductive freedom—not, as it was sometimes perceived, as support for abortion rights *per se*, but, rather, because it believes that reproductive choices should be made by women themselves and not by government. The Association has also stood for reproductive freedom in order to protect members' employment rights. Prior to the Supreme Court's 1973 decision in *Roe v. Wade*, court rulings in a number of states where abortions were illegal had established that the state could deny professional certification to a woman who broke the law by having an abortion, and that education employees who had abortions could be fired for "moral turpitude."[82]

One of the most dramatic examples of NEA's commitment, not to promote or oppose abortions, but to defend reproductive freedom, was the case of *Eckmann v. Board of Education.* In this lawsuit, NEA and its state affiliate in Illinois supported the right of a teacher *not* to have an abortion because having one would have violated her religious beliefs.[83]

Jeanne Eckmann had studied to be a nun before taking up teaching in Marengo, Illinois, northwest of Chicago. In November 1980, while in her early thirties and in her fourth year as a teacher, Eckmann was raped at a motel where she was spending the night while driving back from a religious retreat in Nebraska. Severely traumatized, Eckmann did not report the crime to anyone except her female roommate. In December, Eckmann learned that she was pregnant. She informed her principal, who suggested that she tell no one. In the spring, when Eckmann was afraid that her pregnancy was becoming visible, she took medical leave with the principal's permission.[84]

Late in her pregnancy, however, the president of the school board came to Eckmann's house and told her she would have to resign if she went forward with the birth. He said having a child out of wedlock was immoral. Her choice was clear: have an abortion, which would violate her fundamental religious beliefs, or lose her job.[85]

Eckmann turned to the Illinois Education Association, NEA's affiliate in her state, which asked the school board to drop its threats against her. But on July 20, 1981, the day before her son Gregory was born, Eckmann received a formal "Notice to Remedy," the first step in a process that would eventually lead to dismissal from the school district. The notice said she was "guilty of immorality," and that "your conduct in becoming pregnant outside the state of marriage has lessened your ability to teach and the ability of your students to learn their lessons from you."[86]

Eckmann, having already refused to have an abortion, chose not to take the only other available step to comply with the school board's directive, which would have been to put her son up for adoption. Throughout the fall of 1981, she both raised her son and carried out her teaching responsibilities. In January 1982, the school board finally implemented the threatened firing because she had failed to remedy the "deficiencies" that consisted of bearing and then keeping her child. The board accused her of "irremedial and immoral conduct outside the state of lawful matrimony in a manner which has been open and notorious," and concluded, "You are not qualified to teach, and your dismissal is in the best interests of the school."[87]

The Illinois Education Association challenged Eckmann's firing under a state tenure law that guaranteed that a teacher dismissed for immorality had the right to a hearing by an independent third party. In August 1982, the hearing officer ordered Eckmann's reinstatement with back pay. "There is no evidence in the record that the teacher was an immoral person," he found. "On the contrary, the record indicates that she was an eminently moral person, a religious person and staunch in her beliefs. The charges made against the teacher are not supported by the evidence."[88]

Because the hearing officer did not have the power to provide compensatory damages, Eckmann also took her case to federal district court with NEA support. The court found that the right to bear her child without risking her job was protected as part of the right to privacy established by *Roe v. Wade*. She received a substantial award for damages, although nothing could make up for her psychological suffering. During the proceedings, she was forced to relive the details of the rape, not once, but twice, as school district lawyers tried unsuccessfully to put her and not the school district on trial. Describing this painful legal process later to an Illinois newspaper, she recalled, "I just read the Bible verse, 'Be still and know that I am God.' I wrote it on the palm of my hand. I looked at it whenever things got rough on the witness stand." Even so, she broke down after the four-hour grilling by school board attorneys and had to be hospitalized for six weeks for depression.[89]

Eckmann, like many other plaintiffs in groundbreaking cases, not only established an important legal principle, but also advanced the public debate about fundamental rights. Her case was featured on national network television programs, such as the *Today Show*, and in a feature article in *Family Circle*. It later was the subject of the 1989 made-for-TV movie, "Cast the First Stone."[90]

Another landmark case that dramatized NEA's support for the rights of female education employees was *Cleveland Board of*

Education v. LaFleur.[91] Under a Cleveland, Ohio, school district rule, pregnant teachers had to take unpaid maternity leave beginning at least five months before the expected due date for the child's birth and remain on leave for at least three months after the birth, even if they were fully capable of performing their jobs. The rule had been in effect for nearly twenty years until two junior high school teachers, Jo Carol LaFleur and Ann Elizabeth Nelson, challenged it in federal court. Both were due to give birth during the summer of 1971 and questioned why they had to give up months of income during the spring semester just because they were pregnant.[92]

The district court dismissed their case, holding that the rule was reasonable and constitutional. The U.S. Court of Appeals for the Sixth Circuit reversed the lower court's decision, ruling that the policy violated the Equal Protection Clause of the Fourteenth Amendment. The school district then appealed to the U.S. Supreme Court, which agreed to hear the case, along with a similar case from a Virginia school district. NEA filed an *amicus* brief in support of the teachers' challenge to the pregnancy rule.[93]

The *amicus* brief filed by Chanin and other NEA attorneys said that "NEA strongly believes that rules which force teachers to take a leave of absence at a prescribed stage of pregnancy have no place in the 1970s. These rules are a holdover from another era, when matters relating to sex and childbirth were deliberately kept hidden from children, and when the condition of pregnancy—even in married women—was considered slightly indelicate or impure. In today's world, a rule which forces a teacher to forfeit her job merely because she is pregnant, without regard to her personal physical condition and ability to continue working, is wholly unreasonable and discriminatory."[94]

In January 1974, the Supreme Court agreed with NEA and ruled that the policy violated the Due Process Clause of the Fourteenth Amendment. The Court's decision had special significance for Chanin. Sixteen years earlier, when he was a student at Yale Law School, his wife, Rhoda, had been a teacher in New Haven and the couple's primary income provider until she was forced out of her job because of a similar school board policy on pregnancy. Now, such policies had been declared unconstitutional by the highest court in the nation.[95]

This precedent-setting victory, which shed light on widespread discrimination against pregnant women, helped persuade Congress to enact the Pregnancy Discrimination Act four years later. The law, passed with NEA's support, requires employers to treat pregnancy like any other temporary disability, and prohibits employers from firing, laying off, or refusing to hire women because of pregnancy.[96]

Even though court decisions and an act of Congress established basic protections for pregnant workers, female education employees still turned to NEA for help in challenging restrictions on child-rearing and other familial rights.

One case, *Dike v. School Board of Orange County*, involved the question of whether a teacher had the right to breastfeed her baby during break times at school. Janice Dike, a kindergarten teacher in Florida, gave birth to her daughter just before the December holidays in 1978. She returned to work after the vacation period, and for nearly three months she breastfed her infant during her lunch break because the baby could not go for the whole school day without a feeding. Her husband or babysitter would bring the infant to school, where she would nurse the child in a secure room that was inaccessible to students.[97]

Although no one had complained about Dike's breastfeeding, the principal told her in March 1979 that she was in violation of a school rule prohibiting teachers from bringing their children to work. He ordered her to discontinue the practice, stating that if she failed to do so, she would be disciplined.[98]

In fear of losing her job, Dike agreed to try feeding her baby with formula instead. When that did not work due to allergies, she tried pumping breast milk and leaving it at home to be fed to her baby in the middle of the day. The child did not respond well to that routine and rejected milk from a bottle. Dike then told the principal that she needed to resume breastfeeding and offered to do so in her own camper van in the school parking lot. That would avoid violating the rule that prohibited bringing her child to school.[99]

The school board turned down her proposal because it would violate another rule that provided that teachers were not allowed to leave school premises during the school day. Even though Dike had free time during lunch, the rules effectively barred her from having any contact with her baby while school was in session. Forced to choose between the health of her child or her paycheck, she saw no alternative but to take unpaid leave for the rest of the school year.[100]

NEA and its affiliate, the Florida Education Association, funded the lawsuit on Dike's behalf. The federal district court rejected her complaint, finding that the issue arose "not because the state attempted to forbid an individual from making a private decision to breastfeed, but because the individual made that decision and, thereafter, seeks to impose the consequences on the employer."[101]

Calling the lawsuit "frivolous," the judge also ordered Dike to pay the school district thousands of dollars in attorneys' fees. He indicated that he set the fees at a high level since he expected that NEA and its state affiliate would pay.[102]

Dike appealed the ruling to the U.S. Court of Appeals for the Fifth Circuit, where NEA attorneys succeeded in overturning the lower court's decision. Citing a number of Supreme Court precedents, including *Roe v. Wade*, the appeals court said in its 1981 ruling that "the Constitution protects from undue state interference citizens' freedom of personal choice in some areas of marriage and family life. These protected interests have been described as rights of personal privacy or as 'fundamental' personal liberties." Protected liberties, the court said, include "individual decisions respecting marriage, procreation, contraception, abortion, and family relationships," and, specifically, breastfeeding.[103]

A few years later, another federal appeals court ruled that the right to privacy also means that a teacher may not be fired for getting a divorce. NEA member Linda Littlejohn was a nontenured fifth grade teacher in Calloway County, Kentucky. During her two years of teaching she had received good evaluations, and her principal said her performance was "excellent." She also chaired the school's accreditation programs, which her principal said required "a lot of perseverance and a lot of ability to get along with others."[104]

In the spring of 1982, Littlejohn and her husband of nine years separated, and in July, they divorced. That summer, the school superintendent decided not to rehire her, overruling her principal's recommendation. Believing that the decision was based on the fact that she was divorced, Littlejohn challenged her termination in federal district court with the financial backing of NEA and its affiliate, the Kentucky Education Association. Both the principal and a school board member testified that the superintendent told them his decision was based on the divorce proceedings. Before a jury could undertake its deliberations, however, the court ruled in favor of the school district. The court acknowledged that there "was evidence at the trial that the reason given by defendant for plaintiff's nonrenewal was the fact that she was involved in the dissolution of her marriage," but it held that termination of employment for this reason did not constitute an "impermissible motivation" or a violation of the plaintiff's "clearly established rights."[105]

NEA attorneys took her case, *Littlejohn v. Rose*, to the Sixth Circuit. In 1985, that court reversed the lower court and held that a public school employee may not be fired for getting a divorce. To do so, the court declared, would violate the employee's fundamental right to privacy under *Roe v. Wade* and other Supreme Court decisions.[106]

Although most of NEA's civil rights litigation has been in the employment context, particularly on behalf of teachers and education support professionals, it also has participated in cases involving the rights of students. NEA policy, established by the 2006 Representative Assembly as the latest iteration of earlier policies, provides that the Association "believes that basic student rights include the right to free inquiry and expression; freedom of the press; due process; gender equity; freedom of association; freedom of peaceful assembly and petition; participation in the governance of the school, college, and university; freedom from discrimination; freedom from commercial exploitation, including the payment of sub-minimum wages; and equal educational opportunity."[107]

While there are inherent tensions between the rights of students and the rights of school districts (and their employees), Chanin always believed it would have been the easy route to disregard student rights. But he urged a balance. For one thing, it would be hypocritical for an association that advocates for the fair treatment of school employees not to support such treatment for students as well. He also reasoned that the principles of due process and freedom from discrimination and harassment established in student cases can sometimes be helpful in cases involving the rights of teachers and other staff.

In part because a substantial majority of NEA members are women, the Association has always taken a special interest in protecting female students from sexual harassment and discrimination in schools. To that end, NEA has consistently supported the vigorous enforcement of Title IX of the Education Amendments of 1972, the federal law that prohibits sex discrimination—including sexual harassment—in educational institutions that receive federal funding, which includes all public schools, as well as virtually all colleges and universities.[108]

By filing *amicus* briefs in support of the students involved, NEA played an active role in three landmark student sex harassment cases decided by the Supreme Court in the 1990s. In *Franklin v. Gwinnett County Public Schools*, the High Court in 1992 held that a student suing over sexual harassment and abuse by one of her teachers could win monetary damages under Title IX. In 1998, in *Gebser v. Lago Vista Independent School District*, the Court set a standard for incidents in which schools could be held liable under Title IX for teachers' sexual harassment of students. Damages could be ordered only in cases in which a school district official with authority to take corrective action had been given actual notice of the harassment and had been "deliberately indifferent" to the teacher's misconduct. The next year, in *Davis v. Monroe County Board of Education*, the Court ruled that school districts could also be liable for student-on-student sexual harassment, but only when the same standard from the *Gebser* case was met. The court's rulings sent a message that sexual harassment of students should be treated seriously, even if there were limitations on a school district's liability.[109]

During this period, attorneys from NEA's Office of General Counsel also worked closely with officials from the U.S. Department of Education to draft Title IX regulations, which now require every public school district and higher education institution receiving federal funds to adopt rules prohibiting the sexual harassment of students and to create a procedure that the victims can invoke to complain about the harassment and have the problem resolved. NEA also published handbooks and curriculum guides, including *Flirting or Hurting*, designed to help prevent students from harassing other students and to help school employees recognize and properly respond to instances of student-on-student sexual harassment.[110]

More recently, NEA had an influence on a Supreme Court decision in another landmark case involving the rights of students. The case was brought by 13-year-old Savana Redding, who was strip searched at a middle school in Safford, Arizona. Acting on a classmate's tip that Savana was in possession of a 400 milligram tablet of Ibuprofen, administrators forced Redding to disrobe down to her bra and panties and expose her breasts and pelvic area.[111]

In June 2009, the U.S. Supreme Court ruled eight to one in *Safford Unified School District v. Redding* that the strip search was unreasonable under the Fourth Amendment, which governs searches and seizures. The Court specifically cited an *amicus* brief submitted by NEA, the National Association of Social Workers, and other groups that presented social science research showing that a strip search can cause serious psychological and emotional harm to a student.[112]

As Chanin pointed out in discussing the case with the NEA Board of Directors later that summer, there are several reasons why the Association files *amicus* briefs in Supreme Court cases. There may be a Representative Assembly policy that merits pushing before the Court. Another reason is that NEA either independently or as a part of a broader coalition wants to make its position known about a controversial issue. But sometimes NEA is in a unique position to speak to the issue at stake in a particular case.

That was the situation in *Redding*. Chanin noted to the board that NEA's brief in that case did not cite a lot of court precedents, as such briefs usually do. Rather, it was intended to bring a real-world perspective to the issue of strip searches of students, and it clearly helped convince the Supreme Court majority that the weight of scholarly evidence showed that such searches could result in serious emotional damage to students.

NEA's commitment to civil rights has also been reflected by its involvement in a broad range of litigation dealing with issues other than race and gender.

In the groundbreaking case *Lau v. Nichols*, for example, NEA filed an *amicus* brief urging the U.S. Supreme Court to uphold federal rules requiring school districts to help English language learners overcome barriers so they could fully participate in their school's educational program. Nearly 2,000 students of Chinese ancestry were not receiving English-language assistance from the San Francisco school system. While their lawsuit was rejected by lower federal courts, the Supreme Court agreed in 1974 that the school district's failure to meet the special language needs of such students violated Title VI of the Civil Rights Act of 1964. That provision bars discrimination on the basis of race, color, or national origin in programs and activities receiving federal financial assistance, including public school districts, colleges, and universities.

"Basic English skills are at the very core of what these public schools teach," the Court said. "Imposition of a requirement that before a child can effectively participate in the educational program, he must already have acquired those basic skills is to make a mockery of public education."[113]

In another landmark case involving immigrants' right to an education, NEA filed an *amicus* brief in *Plyler v. Doe*, in which the U.S. Supreme Court held that states may not deny a free public education to undocumented immigrant children. The case began in 1975 when Texas law was changed from guaranteeing free education to anyone who lived in a school district to giving the guarantee only to citizens or immigrants with legal status. Some school districts began to bar undocumented children altogether, while others accomplished the same goal by charging their parents tuition they could not afford and that other families did not have to pay.[114]

The new law was challenged as a violation of the Fourteenth Amendment's Equal Protection Clause. In an echo of the *Dred Scott* decision more than a century earlier that found that slaves and their descendants could not be citizens, the state of Texas argued that undocumented immigrants were not covered by the Constitution because they were not persons legally in this country. After the Fifth

Circuit ruled that the law was unconstitutional, the U.S. Supreme Court agreed to review the case.

NEA's *amicus* brief argued that Congress originally passed the Fourteenth Amendment in 1866, just after the Civil War, to help prevent southern states from maintaining the equivalent of slavery by denying access to education and literacy. To allow states now to treat Hispanic immigrants in a similar way clearly violated the intent of that amendment. The brief also noted that most undocumented immigrants pay taxes but are denied vital public services, such as education, that those taxes support.[115]

In its 1982 ruling, the Supreme Court agreed with NEA's position. In powerful language, Justice Brennan wrote for the Court, "Illiteracy is an enduring disability. The inability to read and write will handicap the individual deprived of a basic education each and every day of his life," and will impose "a lifetime hardship on a discrete class of children not accountable for their disabling status."[116]

The ruling in the *Plyler* case guaranteeing a free public education to undocumented immigrant children is one of the Supreme Court's most far-reaching decisions and has served as an important precedent for other cases as well. For example, when in 1994 voters in California passed Proposition 187, a ballot initiative that would have prohibited undocumented children from attending the state's public schools, a federal district court ruled that the initiative was unconstitutional under *Plyler*.[117]

More recently, the national debate over immigration policies and workplace raids by federal Immigration and Customs Enforcement (ICE) agents has raised new concerns about the treatment of undocumented children. Reflecting its continuing commitment to equal educational opportunities for all children, the 2007 Representative Assembly directed NEA to help ensure that undocumented immigrant children receive the free public education guaranteed by *Plyler*.

In response, Chanin's office prepared a comprehensive memorandum providing advice to NEA members about the educational rights of undocumented students and discussing actions NEA members and affiliates could take to protect those rights. Titled "Immigration Status and the Right to A Free Public Education," the memo was sent to all NEA state affiliates. In August 2009, NEA also joined with the National School Boards Association to publish and disseminate another legal guide titled "Legal Issues for School Districts Related to the Education of Undocumented Children." That booklet provides legal advice on such issues as whether school districts can ask students about their immigration status, whether school officials are required to report undocumented students to ICE officials, and what school districts should do to assist students whose parents have been detained during an ICE raid.[118]

Another particularly moving student rights issue involved the treatment of schoolchildren with acquired immune deficiency syndrome, or AIDS. In the early 1980s, when little was known about the new disease, some parents, teachers, and school boards around the country panicked, adopting drastic policies based more on misinformation and fear than on fact.

The symbol for discrimination against students with AIDS became Ryan White, who in 1984 was a thirteen-year-old attending middle school in Russiaville, Indiana. Given a blood-based medication to treat his hemophilia, White contracted AIDS and was told he had only a few months to live. Although public health officials reassured the community that other students would not be put at risk simply by attending classes with him, a large number of parents and teachers called for White to be barred from school, and the school board and superintendent gave in to such fears.[119]

It took a nine-month court battle for White to win the right to attend school. In an attempt to meet the opposition half way, White and his parents agreed that he would use a separate bathroom and water fountain, as well as plastic eating utensils that would be disposed of each day. Despite these conciliatory (and unnecessary) measures, some parents withdrew their children and started an alternative school.[120] Isolated from his peers and subjected to continuing physical threats, White moved with his family to Cicero, Indiana, to attend high school. Administrators, employees, and students there had been educated about AIDS and were far more welcoming.[121]

As White's situation and other similar cases came to NEA's attention, Chanin and NEA's assistant general counsel Michael Simpson worked with the NEA Health Information Network—an organization founded by NEA in 1987 to promote the health of NEA employees and students—in preparing model guidelines that provided medical, legal, and factual information about dealing with students with AIDS. The guidelines became the basis for a joint document distributed by the National Association of State Boards of Education in cooperation with NEA, the National PTA, federal agencies, and several professional associations of school administrators. This practical, educational material helped NEA affiliates, school districts, and community groups to deal more responsibly with the issue at a time of public panic in many communities.[122]

It was an emotional day on July 4, 1988, when Ryan White, then 17, spoke to the thousands of delegates attending NEA's Representative Assembly in New Orleans to thank the Association for its support of the rights of children with AIDS. He recalled the ordeal he had gone through as an unwelcome student in middle school.

"I was labeled a troublemaker, my mom an unfit mother, and I was not welcome anywhere," he told the delegates. "People would get up and leave so they would not have to sit anywhere near me. Even at church, people would not shake my hand."

At his new high school, he reported, "I'm a normal, happy teenager again. I have a driver's license and a 1987 Chevy. I attend sports functions and dances. I am just one of the kids, and all because the students at Hamilton Heights High School listened to the facts, educated their parents and themselves, and believed in me."

Turning to the future, White said proudly that "I look forward to graduating from Hamilton Heights High School in 1991." He did not make it, succumbing to his disease a few months before his senior prom.[123] NEA helps continue Ryan White's legacy, presenting an award in his honor each year to an affiliate or member who has implemented or supported innovative AIDS prevention education programs.[124]

Because of NEA's commitment to civil rights over the past forty years, including Bob Chanin's personal commitment and his often cutting-edge legal work, gay teachers are now able to pursue their chosen profession without discrimination, female education employees have the right to make decisions about their personal lives without interference from the government or their employers, and students throughout the country have more protection from harassment and violations of their rights.

Part IV |

Great Public Schools for Every Student

"Our mission is to advocate for education professionals and to unite our members and the nation to fulfill the promise of public education to prepare every student to succeed in a diverse and interdependent world."—*NEA Vision Statement*[1]

"NEA is a terrorist organization."—*Rod Paige, President George W. Bush's first secretary of education, speaking to the National Governors Association, February 23, 2004*[2]

"Chanin is the quintessential obnoxious labor lawyer, replete with a thick New York accent and a sarcastic, argumentative demeanor. . . . [But he] is also a masterful orator who makes every second count, wielding total command of his subject matter."—*Clint Bolick, pro-voucher litigation director of the Institute for Justice, in his book* Voucher Wars.[3]

Chapter 8

The Politics of Education

Throughout its history, NEA has been the leading voice for public education in America, and its advocacy for the schools has been guided by several principles. First, quality public schools should be available to every student because education is essential both to achieving the American Dream and to participating fully in our democratic society. Second, public schools should have diverse student bodies in order to produce citizens who are equipped to contribute to our increasingly multicultural society. Third, public schools should be secular, maintaining separation of church and state and respecting the wide array of religious beliefs that can be found in our communities. Fourth, public schools must have adequate and stable funding in order to fulfill their vital mission.[4]

In the years since Bob Chanin first became involved with NEA in the 1960s, the Association has become an increasingly powerful and effective force for these principles, building a grassroots political program that engages hundreds of thousands of education employees throughout the country. As a result, NEA has become one of the chief targets of conservative and right-wing groups that do not share its vision for public schools, but in the Association's view, seek to undermine public education by defunding the public schools, shifting public resources to private schools, censoring the free exchange of ideas within public schools, and requiring taxpayer support for private religious education.[5]

Traditionally, NEA's political work in support of public education consisted primarily of a combination of insider lobbying and public relations—an approach that for many years yielded results. In 1958, for example, NEA played a key role in persuading Congress to enact the National Defense Education Act (NDEA). A response to the Soviet Union's launch the previous year of Sputnik, the first satellite to orbit the earth, the law substantially increased federal support for the public schools.

Sputnik was a technological breakthrough that was thought to pose a major new military threat to the United States. It set off a national debate about the effectiveness of the American educational system. Many public officials became convinced that U.S. schools were falling behind those of other nations, particularly in science education. Navy Admiral Hyman Rickover, who had overseen development of the world's first nuclear submarine, captured the concerns of many when he said that "we have let our educational problem grow much too big for comfort and safety. We are beginning to see now that we must solve it without delay." NDEA increased funding for loans to college students, fostered more instruction in science, mathematics, and foreign languages in elementary and secondary schools, and enhanced vocational and technical training.[6]

After the election of President Kennedy in 1960, NEA worked for an expansion of the federal commitment to education. Three days before Kennedy was assassinated in Dallas, Texas on November 22, 1963, he met in the White House Rose Garden with top leaders of NEA and its state affiliates to discuss that goal. "I hope you will continue to prod us and, occasionally . . . the members of the House and Senate, to see if we can get this job done," Kennedy said.[7]

After Kennedy's death, NEA worked closely with President Johnson to persuade Congress to enact the historic Elementary and Secondary Education Act (ESEA) of 1965. Title I of the act provided unprecedented support to increase educational opportunities for low-income students in inner cities and rural areas. The new law authorized Head Start as a year-round preschool program for low-income children.[8] NEA also helped enact the Higher Education Act of 1965, which provided financial aid programs for needy college students.[9]

Three years later, NEA was instrumental in passing the Bilingual Education Act of 1968, a law that, for the first time, supplied federal support for bilingual programs in the public schools aimed at helping non-native speakers learn English while also maintaining their native language. The act supported teacher training, the development of bilingual instructional materials, and parental involvement programs.[10]

As NEA entered the 1970s, many of its leaders recognized that, despite these legislative successes, the Association's political operation on behalf of public education and education employees was in need of fundamental change. With other organizations and the major political parties developing more sophisticated organizing techniques, NEA needed to involve its members and their families in canvassing, phone banking, and other grassroots action in order to be more effective. Impacting education issues at the federal level required endorsing candidates for national office, a practice that was common among many labor unions, but had been shunned by NEA. Pressure for greater political effectiveness at all levels percolated up from the local affiliates, which were using political organizing increasingly to elect to school boards those candidates who were favorable to the public schools. The transformation of NEA's political program from top-down lobbying as a professional association to bottom-up grassroots action as a member-run union mirrored the other changes in organizational culture brought about by the emergence of collective bargaining and the democratization of NEA's governance.[11]

The transformation, however, did not come quickly or easily. Many within the organization had long thought of political involvement as a rather unseemly endeavor for a group of professional people. They feared that engaging in partisan politics would undermine the Association's ability to be a respected and an effective *national* voice for the nation's schools, their students, and employees. Public education, they argued, was a bipartisan concern and it needed to remain so. Moreover, they simply saw no compelling reason to change. No other entity—including those that had entered the political arena—had even come close to matching NEA's success in legislative advocacy. At the same time, the Association had long held that one of public education's basic functions was to help prepare students to be full participants in a democratic society. Teachers, it believed, needed to be engaged in the processes of democracy as well. The Representative Assembly underscored this in 1956 when it approved a resolution from NEA's Citizenship Committee urging every teacher to exercise "the right and obligation to be an active, informed citizen, with an intelligent concern for the selection of competent public officials, for the issues that are before the voters, and for the decisions that are made by government at the local, state, and national levels."[12]

The Citizenship Committee undertook a wide range of activities to increase the political involvement of teachers generally and NEA members specifically. But for the most part, these were designed to empower individuals or to assist in solving educational problems at the community level through such political involvement. They were not intended to build a political voice for NEA itself.

The election of Richard Nixon to the White House in 1968 recast that thinking. After the enormous gains in federal education programs through the Eisenhower years, the New Frontier, and the Great Society, federal education programs were now in severe jeopardy. Many within NEA saw a clear link between electoral outcomes and education policy. Consequently, in February 1969, the NEA Board of Directors created a task force to explore ways to allow educators, under NEA's sponsorship, to participate legally in political action at the national level.[13]

After more than a year's study, this task force recommended that NEA establish a national political action committee. On June 28, 1970, however, the Board rejected the idea. The opposition came from an unexpected source: NEA's Legislative Commission. The Commission had long been the Association's voice on federal policy matters. Formally, it had five reasons for its opposition: that the proposal was premature, that it could not be successful in the upcoming elections, that coordination with the states was lacking, that uncertainties existed as to its impact on NEA's tax status, and that if the PAC were to falter, NEA's image would be severely tarnished.[14] Behind the scenes, however, some wondered if this opposition was really more the result of concern over whether the Legislative Commission or the Citizenship Committee and a newly formed PAC would have greater sway.

The controversy swirled over the next 24 hours and on June 29, the Board decided to reconsider the issue, ultimately opting to continue to study the advisability and feasibility of forming an NEA political action committee for another year.[15]

Events soon overtook this study, however. Controversial issues and NEA's response to them—such as the Association's decision to oppose President Nixon's nominations of Clement F. Haynsworth and

214

G. Harrold Carswell to the U.S. Supreme Court—moved NEA well into the political arena. All that was left, Allan West would later write, "was the task of setting up the machinery."[16]

Of course, it would be Bob Chanin who was given that task. In some ways, this would have appeared to be a simple endeavor: developing a set of structures and guidelines that would comply with the Internal Revenue Code and the Federal Corrupt Practices Act and assure appropriate coordination with those state political action committees already in place. In reality, it was not an easy venture.

The proposal to create a PAC was opposed by several NEA state affiliates. Some thought that operating a PAC was not in keeping with teachers' professional image, and others did not want financial resources channeled from the state level to the national level. The state affiliates had been major political players in their states for decades, and many had deep reservations about the notion of the national association getting involved in politics in their states.[17]

To address such concerns and build the necessary consensus, Chanin crafted a structure for the proposed PAC that put decision-making power over NEA's federal endorsements and expenditures in the hands of a council made up largely of state affiliate representatives. With that concept in place, the proposal passed at the 1972 Representative Assembly.[18] NEA went on to build this political action committee—which was initially known as NEA-PAC and eventually became the NEA Fund for Children and Public Education—into one of the most visible, involved and successful PACs in America.

That first year, NEA-PAC endorsed 32 candidates for federal office. Twenty-six were elected to office—an 80 percent success rate. In 1974, 282 candidates for the U.S. House of Representatives were endorsed. Two hundred twenty-nine won as did 21 of the 28 NEA-PAC-endorsed candidates for U.S. Senate—another victory rate of approximately 80 percent.

In 1976, NEA made its first foray into American presidential politics, with 265 NEA delegates attending that year's Democratic convention, and NEA making its first endorsement of a candidate for President of the United States. During the next presidential election, NEA would have 302 delegates and 162 alternates at the 1980 Democratic convention—more than the total number of delegates from any state except California, let alone any other interest group. (Some 20 NEA members were delegates and alternates to the Republican convention as well as that year).

NEA's impact on the national political scene was best summed up by Vice President Walter Mondale during that 1980 Democratic convention: "I've learned that if you want to go somewhere in national politics these days, you better get the NEA behind you."[19]

As the visibility of NEA's political efforts increased, its power was readily apparent. The sheer size of its 1980 Democratic convention presence tempted U.S. Senator Daniel Patrick Moynihan, a New York Democrat, to quip, "The Carter delegation is a wholly-owned subsidiary of the NEA."[20] While that actually may not have been the case, NEA's impact was certainly being felt. As *The Wall Street Journal* concluded, "The National Education Association's political clout reflects a new brand of sophisticated special interest politics. . . . It's clear that the NEA has become a force to be reckoned with in the era of 'reform' politics."[21]

As legal counsel to the PAC, Chanin had the responsibility over the years of ensuring that NEA complied with campaign finance and reporting laws. As the Association become a major player on the national political stage, NEA-PAC became a target for constant scrutiny from the Right. Chanin's philosophy was that it was best to err on the side of caution, and as a result, none of the many charges regarding NEA-PAC that have been filed with the Federal Election Commission has ever stuck.[22]

The Representative Assembly became a focal point for events to generate PAC contributions. Playing on his special relationship with RA delegates over the years, Chanin helped build interest and spirit for some of these events. At a meeting of the Board of Directors prior to the 1984 RA in Minneapolis, NEA President Mary Hatwood Futrell announced that she would be a participant in the "Run for Office." That was a "race" involving thousands of RA delegates of all sizes and shapes who would solicit PAC pledges ahead of time from members back home. When a member of the board asked whether Chanin and Don Cameron, the heavy-set NEA executive director, would also participate, the two quickly huddled and announced that, yes, they would be running—in fact, competing against each other—and that board members could raise money from local members who wanted to show their support for one or the other of the two competitors.

Leading up to the RA, contribution pledges for another pair of NEA staff members, Gary Watts and B. J. Yentzer, outpaced pledges for Chanin and Cameron. The latter pair circulated a memo expressing mock disappointment. "We find the ... discrepancy [in pledges] literally beyond belief when the two races are viewed in context," the memo said. "The Watts/Yentzer race is between two individuals who run regularly, have trained arduously, and are reported to be in tip-top condition. The Chanin/Cameron race ... involves two individuals who rarely walk (much less run), are overage and/or overweight, and have been training on Beefeater Gin and Budweiser beer."[23]

When later they considered the stark, cold reality of the rigorous race, Chanin and Cameron came to their senses and devised a plan that would allow them to be involved in the race without actually running.

On the day of the race, the two conspirators snuck out of the hotel where they and the delegates were staying. As some 3,000 RA delegates gathered to run or watch the race, they were greeted by the arrival of a white stretch limousine, from which the chauffeur emerged, opened the trunk, and proceeded to set up a small table, complete with white tablecloth. He then brought out an ice bucket containing a bottle of champagne, popped the cork and filled two glasses with the bubbly. He opened one of the limousine's doors, and out bounded two lean, muscled runners, one with the name "Chanin" on his back, and the other with "Cameron" on his. The obviously experienced runners took their places at the starting line of the race. Meanwhile, the real Bob Chanin and Don Cameron emerged from the limo, each dressed in white tie, tails, and top hat. They moved to the table, picked up the champagne glasses, and toasted each other. Turning to the several thousand gathered delegates, they raised their glasses and proclaimed, "Let the Games Begin." The crowd went wild.[24]

The two surrogates were indeed experienced runners, and some RA delegates participating in the race grumbled as the pair finished first and second. But both were Minneapolis teachers, even if, as Cameron later noted, one was a member of the local AFT affiliate. The real Chanin and Cameron enjoyed their stunt, especially because it added significant contributions to the "Run for Office" total, and hence, for the PAC. As Cameron later put it in a note to Chanin, "After all is said and done, this may have been our most notable contribution to NEA lore."

More recently, the New Jersey delegation to the 2008 Representative Assembly printed T-shirts to sell for the PAC that had a funny caricature of Chanin on the front with the words, "Bob Chanin Caucus." On the back it said, "Show Me Your Amicus Briefs." The T-shirt was presented to Chanin from the floor of the Assembly:

> **From the Floor:** This is for Bob Chanin. Bob, few people earn the title of cult hero in their lifetime. However, Bob, as chief counsel for the NEA, you've dazzled audiences at the RA and persuaded members of the Supreme Court. In recognition of your brilliant rhetoric and your forceful explanations of complex legal issues, we, the members of the Hunterdon County Education Association and NJEA, would like to present you with our first Bob Chanin Caucus T-shirt . . . . (Applause)

> **President Reg Weaver:** All right! . . . Bob, Dennis [Van Roekel, then vice president], and Lily [Eskelsen, then secretary-treasurer], we will wear these in the office tomorrow, all right? (Laughter) Bob, do you want to say something? All right. (Rising applause)

> **Legal Counsel Chanin:** I'm very grateful to NJEA. I did know about the T-shirt and I showed it to my wife. She said, "Nobody in their right mind would pay anything for that." And I said, "You'd be surprised. When it comes to the Political Action Committee or a worthy cause, they'll pay for just about anything." I think this demonstrates that. Thank you all very much. (Applause)[25]

The Chanin T-shirts proved so popular that a second printing was required to meet demand.

The first big test of NEA's new political operation came in 1976 when, for the first time, the Association endorsed a candidate for president—Jimmy Carter. The campaign demonstrated that, as important as PAC contributions might be, NEA's most effective tool for electing candidates was the grassroots work of NEA members and their families who volunteered in the campaigns of candidates for public office. One out of every 72 American adults is an NEA member, and most of them are highly educated and accustomed to conducting discussion as part of their job. When they knock on doors during an election or telephone voters, they generally are far more effective than the typical political volunteer. They are known in their communities and are credible advocates for pro-education candidates and policies. "It is not surprising," said NEA critic Myron Lieberman, "that NEA political operations are often superior to political party operations, especially at the local level."[26]

When Carter decided to run for president, he was an obscure peanut farmer serving his first term as governor of Georgia. Only two percent of American voters had ever heard of him, while the field of other Democratic candidates included six current or former U.S. senators as well as the governors of much larger states such as California and Pennsylvania. A national Gallup poll released on January 26, 1976, showed that even at that point Carter was the choice of only four percent of likely Democratic primary voters.

Recognizing that NEA's broad geographic reach, membership base, and effective advocacy could be of incalculable value in his quest for the presidency, Carter asked to meet with the leaders of NEA's council of large locals, the National Council of Urban Education Associations (NCUEA). Despite his low standing, such a meeting was included on the agenda of the NCUEA conference in Las Vegas. His appearance came near the end of the session and most participants had left to catch their planes before he spoke. He found himself addressing Chanin, Ken Melley, NEA southern regional director Jimmy Williams, and an embarrassingly small group of other national, state, and local association leaders and staff. But it was enough for the candidate to begin a relationship with NEA.[27]

Despite the obstacles he faced, Carter eventually emerged as the Democratic nominee. His lack of experience in national politics turned out to be a major asset in the eyes of many voters at a time when the Watergate scandal that had forced President Nixon to resign had soured Americans on Washington politicians.

As his vice presidential nominee, Carter chose Walter Mondale, a senator from Minnesota and brother of William "Mort" Mondale, who had been the president of the NEA state affiliate in Minnesota. As they sought an unprecedented endorsement from NEA, Carter and Mondale gave their commitment that, if elected, they would establish a cabinet-level U.S. Department of Education, one of NEA's primary legislative goals.[28]

NEA endorsed Carter for president and mounted an all-out mobilization on his behalf. Unlike most national unions, NEA had members who could be active in the campaign in virtually every state, including areas in the South and Southwest where organized labor was weak.[29] When Carter defeated incumbent President Gerald Ford, the new president and his staff had little doubt about the crucial role played by NEA in their victory. "I'm very delighted that the NEA chose to take an active role in politics at that very propitious time," Carter said at a White House reception for the NEA Board of Directors. "I believe that we will get a separate department of education. This is a matter that I considered very carefully before I promised your officers before the election that I would do it."[30]

NEA had sought a cabinet-level Department of Education for more than a hundred years. But the need had become even more urgent after the 1960s, when the existing Department of Health, Education, and Welfare (HEW) took on dozens of new programs as a result of President Johnson's War on Poverty. HEW had within it an Office of Education, but it competed for attention with many other agencies that oversaw social services, and it had no direct voice at cabinet meetings. As President Carter told the NEA board, education "is a subject that rarely arises at a cabinet meeting of your government in Washington. . . . As long as the educational function is buried within a large department with welfare and health, I don't think that education will ever get the visibility that it deserves."[31]

Senator Abraham Ribicoff of Connecticut, the Democratic chairman of the Senate Committee on Governmental Affairs and former HEW secretary under President Kennedy, introduced legislation to consolidate all federal education programs in a new cabinet-level department, including programs that were not currently in HEW. Within the administration, HEW Secretary Joseph Califano, a former domestic policy aide to President Johnson, fought hard against the reorganization, which would dramatically shrink the department he headed. In his memoir, Califano recalled that early in Carter's presidency, he urged the president to rethink his campaign promise to NEA to create a separate federal department. And Califano took glee after an April 1977 White House meeting involving Carter, Vice President Walter Mondale, Califano, and several top NEA leaders. "To my surprise and satisfaction," Califano wrote, "Carter hedged" on the promise.

But the president didn't hedge for long. Hamilton Jordan, Carter's former campaign manager who had become White House chief of staff, reminded senior administration officials that NEA had played a crucial role in the election and that the commitment to create a cabinet-level department had been "complete and unequivocal."[32]

One of the leading forces lobbying against a bill to establish a Department of Education was the AFT. According to Shanker's biographer, Richard Kahlenberg, AFT opposed creation of the separate agency because "Shanker worried that the NEA would dominate the new department," while, as part of the AFL-CIO, AFT would have more influence in the larger, existing department that housed agencies dealing with other services besides education. "Shanker also feared," wrote Kahlenberg, "that a big political victory for the NEA would hurt the AFT in its battles for control in various local representation fights." George Meany, the president of the AFL-CIO, supported AFT in its opposition to the new department.[33]

Other opponents had substantive objections, chiefly that a cabinet-level department would lead to more federal intrusion in education, which traditionally had been a local and state matter. Richard L. Lyman, the president of Stanford University, testified before Congress that "the two-hundred-year-old absence of a Department of Education is not the result of simple failure during all that time. On the contrary, it derives from the conviction that we do not want the kind of educational system that such arrangements produce."[34]

Marian Wright Edelman, founder of the Children's Defense Fund, opposed the bill from another perspective. She was concerned that Head Start, a comprehensive preschool program that includes health and other services, would be relegated to a lower priority if it were subsumed in a new department of education. Ultimately, she was successful in lobbying the House to leave Head Start in what would become the Department of Health and Human Services.[35] And the inclusion of other agencies and services was debated, including the federal school lunch program and Indian education. While the Carter administration had once sought a more expansive new department, it eventually went along with the idea of essentially stripping the education division out of HEW and making that the new department. Senator Moynihan, who had served in President Kennedy's administration, led an effort to derail the bill by loading it up not only with school lunch and Indian education, but also with the National Science Foundation and other federal agencies. Such a broad portfolio for the department would never win over a majority of lawmakers. But Moynihan's amendment failed, and the Senate approved its bill in April 1979.[36]

The bill faced a tough battle in the House. It came out of the House committee by only one vote and passed the full House by only a four-vote margin. A week after the House vote, Carter fired Califano, with whom he was dissatisfied for a number of reasons, including his work against the president's effort to create a federal Department of Education.[37] The two chambers approved a conference report in September, and on October 17, 1979, Carter signed the bill into law. He nominated Shirley Hufstedler, a federal judge from Los Angeles with no previous education experience, as the first U.S. secretary of education.

Carter did not have much time in office to get the new department up and running. It was May 1980 by the time the department actually came into being. Six months later, Ronald Reagan defeated Carter in the presidential election.[38]

President Reagan did not want the new department to succeed. In fact, as a presidential candidate, he had promised that, if elected, he would ask Congress to reverse course and abolish this new creation. Like NEA, Reagan believed that a cabinet-level Department of Education was likely to push successfully for increased spending and stronger federal standards for education, but unlike NEA, he thought that was a bad idea. "We will respect the rights of state and local authorities in the management of their school systems," stated the Republican Party Platform on which Reagan ran."[39]

In addition to abolishing the new department, the central plank of Reagan's platform on education was to shift public resources to private education—chiefly through the mechanism of tuition tax credits. For the first time, families would receive money from the federal government in the form of tax credits for tuition paid to private schools, including religious schools. With such tax credits, Reagan's platform said, families could "choose for their children those schools which best correspond to their own cultural and moral values. In this way, the schools will be strengthened by the families' involvement, and the families' strengths will be reinforced by supportive cultural institutions."[40]

Reagan never was able to convince Congress to eliminate the Department of Education, but during his eight years in office, he was successful in cutting federal education funding in real terms by 11 percent. Eliminating the department would remain a goal of many Republicans for years to come.[41]

Unable to abolish the Department of Education, Reagan began to use it to promote his goal of shifting public resources to private schools. In August 1981, the department that he now controlled announced that it intended to establish a commission to study the quality of learning and teaching in the nation's schools. The 18-person commission was chaired by David Gardner, president of the University of Utah; its vice chair was Yvonne Larsen, immediate past president of the school board in San Diego, California. No representative of NEA or AFT, the two leading organizations of education employees, was included.[42]

In April 1983, the commission issued a highly publicized report, "A Nation at Risk," that helped create a sense of crisis over public education. The report famously warned that the American school system was plagued by a "rising tide of mediocrity" and that problems in public schools threatened "our very future as a nation."[43]

"If an unfriendly foreign power had attempted to impose on America the mediocre educational performance that exists today, we might well have viewed it as an act of war," the report warned.[44]

The report called for more focus on the basics, higher standards, tighter discipline, longer hours in class, and more homework. It also advocated basing teacher pay, tenure, promotions, and retention on performance, and removing inadequate teachers who could not improve.[45]

At a White House ceremony to present the report to the news media, surrounded by members of the commission, Reagan attacked the public schools in strong language. "This year our country will spend $215 billion for education," he said. "We spend more on education at all levels than any other country in the world. But what have we bought with all that spending?"

According to Reagan, the report demonstrated that public schools were failing, in part because of increased "federal intrusion" in local matters:

> I was interested to see that you noted the almost uninterrupted decline in student achievement in the scores during the past two decades, decades in which the federal presence in education grew and grew.
>
> Your report emphasizes that the federal role in education should be limited to specific areas, and any assistance should be provided with a minimum of administrative burdens on our schools, colleges, and teachers.

Reagan asked for the support of all Americans to implement the report's recommendations, which, he suggested, included not only tuition tax credits but also school vouchers, which would give individual families public funds to spend on tuition at private elementary and secondary schools.

> We'll continue to work in the months ahead for passage of tuition tax credits, vouchers, educational savings accounts, voluntary school prayer, and abolishing the Department of Education. Our agenda is to restore quality to education by increasing competition and by strengthening parental choice and local control. I'd like to ask all of you, as well as every citizen who considers this

report's recommendations, to work together to restore excellence in America's schools.[46]

It so happened that none of the pet goals Reagan listed actually appeared anywhere in the report's recommendations, but he had the power as president, not to mention his masterly communications skills, to frame the public debate. In the years that followed, he and many other politicians of both parties continued to refer to the Nation at Risk report as they called for changes to fix the "failing public schools."[47]

In response to Reagan's impact on public opinion, NEA President Mary Hatwood Futrell argued within the Association's top leadership that the organization ought to acknowledge serious problems in public education, even if schools weren't failing, and use the report as an opportunity to build political support for improving the system. By showing some openness to change, NEA could play a role in shaping reforms. If, on the other hand, the Association simply defended the status quo, it could become irrelevant in the ongoing debate about education reform.

Other members of NEA's nine-person Executive Committee strongly disagreed with Futrell, including future NEA President Bob Chase, a junior high school teacher and former president of the Connecticut Education Association. NEA should respond by defending the record of the public schools, Chase said, and concentrate its efforts on protecting education employees and winning increased resources for the existing system.[48]

Chase and others who agreed with him prevailed. NEA responded to the report in several ways. One was to argue that the whole premise that America's public schools were failing was false. This response was eventually summarized in a book called *The Manufactured Crisis* by two researchers: David Berliner, a professor at Arizona State University, and Bruce Biddle, a professor at the University of Missouri. Their study provided statistics to show that student achievement in America was not declining; America was not falling behind in math and the sciences; teachers were not poorly prepared; spending was not increasing without producing improved results; and members of the public were not dissatisfied with the schools in their communities. "Many of the myths seem to have been told by powerful people who—

despite their protestations—were pursuing a political agenda designed to weaken the nation's public schools, redistribute support for those schools so that privileged students are favored over needy students, or even abolish those schools altogether," the professors wrote. "To this end, they have been prepared to tell lies, suppress evidence, scapegoat educators, and sow endless confusion."[49]

Recognizing that some kind of proactive response to "A Nation at Risk" was necessary, the 1984 Representative Assembly adopted "An Open Letter to America on Schools, Students, and Tomorrow" that proposed nine principles for the public schools. Those principles focused on, among other things, higher expectations for students, equal access and opportunity, a stronger role for teachers in decision making, professional compensation for school staff, improved teacher training, and adequate funding.[50]

A second response was to challenge some of the Nation at Risk report's most troublesome recommendations. Representative Assembly resolutions strongly opposed the idea of merit pay, arguing that it would result in a teacher compensation system based not on qualifications, knowledge, or years of service, but on an administrator's subjective attitudes and biases toward each teacher. While merit pay in concept sounded attractive to many people, NEA feared that in implementation the practice would undermine twenty years of progress achieved through collective bargaining that limited the "power" of administrators to engage in favoritism. Paying a few teachers more, based on "merit" as perceived by an administrator, could be used by school boards to relieve the pressure to raise pay for all teachers to adequate levels. Merit pay, moreover, would be likely to create divisiveness among teachers, undermining the spirit of teamwork and mutual support so essential for effective schools. Any attempt to create a supposedly "objective" measure of merit through standardized testing of students would be fraught with problems, including whether such tests truly measure progress in student learning or whether test results are affected by students' economic and social environment, factors over which teachers have no control.

A 1985 NEA research report summarized the Association's position in favor of maintaining the public schools' traditional "single salary schedule" based on the dual criteria of college education and years of teaching experience:

> The single salary schedule persists as the dominant method, not by fiat, but because of its merits. The salary schedule based on training and experience won out in competition with less objective teacher pay systems characterized by discrimination in compensation based on gender, race, and a host of other subjective considerations. It won out because of its ease of administration and low operating costs. It won out because of its compatibility with sound principal-teacher relationships and teacher collegiality. It won out because it supports the basic structure of the occupation.[51]

Speaking for AFT, meanwhile, Al Shanker responded to "A Nation at Risk" with a more conciliatory approach. He publicly supported the report's call for greater accountability, and said that merit pay could be acceptable under the right conditions.[52] Reagan showed his appreciation for the support by inviting Shanker to meet with him at the White House, and, in turn, Shanker invited Reagan to speak at AFT's national convention in July 1983.[53]

Reagan's speech to AFT was perhaps the only time in American history that a U.S. president used the convention of one union to attack another union. The president listed a series of issues on which he and AFT agreed—in pointed opposition to NEA. By way of example, he noted that he and AFT strongly supported stricter student discipline policies in the schools; NEA wanted to balance that with concerns about due process and disparate treatment of students of color. He and AFT were opposed to requirements supported by NEA for bilingual education for English language learners.

Reagan went so far as to attack NEA for producing curriculum guides for teaching about race that, in his view, suggested America was a racist society. He commended AFT "for its ringing condemnation of those organizations, one of which I referred to earlier, who would exploit teaching positions and manipulate curriculum for propaganda purposes. On this last issue, you stand in bright contrast to those who have promoted curriculum guides that seem to be more aimed at frightening and brainwashing American schoolchildren than at fostering learning and stimulating balanced, intelligent debate."[54]

In Chanin's view, "A Nation at Risk" caused an abrupt change in the political climate for public education. The schools, he told one state association audience in 2000, had largely been ignored by the general public, but they were all of a sudden under close scrutiny "and were found to be wanting. Critics predicted that shortcomings of public education would compromise America's economic security and world leadership, and teachers became easy targets of blame."[55]

An initial wave of reform swept through many states as lawmakers reacted to the alarm sounded by the Nation at Risk report. California and Florida enacted Master Teacher programs. These and similar programs in other states, were meant to identify and reward exemplary teachers—and to some degree weed out those who did not measure up.

The greatest direct impact of "A Nation at Risk" came in southern states, where there were no collective-bargaining laws for education employees. Shortly after the report was issued in 1983, the 37-year-old Democratic governor of Arkansas, Bill Clinton, established an education standards panel, headed by his wife, Hillary Rodham Clinton, to hold hearings on how to respond to the crisis in the state's public schools. Picking up on the national commission's theme that incompetent teachers were a major problem, the Clinton panel recommended that, in order to keep their jobs, all "in-service" teachers—teachers who had already been working in the classroom for years—should be required to pass a paper-and-pencil test on basic skills such as English and mathematics. At Governor Clinton's insistence, the proposal was enacted into law by the Arkansas legislature, to be implemented for the 1984-85 school year.[56]

The new requirement created a storm of protest from Arkansas teachers and the NEA state affiliate, the Arkansas Education Association (AEA). A 12-year veteran teacher, Lura Holifield, expressed the outrage shared by many AEA members in a letter to her local newspaper:

> If I am unqualified and need to prove my worth, then I demand to be tested on the 12 years of experience I have had. . . . I would suggest the Communication Skills section of the test include multiple-choice items dealing

with . . . how to explain to a class of fifth-graders why one of their classmates died before school that morning; how to respond to a 14-year-old that confides in me that she is pregnant; how to help another who wants to commit suicide; how to comfort a child crying because . . . his parents just separated; and what to say when told: "I'm sorry but we are having a revenue shortfall and we'll have to cut your pay on your last check.". . . If the legislature can devise a test that can accurately measure what a teacher or administrator does every day, I'll be glad to take it. . . . Forgive me, Mr. and Mrs. Clinton, if I sound bitter and hurt by your assessment of my job performance, but I am.[57]

AEA Executive Director Kai Erickson told reporters that a paper-and-pencil test would not identify teachers "who cannot communicate with their students or conduct themselves effectively in a classroom." If there are teachers who lack basic skills, Erickson added, they should be "helped to upgrade themselves, not driven from their jobs after being adjudged as satisfactory by the normal evaluation procedures over so many years."[58]

NEA sent an investigative committee of educators from around the nation to Arkansas to assess the ramifications of the law for other states. The team asked to meet with Governor Clinton, and he agreed, as long as the discussion was open to the news media and the public. The first question the visiting educators asked the governor was whether his proposal for testing was motivated more by political posturing than sound educational policy. "No politician in his right mind enjoys the kind of controversy this has generated," Clinton replied. "This has caused me a great deal of pain."[59]

Clinton explained that he needed to establish the testing requirement in order to gain public acceptance of other provisions of the legislation that would increase the state sales tax to fund education and, in particular, higher salaries for teachers. At the time, Arkansas ranked last among all states on per-pupil spending for the public schools and next to last in teacher salaries.[60]

NEA's investigative committee told Clinton that the testing requirement had undermined teacher morale as well as student and community respect for teachers. Clinton responded that any such effects were not his fault, but AEA's.

"If they had said, 'We're more than happy to take it, let's just rear back and show them,' then that dip in public respect for teachers would have lasted about three days," he told the *Arkansas Gazette*. "Then, public confidence in teaching would have taken off like a skyrocket. As it was, the [AEA] reaction confirmed the attitude that something had to be done."[61]

At the urging of its angry members, AEA—with NEA support and involvement—challenged the testing law in federal court under Title VII of the Civil Rights Act of 1964. AEA charged that the employment test was culturally biased against African American teachers. AEA lawyers eventually concluded that the case was not likely to succeed, however, because there were no evident disparate results between black and white teachers. The suit was withdrawn in 1987.[62] More than 37,000 teachers took the test, and 3.6 percent were unable to pass.[63]

NEA had more success with litigation against a similar test for in-service teachers adopted in Georgia in 1985. The Georgia test asked experienced teachers questions about the broad field in which they were already certified to teach. As compared with Arkansas, the performance of black and white teachers differed markedly in the Georgia tests, with 62 percent of black teachers failing the test while only 12 percent of white teachers failed it. In October 1986, the Georgia Association of Educators (GAE), backed by NEA, filed suit in federal district court under Title VII, charging that the test was racially biased and not sufficiently related to teachers' actual job requirements.[64]

In March 1988, GAE reached a court-approved settlement with the state. Conditions of the settlement determined that: in-service teachers who failed the test would receive a $6,000 study grant; an advisory committee would be established to monitor and evaluate the test; and the scope of the test would be narrowed to align more closely with the subject matter each teacher actually needed to know. Biology teachers, for example, would no longer be tested on physics, and vice versa.[65]

The NEA-funded lawsuits in Arkansas and Georgia apparently persuaded decision-makers that testing veteran teachers was an ineffective means of enhancing teacher quality. Since the 1980s resolution of the litigation in Georgia, no other state has initiated a program to test in-service teachers.[66]

The drumbeat from those who saw the teacher unions and collective bargaining—and particularly NEA—as a major cause of the problems of public education continued to grow louder in the 1990s. *The Wall Street Journal*, for example, was unrelenting in its editorial-page criticism of the teachers' unions. "Both the NEA and the AFT promote policies that protect the jobs of incompetent or poor teachers at the expense of those who would improve the system," said a July 13, 1993, editorial about the budding school voucher movement. "The status quo stultifies the efforts of great teachers, but it also provides protected employment for all union members." The newspaper would return to such themes time and again in the 1990s and 2000s.

In 1993, meanwhile, *Forbes* magazine published a cover story with the headline, "Suffer the little children: How the National Education Association corrupts our public schools." Inside the upscale business magazine, another headline read: "The National Extortion Association?" The magazine made clear that its gripe with NEA was that it "fights all voucher and choice proposals that might allow students to escape to a private school." As noted earlier, *Forbes* complained that NEA's UniServ staff constitutes "the largest field army of paid political organizers and lobbyists in the U.S., dwarfing the forces of the Republican and Democratic national committees combined." The chair of the National Taxpayers Union, which fights against funding for public education and other public services, was quoted as complaining that "wherever we go, the NEA is our main opponent." Surrounding the references to NEA's policy positions was a heavy dose of invective that belied any pretense of journalistic objectivity. The office building NEA owns in Washington, D.C., was described as "breathtakingly palatial." The Association's stands on social justice were labeled "NEA's streak of left-wing looneyism." NEA's attempts to affect public policy on education were called "alien to American constitutional principles of equal protection and republican government."

Chanin, too, rated a mention. The magazine described NEA as "a political science textbook case" of "the tendency of membership organizations to degenerate from democracies into elite-driven groups serving the interests of their leaders. Indeed, one of the most powerful NEA leaders has never been a classroom teacher at all: longtime general counsel Robert Chanin, who has been generously allowed to go off staff to work from a major labor law firm and won't reveal his income."[67]

The significance of the *Forbes* article went beyond the circulation of the magazine itself, as other right-wing groups distributed copies throughout the country in fundraising appeals. "I'd like to be able to put this exposé into the hands of the teachers, parents, journalists, editors, news directors, and elected officials who need to read it," wrote the head of the National Right to Work Committee, an anti-union group, in an appeal to his members. "But that means printing and mailing up to as many as 200,000 more copies of this article—which will cost a fortune. So I'm writing to ask for your help."[68]

The *Forbes* article also touched on another issue that has been significant to NEA's organizational and political power and a target for its critics: "agency shop" arrangements, in which bargaining-unit employees who do not wish to join the association that is recognized as the exclusive collective-bargaining representative still must pay their "fair share" of costs related to collective bargaining, since these workers also benefit from the process. Such arrangements led to several U.S. Supreme Court cases over the years, including one argued by Chanin in 1990.

The principle of agency-shop arrangements in the public sector has its roots in the "union shop" of the private sector, which requires every employee in the bargaining unit, as a condition of employment, to become a member of the union recognized as the exclusive collective-bargaining agent. The union has the responsibility of fair representation of all members of the unit, and the problem of "free riders" who would benefit from the negotiated agreement without paying for representation is eliminated. Finding that union shop arrangements serve the compelling government interest of promoting labor peace in the private sector, the U.S. Supreme Court upheld such union-shop arrangements in two seminal cases in the 1950s and early 1960s.[69] In deciding those cases, the court reduced the union shop to its financial core—issues such as payment of dues, initiation fees, and assessments—and concluded that neither First Amendment freedom of speech nor freedom of association was infringed by requiring that all employees in the bargaining unit contribute to the cost of negotiating and administering a collective-bargaining agreement. Although it said that constitutional problems might exist if the union were to use the exacted fees for "political causes" over the objection of dissenting employees, the Court found it unnecessary to address those problems in the private-sector cases because the union-shop fees were only being used for purposes related to collective bargaining.[70]

The first public-sector agency shop case to come before the U.S. Supreme Court arose in Michigan, which had adopted a labor law allowing an exclusive collective-bargaining agent for public employees to negotiate such an arrangement. In 1967, the Detroit Federation of Teachers (DFT), an AFT affiliate, had been certified as the bargaining agent for that city's teachers and had negotiated an agency shop arrangement. Louis Abood was one of several Detroit teachers who refused to join or pay an agency shop fee to DFT.

Abood and his fellow nonunion members objected to the DFT collecting agency-shop fees for collective bargaining. They also objected to certain "economic, political, professional, scientific, and religious" activities and programs of the federation.[71] A Michigan state appellate court upheld the agency-shop arrangement under the First Amendment. It ruled that while the requirement that the objecting teachers pay for the union's political causes could raise constitutional concerns, the teachers in this case had not notified the union of their specific objections, and thus they could not recover any of the fees at issue in the litigation.[72]

The teachers took their case to the U.S. Supreme Court, where NEA joined with the Detroit school system and the DFT in defending the agency-shop arrangement. In an *amicus* brief filed by Chanin and deputy general counsel David Rubin, NEA argued for the basic legality and necessity of the agency-shop arrangement in the public sector. "If a union shop or agency shop arrangement, insofar as it requires all employees in the bargaining unit to contribute to the cost of bargaining, policing, and administering the collective agreement, infringes at all upon First Amendment rights, the infringement is marginal and outweighed by the important and substantial interests [that the Court had recognized in the private sector] in insuring basic equity, labor peace and stability, and effective collective bargaining," the NEA brief said.[73]

"A different result might be reached if the exaction of fees were to be used to support political causes to which the employee is opposed," the brief continued, noting that the High Court had ruled in private-sector cases that such fees were not permitted.[74]

On May 23, 1977, the Supreme Court issued its opinion in *Abood v. Detroit Board of Education.* It upheld agency-shop arrangements in the public sector insofar as nonmembers' fees went to finance collective bargaining and contract administration. The state, however, may not condition employment as a public school teacher or other public-sector employee on the requirement that the employee contribute to a union's ideological activities unrelated to collective bargaining with which he might not agree, the Court said.[75]

Although the overall judgment in the case was unanimous, in an opinion signed by five of the justices, Justice Potter Stewart offered a bit of understatement about the Pandora's box that the Court was opening in this area of the law: "There will, of course, be difficult problems in drawing lines between collective-bargaining activities, for which contributions may be compelled, and ideological activities unrelated to collective bargaining, for which such compulsion is prohibited."[76]

In reporting on the decision, *The Wall Street Journal* said that "the 'right to work' forces that supported the anti-union Detroit teachers did score some points with three members of the court. Justice Lewis Powell, joined by Chief Justice Warren Burger and Justice Harry Blackmun, argued that the court had incorrectly placed the burden on the employes [sic] to prove that their rights had been violated. . . . They said that the state should have to prove that any union dues or fees it requires of nonunion members 'are needed to serve paramount governmental interests.'"[77]

The table had been set for major battles throughout the next three decades over where to draw the line between chargeable and non-chargeable expenses. But the basic ruling upholding agency fees for bargaining-related expenses was an important victory for NEA and other public-sector unions.

For the next several years after *Abood*, NEA and other public-sector unions worked to develop procedures to draw the line between those expenses that could be charged to objecting nonmembers and those that could not. In 1985, the issue of agency fees and the teachers' unions returned to the Supreme Court. Annie Lee Hudson, a Chicago teacher who was not a member of the AFT-affiliated Chicago Teachers Union, objected to the agency fee the union charged her, believing some of her fee was going for costs not related to collective bargaining. She sent a letter to the union demanding detailed financial information about how the fee was calculated. The union invited Hudson to its offices so she could review union financial records, but Hudson and three other nonunion members sued over their fees instead. The nonmembers lost in federal district court, but a panel of the U.S. Court of Appeals for the Seventh Circuit ruled that the union's review procedure was inadequate, and that any rebate which allowed the union temporary use of money for activities that violated the nonmembers' rights was unconstitutional.[78]

In an *amicus* brief filed when the case reached the U.S. Supreme Court, Chanin pointed out that NEA had adopted a procedure which it believed met the constitutional concerns involved. For any nonmember who objected to the use of his or her agency fee, the Association established an escrow account for a portion of the objecting employee's agency fee, then hired an arbitrator to be an "umpire" to determine which costs related to collective bargaining and which did not.[79] On March 4, 1986, the Supreme Court ruled unanimously in *Chicago Teachers Union v. Hudson* that the public-employee unions had to adopt stronger procedural safeguards to ensure that nonmembers' agency fees were not spent on noncollective-bargaining related activities to which they objected. Without specifically commenting on the NEA procedure, the Court alluded to the key components of that procedure, stating that unions must provide nonmembers with a detailed explanation of how their agency fees were calculated, must provide them with a prompt way of challenging their fees in impartial arbitration, and must place disputed fee amounts in an interest-bearing escrow account.[80]

The Wall Street Journal said the ruling would likely "force some changes in the way public unions operate," and it quoted Chanin as saying, "The problem is going to be how to set up arbitration and who pays for it."[81] In a 60-page memorandum a few weeks after the ruling, Chanin and his Bredhoff & Kaiser colleague Bruce Lerner dissected the decision, stating that "there are at this juncture few definitive solutions to the problems raised by *Hudson*." The ruling raised a host of practical questions about association budgets, notices to objecting fee-payers, arbitration procedures, and so forth, the memorandum said. "Although the requirements set forth in *Hudson* for a constitutionally acceptable procedure for collecting agency fees are on their face relatively straightforward, the Court obviously did not give much thought to the practical problems involved in complying with these requirements," it concluded.[82]

NEA and its affiliates worked through those practical problems over the next few years. But groups such as the National Right to Work Legal Defense Foundation stepped up their efforts in opposition to agency-shop arrangements. These opponents viewed such arrangements as "compulsory unionism," and they attacked NEA and other public-sector unions in state legislatures and in the courts.

By 1990, the next important battle over agency fees in the public sector reached the Supreme Court. The case involved six faculty members at Ferris State College, a state institution in Big Rapids, Michigan. Faculty members at the college were represented in collective bargaining by the Ferris Faculty Association (FFA), an affiliate of both the Michigan Education Association (MEA) and NEA. Faculty members who declined to join the FFA were charged an agency fee of $248 for the 1981-82 academic year, an amount that was the same as annual dues for FFA members, and included payments to FFA, MEA and NEA. The dissenting faculty members filed a lawsuit under the First and Fourteenth Amendments which alleged that much of their agency fees went for activities that were not related to collective bargaining. And they objected to any portion of their fees being paid to MEA or NEA for activities that did not directly involve employees in the FFA bargaining unit.[83]

A federal district judge analyzed the activities of FFA, MEA, and NEA included in the agency fee and ruled that many were not chargeable to the nonmembers. He also held that at least some expenses for activities of the state and national associations that did not relate specifically to the FFA bargaining unit, such as the costs of sending members to conventions, most of the costs of the state association's magazine, and expenditures by NEA on bargaining and negotiation support activities, were chargeable. He knocked the per-person agency fee for the year in question down to $28.59.[84] The U.S. Court of Appeals for the Sixth Circuit affirmed, and the nonmembers appealed to the Supreme Court. On November 5, 1990, Chanin argued the case for NEA and its state and local affiliates in *Lehnert v. Ferris Faculty Association*, going up against Raymond LaJeunesse, the lead counsel of the National Right to Work organization.

"The First Amendment requires a proven, compelling governmental interest to infringe on the nonmember's right not to associate with this union and in any way support any of its activities," LaJeunesse told the justices. "And the only compelling governmental interest that's been identified by this Court is reimbursing the union for its costs of performing its statutory functions as exclusive representative of the bargaining unit." This, he contended, meant nonmembers could not be charged for the state and national affiliates' expenditures that were not incurred for the direct benefit of the nonmember's bargaining unit.[85]

Chanin, making his fourth argument before the Supreme Court, told the justices: "The courts below held that the petitioners may be charged for the cost of certain activities engaged in by MEA and NEA. Because these activities did not directly involve the collective-bargaining process at Ferris State College, petitioners contend that they are in effect being asked to subsidize employees in other bargaining units represented by MEA and NEA—to pay for service provided to these other employees which is of no benefit to the members in their own bargaining unit. The petitioners are wrong."

One of the justices interrupted: "They don't say 'is of no benefit.' They say [the questioned activities do] not pertain to their bargaining process."

"They're wrong. They're wrong on that as well, Your Honor," Chanin replied, with such conviction that he prompted a ripple of laughter in the courtroom.[86]

Later in the argument, Chanin was making the point that the designation of a union as the bargaining agent brought responsibilities that often required the services of the state or national association's expertise, such as that of "lawyers, expert negotiators, economists, a research staff, as well as general administrative personnel."

"What has happened here is by selecting as a bargaining representative a local union that was affiliated with larger parent organizations, the majority of employees in the Ferris College bargaining unit have chosen to provide and fund certain of those responsibilities on a unit . . . a cross-unit basis with a sharing of the risks in which all of the people who benefit, the members and the fee payers, are charged a periodic uniform flat fee," Chanin added. This prompted some mock disbelief from Justice Antonin Scalia, who would prove to be sympathetic to the objecting nonmembers in this and later agency fee cases:

> **Justice Scalia:** You certainly make the union movement sound like a very business-like operation. I've always heard it called "the movement." I thought that people in one union would contribute to the international [i.e. national union] because they believed in unionism. They don't care whether they're getting back penny for penny an investment that they're making in the international. There's none of that here?
>
> **Chanin:** Your Honor—
>
> **Justice Scalia:** This is strictly a business operation?
>
> **Chanin:** It hurts me . . . it hurts me to say that— [Laughter] . . . that is not the sole basis for affiliation. It is partially there, and it is part of why people join unions—
>
> **Justice Scalia:** Of course it is.
>
> **Chanin:** But unionism is a competitive area. There are unions competing on a day-to-day basis for the allegiance of employees. The ones who get those employees, the ones

who are voted in, are the ones who can deliver when they are called upon. And delivery in a collective bargaining sense means when a local has a crisis, a crisis beyond its own means to deal with, the parent organizations are there. They are there with what the Court referred to in *Abood*, the lawyers, the negotiators, and the research people. . . .[87]

The Supreme Court took the case under advisement, and it would be nearly seven months before it would issue a decision. The reasons became clear the day the decision was handed down.

On May 30, 1991, Justice Harry Blackmun announced the judgment of the court. In most Supreme Court cases, the author of the majority opinion gives a sort of executive summary, sometimes reading excerpts for as long as 10 or 15 minutes. But in *Lehnert*, the court issued four separate opinions.

"The case [does] not easily lend itself to announcement from the bench," Justice Blackmun said that day. "I think it suffices to say that certain nonmember faculty objected to particular uses by the unions of their service fees and filed suit under federal statutes claiming violation of their rights under the First and Fourteenth Amendments. The District Court held that certain of the expenditures were constitutionally chargeable to [the nonmembers], and the Court of Appeals affirmed. In an opinion filed with the Clerk today, we affirm that judgment in part and reverse it in part, and remand the case. The details are complex and are revealed, we hope, by the opinion."[88]

Blackmun was not understating the complexity of the decision. Although he wrote the main plurality opinion, he secured a fifth vote to command a majority for only parts of his opinion.[89]

The bottom line was that eight justices agreed that nonmembers could not be charged for the lobbying activities of the union, unless the lobbying was very narrowly aimed at, say, persuading a state legislature to approve or implement a local union contract. "The state constitutionally may not compel its employees to subsidize legislative lobbying or other political union activities outside the limited context of contract ratification or implementation," Blackmun said in a part of his opinion signed by three other justices. Justice Scalia issued his own opinion, signed by three other justices, which agreed that only narrowly focused lobbying could be charged to nonmembers, though he proposed a legal test for analyzing the issues different from the one Blackmun proposed. Eight members of the court also disapproved of charging nonmembers for certain litigation and public relations expenses that were not directly tied to bargaining issues.

On the key issue in the case—highlighted by the above quoted colloquy between Justice Scalia and Chanin—all nine justices upheld the use of agency fees for the costs of the local union's affiliation with the state and national associations. "The essence of the affiliation relationship is the notion that the parent will bring to bear its often considerable economic, political, and informational resources when the local is in need of them," Blackmun said. "Consequently, that part of a local's affiliation fee which contributes to the pool of resources potentially available to the local is assessed for the bargaining unit's protection, even if it is not actually expended on that unit in any particular membership year."[90] Even Justice Scalia apparently had been persuaded by Chanin's advocacy, noting Justice Blackmun's holding on this critical point and declaring that "I think that resolution is correct."[91]

Five members of the court agreed among the different opinions that the costs of sending delegates to national union conventions and meetings could be charged, as could the costs of reporting on chargeable activities in a national union magazine. Finally, five justices upheld the chargeability of certain FFA activities that had been carried out in preparation for a possible illegal strike.

Such a complex—and splintered—opinion was certainly open to several interpretations and continuing analysis, and when it was released, both sides claimed victory.

"On balance, it was more of a victory for nonunion employees than a loss," Raymond LaJeunesse told *Education Week*. "Lobbying was probably the largest issue. We consider that part of it a victory."[92]

Chanin, meanwhile, told the same publication that the *Lehnert* decision was a "mixed bag, [and] we got the bigger part of the bag."

"We're overjoyed," he continued. "We have a 9-to-0 vote on the critical issue: every justice said you can charge for parent-organization expenses."[93]

A memo prepared later that summer by the NEA Office of General Counsel and Bredhoff & Kaiser concluded that "on balance, we consider the outcome in *Lehnert* to be quite satisfactory. . . . The decision is not entirely favorable, however, and the position taken by a majority of the justices with regard to legislative lobbying and other political activity, public relations activity, and out-of-unit litigation will require NEA and its affiliates to make certain revisions in their pre-*Lehnert* chargeability calculations."[94]

NEA and other public-sector unions would continue their battles with the "right to work" forces throughout the 1990s and into the new century, on agency fees and other issues. The complexity of the agency-shop arrangements sometimes led to questions about whether the battles were worth the effort. Chanin's answer was always an unequivocal yes. For one thing, there was a matter of principle, he said. It was simply right that those who benefit from the collective-bargaining process pay their fair share.

Additionally, revenue from agency fees was not insignificant. For example, in fiscal year 1991-92—around the time the *Lehnert* case was decided—NEA received some $2 million from 34,000 fee-payers. That was an amount equal to dues income from slightly more than 20,000 active members, about the number in a medium-size state affiliate at the time. Agency fees also provided substantially more income to state and local associations, Chanin noted.

Moreover, the economic value of the agency fee was not reflected simply in the amount collected. When employees are subject to the nonmembers' fees, many decide to join the Association as full dues-paying members. And the agency fee arrangement tended to limit competition from organizations that might challenge the NEA-affiliated association as the recognized bargaining agent, Chanin believed.[95]

Far from the intricate legal battles over agency fees, meanwhile, NEA supported Bill Clinton for president in 1992, despite his push as governor of Arkansas for in-service teacher testing. It also supported him in his 1996 re-election bid. Political attacks on NEA gained their highest public profile when the 1996 Republican presidential nominee,

Senator Bob Dole of Kansas, devoted a passage in his nationally televised prime-time acceptance speech at the Republican National Convention to a direct attack on NEA and teacher unionism. His opposition to NEA renewed his party's call for school vouchers that would divert public funds to subsidize private schools. His words rallied his supporters to the continuing attack:

> We're not educating all of our children. Too many are being forced to absorb the fads of the moment. Not for nothing are we the biggest education spenders and among the lowest education achievers among the leading industrial nations.
>
> The teachers' unions nominated Bill Clinton in 1992. They're funding his re-election now. And they, his most reliable supporters, know he will maintain the status quo.
>
> And I say this—I say this not to the teachers, but to their unions. I say this, if education were a war, you would be losing it. If it were a business, you would be driving it into bankruptcy. If it were a patient, it would be dying.
>
> And to the teachers unions, I say, when I am president, I will disregard your political power for the sake of the parents, the children, the schools and the nation. I plan to enrich your vocabulary with those words you fear— school choice. . . .
>
> There is no reason why those who live on any street in America should not have the same right as the person who lives at 1600 Pennsylvania Avenue—the right to send your child to the school of your choice. [96]

By "school choice," Dole and the Republican Party in 1996 generally meant "private school vouchers."

Attacks like these helped convince Bob Chase, who became NEA president in September 1996, that it was time for NEA to position itself aggressively in the forefront of education reform in order to maintain voters' support for the public schools and education employees' pay and benefits. By working more closely with school boards and administrators, the organization could improve its image with the public as a constructive contributor to educational quality. Chase said that his opposition to Mary Futrell when she had made the same argument 12 years earlier was "the biggest mistake of my career."[97]

Chase commissioned an internal NEA report to argue the need for what he called "New Unionism." Completed in January 1997, the report was called "An Institution at Risk," playing off the title of the Reagan-era report on the state of education in America. Based on focus groups of teachers as well as interviews with the leaders and staff of NEA and its state and local affiliates, the report contended that "there appears to be a sizable number of new or potential new members of NEA who want to hear what the organization has to offer in terms of professional development, who are less concerned with traditional collective-bargaining issues, and do not believe it is a player in terms of ensuring quality public education."[98]

Meanwhile, the report said, "NEA's adversaries have been more effective at advancing their messages and initiatives, and have succeeded in putting the Association on defense—and keeping it there. The NEA needs to make the opposition explain why it does not like the NEA's ideas—not the other way around."[99]

Chase believed that establishing a better image for NEA as a positive force for change required a dramatic and visible break from the past. In February 1997, he gave a ground-breaking speech at the National Press Club, promising that NEA was going to "reinvent" itself as it had once before:

> In the 1960s, we took a rather quiet, genteel professional association of educators and we reinvented it as an assertive—and, when necessary, militant—labor union. . . . We accepted the industrial premise—namely, that labor and management have distinct, conflicting roles and interests . . . that we are destined to clash . . . that the union-management relationship is inherently adversarial. These industrial-style, adversarial tactics simply are not suited to the next stage of school reform.

> While the vast majority of teachers are capable and dedicated professionals who put children's interests first, there are indeed some bad teachers in America's schools, and it is our job as a union to improve those teachers or—that failing—to get them out of the classroom.

> While NEA does not control curriculum, set funding levels, or hire and fire, we cannot go on denying responsibility for school quality. We can't wash our hands of it and say 'that's management's job.' School quality—the quality of the environment where students learn and where our members work—must be our responsibility as a union. . . . Instead of contracts that reduce flexibility and restrict change, we—and our schools—need contracts that empower and enable. . . .
>
> I say to the traditionalists in NEA's ranks—to those who argue that we should stick to our knitting, leaving education reform to others: you are mistaken.[100]

Chanin understood Chase's goal of dramatizing NEA's commitment to educational quality, but he felt that the speech had two fundamental flaws. It ignored the fact that, from the earliest days of collective bargaining in the 1960s, he and other negotiators had sought—and sometimes achieved—"contracts that empower and enable," in that they gave teachers influence over policy issues that previously had been management's sole prerogative.[101] As Chanin said in a 2002 speech to the Indiana State Teachers Association:

> Every one of dozens of local associations that I worked with in the 1960s and 1970s put on the bargaining table proposals to reduce class size; hire more librarians, counselors, and reading specialists; update textbooks; and otherwise improve the quality of education provided to students. When school districts refused to collectively bargain because they said these were 'matters of educational policy,' we went to court, and when courts agreed with school districts, teachers often went on strike.
>
> To be sure, NEA's concept of 'new unionism' involves different ways of dealing with certain problems that confront public education, and may require education employees and their associations to take more responsibility for assuring that there is a qualified teacher in every classroom—but I think we do a great disservice to those who came before to suggest that they only saw collective bargaining as a way to improve their salaries, fringe benefits, and working conditions.[102]

More fundamentally, Chanin believed that Chase's speech did not adequately address the complex tension between education reform and the rights of education employees under collective bargaining. Indeed, he had essentially addressed Chase's speech five years before Chase gave it.

In a speech delivered in March 1992 to leaders of NEA and its affiliates, Chanin discussed the importance of making sure that decades of achievements in education employees' rights through collective bargaining would not be undone in the name of education "reform." At the time, there was much discussion about changes such as site-based decision-making (turning over more decisions to committees of administrators, teachers, and parents at each school); peer review (involving teachers in job performance evaluations of other teachers); and mentor teacher programs (using more experienced teachers to develop the skills of other teachers on an ongoing basis). In some cases, experiments with such innovations raised the possibility of conflict with teachers' rights achieved through collective-bargaining agreements.

The essential question, Chanin said, was this: "Can an education reform movement that is premised on a sharing of common interests, mutual trust, and consensus building find happiness in a system of labor relations that is inherently adversarial in nature?" He continued:

> The principle of seniority is the cornerstone of American labor relations, in both the public and private sectors. Seniority provides an objective standard by which employment decisions can be made, as opposed to unilateral and often arbitrary employer action. . . .
>
> But how can we deny that seniority. . . reduces what some consider to be 'managerial flexibility' in the operation of school systems?. . . Contract provisions for seniority-based layoffs, transfers, and assignments prevent the type of less structured, performance responsive system of personnel administration that many believe is essential to meaningful education reform. . . .
>
> In addition to seniority, another basic precept of collective bargaining is that there be a clear distinction between rank-and-file employees and management. Unionism assumes that the interests of labor and management are

antithetical, and that it is necessary to have a completely autonomous organization in order to adequately represent the employees' interests. . . .

But this philosophy of conflict—with all of its spin-off ramifications—casts a shadow on the type of shared responsibility that is essential to site-based decision making, peer review, mentor teacher programs, and other arrangements that some see as the hallmark of meaningful educational reform.

Indeed, to some the very nature of collective bargaining agreements is problematic for education reform. Collective-bargaining agreements are formulated with the express purpose of reducing 'flexibility' and uncertainty of action so that there are fewer opportunities for mistreatment of employees. . . .

In this era of paradigm shifts, supporting the status quo in regard to anything is somewhat out of fashion, but the status quo in collective bargaining does not mean preserving static practices. Collective bargaining is an inherently developmental process that has the capacity to evolve and adapt to new circumstances and changes in environment. Nor does one have to be a futurist to recognize the direction of change or to identify those aspects of traditional collective bargaining that will have to be adjusted in order to accommodate the education reform movement. . . .

To begin with, the present scope of collective bargaining, which is generally limited to salaries and working conditions and makes educational policy a management prerogative, will have to undergo change. There is increasing recognition that, in a service industry like education, where the work of individual employees is the product that the enterprise provides to its student clients, virtually any educational policy has a direct and immediate impact on the working conditions of teachers. If teacher unions are to play a meaningful role in education reform, and if teachers are to be change agents, collective bargaining will have to embrace many issues that traditionally have been reserved for unilateral school board action. . . .

246

Moving to a related point, the growing tendency to define 'professionalism' in terms of collegial assistance and mutual responsibility for the quality of education can be expected to keep issues such as peer review, mentor teaching, site-based decision-making, and so forth, at the forefront of the education reform movement. These arrangements will require the parties to rethink current concepts regarding 'managers' and 'supervisors' for purposes of bargaining unit structure in the short run and the right to collective bargaining in the long run. . . . We will probably see in the public sector an increased blurring of the traditional distinction between labor and management as rank-and-file teachers are called upon from time to time to perform supervisory and managerial functions.

Forums for collective bargaining will probably undergo changes as parties find that formal at-the-table collective bargaining is better for some things than for others—that it is best suited for dividing resources and making work rules, but less well-suited for dealing with educational problems or devising new educational programs. . . .

As parties move beyond work rules and attempt to address educational problems and develop educational programs, there inevitably will be increasingly more problem solving and labor-management cooperation—which I might note is not a phenomenon foreign to the current adversarial system of collective bargaining. Labor/management cooperation is not something to be accepted or rejected on the basis of *a priori* principles, but rather a tactic to be used where it works and rejected where it does not work.

There is evidence to suggest that this process of evolution and adaptation is already underway—that unions and school boards in at least some school districts are developing new rules to govern their relationship. . . . It may just turn out that, at least in many school districts, we can indeed have the best of both worlds—meaningful education reform within the framework of the current adversarial system of collective bargaining.

By the same token, however, I am not so naïve or Pollyannaish as to rule out the possibility that these two tracks—collective bargaining and education reform—may on occasion cross. As the education reform movement progresses, proposals may be developed that are . . . objectionable to NEA only because they do not adequately protect the collective bargaining rights of education employees. Accommodation may prove impossible, and NEA may be forced to do in this context what it has been forced to do in other contexts, such as school desegregation. That is, to make a choice it would rather not have to make—to perhaps establish priorities between its commitment to education reform and its commitment to collective bargaining. . . .

Should this become necessary, for me, the choice is relatively clear, for two reasons. First, because I believe very deeply in the concept of collective bargaining, but primarily because I remember what things were like before we had collective bargaining. . . . It is my cynical view that the basic attitudes of many, perhaps most, school board members and administrators have not changed very much in the past twenty-five years. I firmly believe that if we back away from exclusive recognition, seniority, grievance arbitration, and the other protections that the current collective bargaining structure gives us, we will most assuredly—and rather promptly—find ourselves subject to the same authoritarian structure and in the same subservient status that we were prior to the advent of collective bargaining. . . .

I am fully aware of the need to improve the quality of education in order to save public education, and the need for NEA to be deeply involved in that effort in order for NEA to remain relevant, but I do not believe that education reform should be achieved at the expense of employee rights. . . . Education employees have achieved, through collective bargaining, important and well-deserved rights. We cannot allow these rights to be taken away in the name of education reform, and we must resist any attempt to weaken collective bargaining.[103]

As controversial as "New Unionism" was in parts of the organization, Chase's other initiative to "reinvent" NEA was even more challenging: a proposed merger with the American Federation of

Teachers.

The issue of such a merger had arisen before. It was first proposed by AFT in October 1968, only to be promptly and thoroughly rejected by both the NEA Executive Committee and the NEA Board of Directors.[104] Rebuffed at the national level, AFT turned its attention to the state and local levels, where the merger concept received a more sympathetic response from some NEA affiliates. In a few instances, these resulted in formal negotiations and, in some, the actual consummation of merger. The first of these was in Los Angeles, where Chanin was asked to assist in melding the two local entities and helped construct a unique organization meeting the needs of NEA, AFT, the AFL-CIO, NEA's state affiliate (the California Teachers Association), AFT's state affiliate (the California Federation of Teachers), and the local associations involved. A small number of other locals followed suit, albeit all with different structures that Chanin helped design to meet each individual situation. Of greatest impact, however, was the 1972 merger of the NEA and AFT state affiliates in New York, creating a massive 250,000-member joint NEA/AFT affiliate: the New York State United Teachers (NYSUT).

Despite having rejected AFT's invitation to enter into national merger talks, NEA had no official policy about either merger or the broader question of AFL-CIO affiliation—an essential issue, inasmuch as AFT was an AFL-CIO affiliate and all of its locals were consequently affiliates of the AFL-CIO. Deeply troubled by the growing entanglements of NEA affiliates with both AFT and the AFL-CIO, the NEA Executive Committee asked Chanin to put together a policy that would clearly delineate what the Executive Committee saw as the appropriate approach to the question of mergers, safeguarding the Association's fundamental principles and assuring that future local mergers were in accord with NEA's positions and interests.

The framework Chanin constructed reflected the prevailing sentiment at the time as well as his own view that state or local mergers should not take place "unless and until" a national merger was also effected. His view was based on three fundamental concerns. First, it would be "totally illogical" to have merged state or local affiliates while the parent organizations were continuing to compete. This would set up a counter-intuitive and paradoxical situation—one, for instance, in which the national dues paid by the merged affiliate might well be used by the two parent organizations to fight each other. Second, the terms and conditions of such state and local mergers could develop a pattern or create structures that would limit the flexibility of both NEA and AFT to forge an appropriate national merger if they decided to do so in the future. And third, if such mergers continued, they might well reach a political tipping point at which there would be enough merged affiliates to force NEA into a national merger over significant opposition from much of its membership, thus splitting the Association and undermining its cohesion and effectiveness. A better approach, Chanin believed, would be for the Representative Assembly to look at the issue of merger from a broad, national, organization-wide perspective, unlimited by preconditions established by state or local affiliates and without the undue influence of affiliates already aligned with AFT or the AFL-CIO.

The 1972 Representative Assembly agreed and adopted the Chanin-crafted framework. Of particular consequence was that this new policy, while grandfathering in those existing state and local mergers, acknowledged the intense and widespread organizational opposition to AFL-CIO affiliation and mandated that "in the future, NEA and its affiliates will not enter into a merger requiring affiliation with the AFL-CIO."[105]

While the overwhelming majority of NEA affiliates and members appeared to support this position, there was some criticism of NEA for its apparent unwillingness even to talk to AFT about the merits of a national merger. To meet this criticism, the following year's RA authorized NEA to enter into merger negotiations with AFT, but only under certain very clear and unequivocal conditions. Any merged organization would have to embody three basic principles: 1) no affiliation of any type with the AFL-CIO; 2) guaranteed minority group participation in the governance and operation of the merged organization; and 3) the use of the secret ballot to elect officers or change any of the governing documents of the merged organization.[106]

Pursuant to this policy, national merger negotiations began in October 1973. Inasmuch, however, as the NEA negotiating team had absolutely no flexibility with regard to these issues, and because the

AFT negotiators were unwilling to countenance a merged national organization that did not have AFL-CIO affiliation, the negotiations were doomed to failure. By February 1974, the talks were formally put to an end. "The impasse," incoming NEA president James Harris concluded, "was inevitable."[107]

After it became apparent that the merged New York state organization—whose members had been paying full dues to both national organizations in the anticipation of an eventual merger between the two national entities—would not have a single national parent organization for the foreseeable future, a choice between NEA and AFT became inevitable. NYSUT began moving toward AFT, ultimately disaffiliating from NEA in 1976 and retaining AFT as its sole national affiliate. NEA immediately established a new state association in New York, but it had only 20,000 members, compared with the more than 200,000 in NYSUT. NEA also went to court challenging the disaffiliation. One small consolation was that as a result of a provision Chanin had inserted in the original merger agreement, the litigation was eventually settled with NEA receiving a one-time payment of some $6 million in dues from NYSUT.

With the New York debacle still ringing in its ears, the 1976 Representative Assembly—with hardly a dissenting vote—reaffirmed its prohibition against mergers requiring AFL-CIO affiliation at the national, state, or local level, and sent a strong message that it would rigorously enforce that prohibition.[108] For all intents and purposes, this posture put an end to any future merger discussions—at least for a while.

Over the next twenty years, the NEA/AFT relationship would be complex and often changing. For much of that time, the two organizations were keen competitors, battling over representational rights, members, and policy differences. On occasion, however, they were also allies on national legislative, political, and policy matters. This became increasingly true as the two unions, indeed as American public education, came under attack.

By the time Keith Geiger was elected NEA president in 1989, the assault by the right wing on NEA and other unions was virtually unrelenting. A few weeks after Geiger's election, Chanin was having dinner with NEA executive director Don Cameron and Ken Melley, who at that time was NEA's director of government relations. The three agreed that it made little sense to maintain the unwritten taboo against even discussing merger within NEA's governing bodies given the threats facing the two organizations. Cameron subsequently raised the issue with Geiger, who had been thinking the same thing.[109] The issue continued to percolate, culminating with a directive from the 1992 RA for a re-evaluation of the 1976 anti-merger policy. That review took place during the 1992-93 year, and, based on its results, the 1993 RA authorized NEA to enter once again into merger talks with AFT. Significantly, the 1993 policy modified the position taken earlier with regard to AFL-CIO affiliation—instead of an absolute prohibition, it gave NEA some flexibility to "explore whether some type of affiliation relationship with AFL-CIO is compatible with the goals and objectives of NEA and its affiliates."[110]

National merger negotiations began in September 1993. Both sides were committed to trying to hammer out an agreement, but after 18 months of negotiations, the talks finally broke down in December 1994. The two teams simply were not able to make meaningful progress on certain critical issues, including AFL-CIO affiliation, term limits for the new organization's officers (NEA had a strong belief in the need for such limits; AFT, led by Al Shanker since 1974, did not), and how to resolve the incompatibility of certain membership categories, particularly AFT's members who worked in fields other than education.[111]

Bob Chase, who had been Geiger's vice president for seven years and had succeeded him in 1996 as NEA president, saw a resumption of merger talks as another means of reinventing NEA. His goal was to create a new organization dedicated to providing a quality education for every child in America—an organization better, not just bigger, than either NEA or AFT alone.

Chase had built a strong relationship with Sandra Feldman, who had become AFT president following Al Shanker's death in February 1997. He believed the time was right to move forward once again, and merger talks soon resumed. The two negotiating teams made considerable progress and by the summer of 1998 had fashioned a statement of "principles" that, if approved by the two unions' national governing bodies, would authorize the drafting of an appropriate constitution and bylaws for the new organization. These "Principles of Unity,"[112] which were presented to the 1998 Representative Assembly in New Orleans, needed a two-thirds majority to pass. They failed to gain the support of even half the delegates, receiving only 42.1 percent of the vote.[113] There were numerous reasons for the defeat: the lack of a compelling case to abandon the more than 100-year-old NEA for a new and uncertain entity; comfort with the status quo; antipathy to the AFT and the AFL-CIO; the specific terms of the agreement regarding the governing structure, the method of voting, and the membership make-up of the merged organization; and, most basically, the fundamental differences in culture between the two organizations.[114]

While the Principles of Unity had been defeated, however, NEA and AFT had built a new relationship in the process of negotiating them. Chase did not want to let that relationship wither, and he needed a way to reunite NEA after the divisions created by the Unity debate. Not unexpectedly, he turned to Chanin for help.

Chanin helped craft a new set of positions and policies that assisted in healing the wounds from the merger battle. A plan was developed on how the two organizations might work together in the absence of a merger.[115] A national jurisdictional agreement was forged with AFT prohibiting the "raiding" of bargaining units that are represented by affiliates of the other organization and the solicitation of each others' members, and assisting state affiliates in fashioning similar state-based understandings.[116] An "NEAFT Partnership" was created to enhance NEA and AFT collaborative work on behalf of public education, school employees, and the students they served.[117] And guidelines were adopted allowing the mergers of NEA and AFT state affiliates in the absence of a national NEA-AFT merger.[118]

The philosophy behind having a national merger precede state and local mergers had not changed. But the world had. A number of NEA state affiliates had made significant movement toward merging with their AFT counterparts in the expectation of the Principles of Unity passing. They were simply too far along to stop. These affiliates believed in the underlying assumption that had led to Chase's reopening of merger discussions: the organizations would be stronger, would be better able to represent their members, and would be able to address the needs of the students they served more effectively by being together rather than apart. These were not just academic beliefs. They stemmed from the affiliates' own pressing, state-specific situations and needs—needs that the NEA leadership knew had to be addressed.

By 2010, NEA and AFT had four merged state affiliates (in Florida, Minnesota, Montana, and New York) with a joint NEA-AFT active membership of almost 618,000, as well as 15 merged local affiliates (in nonmerged states) with a combined NEA membership of more than 52,000. In total, some 670,000 NEA members were in merged states or locals—almost one out of every four NEA active members—23 percent.[119] From the AFT perspective, 57 percent of AFT's education employee members were NEA members as well.

As NEA's relationship with AFT evolved, so too did its relationship with the rest of organized labor. Even while NEA and the AFL-CIO maintained a clear separation at the national level, NEA affiliates often worked closely with their AFL-CIO counterparts at the local level to address local issues. The main vehicle for local collaboration was the federation's 600 or so central labor councils (CLCs)—local coalitions of AFL-CIO unions. In some instances, this relationship was very informal; in others NEA locals were participating members, paying dues, holding office, and voting on CLC policies. There was only one thing wrong with this—it violated the AFL-CIO constitution, which required a local to be an AFL-CIO affiliate to be part of a CLC. To a large extent, the federation followed a "don't ask, don't tell" policy. As it became aware of violations of this rule, however, the AFL-CIO chose to enforce it. As a consequence, some NEA locals and other non-AFL-CIO locals were kicked out of the central labor councils.

In 2003, this happened to NEA's local affiliate in Louisville, Kentucky. At the request of that affiliate, the Jefferson County Teachers Association (JCTA), NEA began looking for ways to address the situation. A special committee of local, state, and national leaders and staff was created to advise the NEA Executive Committee on appropriate approaches to solve the problem. Chaired by then-vice president Dennis Van Roekel, with Chanin serving as its counsel, the committee came up with some innovative methods to address the situation. Based on its guidance and subsequent Executive Committee action, NEA began discussions in December 2004 with the AFL-CIO regarding the participation of NEA local affiliates in the activities of AFL-CIO local central bodies.

NEA's negotiating team consisted of Van Roekel, Chanin, NEA deputy executive director John Stocks, NEA director of governance and policy Michael Edwards, and Stan Johnson, president of NEA's Wisconsin state affiliate. Representing the AFL-CIO were its secretary-treasurer Richard Trumka, chief of staff Robert Welsh, and Jon Hiatt, the general counsel. These discussions culminated with the NEA/AFL-CIO Labor Solidarity Partnership Agreement, which was approved by the NEA Board of Directors and the AFL-CIO Executive Council in February 2007.[120] The purpose of the agreement was to facilitate greater cooperation between NEA local affiliates and AFL-CIO local affiliates in dealing with local issues. Under its terms an NEA local affiliate may join the AFL-CIO as a Directly Affiliated NEA Local ("DANL"). This is a unique affiliation relationship, requiring the approval of NEA, the AFL-CIO, and the respective NEA state affiliate. It provides a DANL with the same rights and obligations as any other directly affiliated AFL-CIO local union, including protection against raiding by other AFL-CIO unions. The AFL-CIO, however, has no oversight powers or control over a DANL. The federation's sole power is the ability to revoke the local's membership in a CLC and its affiliation with the AFL-CIO.[121]

Adoption of this agreement signaled a significant shift in the relationship between NEA and the AFL-CIO. It was, in the words of then-AFL-CIO president John Sweeney, "historic." "In my opinion, the AFL-CIO/NEA agreement is the most important step forward for the labor movement since the merger of the AFL and the CIO in 1955."[122] It is worth noting that the two men who led the negotiations creating this partnership—Dennis Van Roekel for NEA and Richard Trumka for the AFL-CIO—would soon become the presidents of their respective organizations.

As a result of the Labor Solidarity Partnership program, by 2010 twenty-one NEA locals representing some 30,000 NEA members were AFL-CIO members. They were not alone. Another 670,000 were members by virtue of being in merged NEA-AFT state or local affiliates. In 1998, there were virtually no NEA members who were also in the AFL-CIO. As of July 2010, almost 700,000 NEA members were members of the AFL-CIO as well.[123]

Chapter 9

Chanin v. Vouchers

The hard choices that stemmed from the debate over "new unionism" became the focus of a series of special NEA committees appointed by Bob Chase and subsequent NEA presidents in the years that followed. These committees, to which Chanin served as advisor, proposed changes in NEA policies that ultimately were adopted by Representative Assemblies. The policy documents, in the drafting of which Chanin played a major role, covered performance pay (2000), charter schools (2001), distance education (2002), and early childhood education (2003). Each new policy reflected an evolution in NEA's positions to accommodate changing times.[124] On one issue, however, NEA and its affiliates strongly believed that no accommodation was appropriate or possible. That issue was publicly funded vouchers for private school tuition.

Beginning in the 1990s, vouchers became the seminal point of conflict between NEA and those it viewed as undermining public education. The "Voucher Wars," as voucher advocate Clint Bolick named the conflict, became an intense focus of Chanin's work for at least a decade. It was a defining issue in the national debate over improving public education.[125]

Debates and tensions over public aid to American private education date to the 19th Century. Notwithstanding the First Amendment's so-called Establishment Clause, which says, "Congress shall make no law respecting an establishment of religion," or Thomas Jefferson's views about the need for a "wall of separation" between church and state, periodically in the early history of the United States, private and religious schools actually received generous public funding. This occurred before the notion of public "common schools" as we know them today was fully formed.[126] In New York City, funding for religious schools was cut off by the 1820s as the public schools came under Protestant influence. The rise of Catholic immigration led to tensions over readings from the

King James Version of the Bible in public schools, and many Catholics chose to build their own parochial schools. By the 1870s, as Catholic dioceses sought public funds, a movement emerged to deny public funding to "sectarian schools." U.S. Representative James Blaine of Maine, a Republican with presidential aspirations, proposed a federal constitutional amendment that would prohibit the states from allowing public money to "ever be under the control of any religious sect." The amendment failed in Congress in 1876, but it propelled a movement that promoted similar language in state constitutions. Congress insisted for the next several decades that states entering the Union prohibit aid to religious schools, and several older states added so-called "Blaine" language to their constitutions.[127]

The modern era of Establishment Clause doctrine began with the U.S. Supreme Court's 1947 decision in *Everson v. Board of Education of Ewing*.[128] In that case, the court upheld a New Jersey law that allowed school districts to pay the transportation costs of all pupils, including those attending religious schools. The court's complex opinions in the case said both that "No tax in any amount, large or small, can be levied to support any religious activities or institutions," and that government "cannot exclude individual Catholics, Lutherans . . . or the members of any faith, or lack of it, from receiving the benefits of public welfare legislation." The former became known as the "no aid" principle, while the latter was known as the "nondiscrimination" or "neutrality" principle.

The nondiscrimination principle won out in *Everson*, but by the 1970s the High Court stressed the no-aid principle in cases that included *Committee for Public Education and Religious Liberty v. Nyquist*,[129] which struck down a New York State program of tuition reimbursement for parents whose children attended religious schools.[130]

NEA has long had numerous objections to private school vouchers. Public schools are one of the foundations of a democratic society, bringing together Americans of diverse backgrounds and providing access to the American dream for all. By using taxpayer money to subsidize private school tuition, voucher programs drain funds from the public schools, and impair their capacity to promote social equality through education. As Chanin said in a May 2000 cover story in *The*

American Lawyer that focused in large part on his anti-voucher legal efforts, "Vouchers . . . are never going to be the way the vast number of children in our country are educated. Unless we improve the inner-city public school systems, we don't solve the problem."[133] In addition, NEA has objected to the government provision of vouchers for use at private religious schools because it strongly believes that the voucher program violates the separation of church and state, both as embodied in the U.S. Constitution's prohibition against government establishment of religion and in various forms in many state constitutions.

The leading forces promoting vouchers, on the other hand, have sought to break what, in their view, is the monopoly of public schools, introduce competition into the market for educational services, and empower parents, especially those in the inner cities, to have a choice of schools for their children.

In their earliest efforts, before the voucher idea began to win approval as a policy measure in a few states, the religious right and other pro-voucher forces sought to mandate the use of vouchers as a legal remedy. In one such case, *Mozert v. Hawkins County Board of Education*, the effort was made in the name of religious freedom. In December 1983, seven fundamentalist Christian families in a rural county in Tennessee filed suit in federal district court, claiming that certain readings that were part of the school curriculum conflicted with their religious beliefs and thus violated their right to religious freedom under the First Amendment. When school authorities refused to excuse their children, the parents removed their children from the public schools and then sued the school district for money to pay for their private school education.[131]

Their case was argued by Michael P. Farris, an attorney who later became an unsuccessful Republican candidate for lieutenant governor of Virginia. The author of such Christian books as *How a Man Prepares His Daughters for Life*, he was also a Baptist minister and founder of Patrick Henry College in Purcellville, Virginia, whose mission is "the transformation of American society by training Christian students."[132]

Based upon the testimony in the district court, the U.S. Court of Appeals for the Sixth Circuit explained the basis for the parents' objection to the curriculum:

These ranged from such familiar concerns of fundamentalist Christians as evolution and "secular humanism" to less familiar themes such as "futuristic supernaturalism," pacifism, magic and false views of death. . . . [One parent] felt that a passage entitled "Seeing Beneath the Surface" related to an occult theme by describing the use of imagination as a vehicle for seeing things not discernible through our physical eyes. She interpreted a poem, "Look at Anything," as presenting the idea that, by using imagination, a child can become part of anything and thus understand it better. [She] testified that it is an "occult practice" for children to use imagination beyond the limitation of scriptural authority.[133]

* * *

[Another parent] also found objectionable passages in the readers that dealt with magic, role reversal or role elimination, particularly biographical material about women who have been recognized for achievements outside their homes, and emphasis on one world or a planetary society. Both witnesses testified under cross-examination that the plaintiff parents objected to passages that expose their children to other forms of religion and to the feelings, attitudes and values of other students that contradict the plaintiffs' religious views without a statement that the other views are incorrect and that the plaintiffs' views are the correct ones.[134]

The federal district court agreed that the families' First Amendment right to free exercise of religion had been violated and awarded the reimbursement of more than $50,000 in public funds for private school tuition costs that the parents had incurred.[135]

When the case went to the Sixth Circuit, Chanin and his colleagues wrote an *amicus* brief on NEA's behalf. As the brief framed it, "[T]he question that properly should be posed is whether the state's compelling interest in providing a system of public education that fosters pluralism, a tolerance of diversity, a capacity for critical thinking, and other fundamental democratic values is subverted by allowing plaintiff students to opt out of the Hawkins County School District's reading program." If parents do not want their children to be exposed to values that are "central to the mission of public education," the brief argued, "they have the alternative of educating their children in private schools or through home study," but not at public expense.[136]

The appeals court agreed with NEA's position, overturning the district court's decision in August 1987. Requiring students to use curriculum materials that resulted in exposure to others' ideas did not constitute a violation of the First Amendment because it did not require students to change their own beliefs, the court said. It found that, "There was no proof that any plaintiff student was ever called upon to say or do anything that required the student to affirm or deny a religious belief or to engage or refrain from engaging in any act either required or forbidden by the student's religious convictions."[137]

In 1992, pro-voucher attorney Clint Bolick filed several lawsuits that took a different approach in seeking public money for private school tuition. He filed a lawsuit in the state court in Cook County, Illinois, charging that the Chicago public schools had failed to provide "efficient" and "high quality" public education as required by the Illinois state constitution. As a remedy, he asked the court to order the state to give students vouchers for tuition at private schools. In March 1993, the court dismissed the case, noting that "courts should not attempt to decide questions that rightfully belong to the legislature."[138]

Bolick filed a similar case in Los Angeles, charging that students were being denied their "fundamental right" to a public school education under the California constitution and, therefore, should be provided private school vouchers. In June 1993, a state Superior Court judge threw out that case, noting that the California constitution prohibits the expenditure of state money on private schools.[139]

These legal efforts to secure vouchers as a court-ordered remedy for parents had always been unrealistic. But in the late 1980s and into the 1990s, the voucher movement began to make inroads with policymakers. And as a few states established experimental voucher programs, private efforts emerged not only to lobby for them, but to help defend them in court as well.

Bolick, who strategized for the voucher movement as a vice president of the Institute of Justice in Washington, D.C., during much of this time, proudly recounted in his book *Voucher Wars* that legal strategies to defend voucher laws were funded by some of the wealthiest donors to other right-wing causes in America. A major benefactor was John Walton, one of the heirs to the Wal-Mart fortune. Other funders of the voucher campaign included Charles and David Koch, oil magnates listed by *Forbes* magazine among the ten richest Americans;[140] Pierre S. du Pont, IV, an heir to the du Pont chemical fortune; and the Lynde and Harry Bradley Foundation, whose board included industrialists, right-wing political activists, and the head of an independent group of Roman Catholic schools in Milwaukee, Wisconsin.[141]

The pro-voucher forces funded a nationally coordinated campaign, identifying states in which they thought the political environment and the courts would be hospitable to their cause. Chanin followed wherever they went and, for more than a decade, traveled from coast to coast to argue before state supreme courts, federal appeals courts, and, ultimately, the U.S. Supreme Court.[142]

The first battleground state was Wisconsin. Chanin was called in after the state legislature, in July 1995, expanded what had been a small voucher program in Milwaukee. The state had enacted the initial program in 1990, but it had been limited to just 1,000 students, and only nonsectarian schools could participate. Nevertheless, the program drew nationwide publicity, much of it focused on State Representative Polly Williams, a black former welfare mother who was its chief sponsor in the state legislature. Williams, a Democrat from Milwaukee who had pulled her own children out of that city's public schools years earlier, bucked her party and many traditional liberal interests by promoting the voucher program, an activity for which she was lionized in *The Wall Street Journal* and on "60 Minutes" and praised by President George H.W. Bush. "Williams mixed a dose of Milton Friedman and a dose of Malcolm X to come up with the nation's first urban school choice plan," Bolick observed.[143]

Williams and her allies ended up retaining Bolick and the organization he was with at the time, the Landmark Legal Foundation, to help defend the voucher program on behalf of parents who intervened in a lawsuit brought by the teachers' unions and other groups. Again, this first program did not authorize vouchers to be used at religious schools, but the battle laid the groundwork for a much bigger confrontation to come. In 1992, the Wisconsin Supreme Court upheld the program against various claims under the state constitution.

In 1995, with support from Republican Governor Tommy Thompson, as well as Polly Williams, the state expanded the program from 1,000 to 7,000 pupils, and, for the first time, permitted religious schools to participate.[144]

Chanin filed a lawsuit in state court on behalf of the NEA affiliate in Milwaukee and other plaintiffs, alleging that the voucher program diverted tax dollars from the Milwaukee public schools to pay tuition for students to attend private schools, the vast majority of which were affiliated with a religious institution and included religious education and worship in their programs. This, the complaint contended, violated the prohibition against any government "establishment of religion" in the First Amendment of the U.S. Constitution and its counterpart in the Wisconsin Constitution, which prohibited the government from advancing religion.[145]

Governor Thompson, who had championed the Milwaukee voucher program and was attempting to ride it to national political prominence, filed a petition to bypass the lower state courts and take the case directly to the state supreme court, where he expected to win easily.[146]

The argument was held on February 27, 1996, before six of the seven justices on the Wisconsin Supreme Court. (The seventh justice recused herself for an unexplained reason.) Bolick had created a circus atmosphere outside the courtroom, bringing hundreds of nuns, priests, and families whose children attended religious schools to put on a show for the substantial press corps that was present. The cable channel Court TV covered the argument, perhaps in part because Governor Thompson had enlisted Kenneth W. Starr to argue the case on the state's behalf. Starr had served from 1983 to 1989 as a U.S. Court of Appeals judge, appointed by President Reagan, and for four years as U.S. solicitor general under President George H.W. Bush. The latter position principally involved making arguments before the U.S. Supreme Court on behalf of the administration and the federal government. At the time that he argued the Milwaukee voucher case,

Starr was a noted "hired gun" appellate lawyer, constantly in the news because he was also serving as independent counsel investigating the Whitewater case, which involved financial dealings by Bill and Hillary Clinton in the 1980s.[147]

The courtroom faceoff in Madison was also the first of several which Bolick and Chanin would have over vouchers. At least a generation older than Bolick, Chanin was the much more experienced of the two in litigation. The series of confrontations between the two legal advocates, from state trial courts to state supreme courts and federal district and appeals courts, left some battle scars, as Bolick recounted in *Voucher Wars* and as presented in two national magazine profiles describing the long-running courtroom duel.[148]

"Over the years, I would grow to know Chanin well," wrote Bolick, who, in addition to his legal work and voucher advocacy, was a prolific writer on libertarian issues in the op-ed pages of *The Wall Street Journal*. "To put it mildly, first impressions were, for me, off-putting. Chanin is the quintessential obnoxious labor lawyer, replete with a thick New York accent and a sarcastic, argumentative demeanor. He wags his finger at the court and refers to judges as 'Yawawna.'"[149] But Chanin "is also a masterful orator who makes every second count, wielding total command of his subject matter," Bolick continued. "Over six years of litigation and myriad encounters, I grew to admire him, despite myself. The guy is good. He's an ethical lawyer who is interested in cutting to the chase. And he represents his clients with zeal."[150]

The Wisconsin Supreme Court devoted two hours to the oral arguments, with Starr, Bolick, and another lawyer arguing to uphold the voucher program, and Chanin arguing against it.

The expanded choice program was "a garage door" that could open up to an explosion of religious-school vouchers, Chanin said. "When does it stop? When you have side-by-side systems of [government-funded] public and private education?"[151]

It turned out that Governor Thompson had miscalculated in his expectations of an easy victory before the state high court. The court split three to three, and sent the case back to the trial court to start all over again. The court also granted the Association's motion for a preliminary injunction preventing implementation of the expanded voucher program while the trial court heard the case.[152]

The plaintiffs prevailed in the trial court, and then in the state court of appeals. In early 1998, the case returned to the Wisconsin Supreme Court. The composition of the court had changed since 1996, however. One of the three justices who had voted against the voucher program had retired and had been replaced by a Thompson ally.[153]

Starr was scheduled to present the governor's case again at the oral argument on March 4, 1998, but by this time his duties as the Whitewater independent counsel had intensified, and he was in the middle of conducting a grand jury inquiry into President Clinton's affair with one-time White House intern Monica Lewinsky. He sent a notably understated letter to the Wisconsin court that simply said that he was "otherwise occupied."[154] In his stead, the state was represented by Jay Lefkowitz, a young partner at Starr's Washington law firm.

Once again, Bolick managed to create what John Witte, the University of Wisconsin professor selected by the state to evaluate the voucher program, termed "school choice theater."[155] Bolick had arranged for busloads of voucher students, neatly dressed in their school uniforms, to rally on the steps of the courthouse, carrying signs that said "What about the kids?" "NEA doesn't care about children," and so forth. And, as usual, in addition to their constitutional arguments, Bolick and the other pro-voucher lawyers argued the purported educational merits of the voucher program, attempting to persuade the judges that vouchers were good public policy. "This program is one part of a very large and aggressive effort to rescue children in the Milwaukee public schools," Bolick told the court.[156]

Chanin again argued the case against the voucher program. Although well versed in the educational pros and cons of vouchers, he believed that such policy arguments had no place in voucher litigation, and he had consistently refrained from responding in kind. But this time—at the very end of what would be his final argument before the Wisconsin Supreme Court—he departed from the usual script:

> In the few minutes I have left, I would like to totally shift
> gears. I have been involved with the amended choice plan
> for almost three years. I have invested endless hours in

research and analysis, and have argued before the Wisconsin courts on three separate occasions. Barring review by the United States Supreme Court, this is my last hurrah. And with the indulgence of the Court, I would like to take a moment of what might be termed personal privilege. Throughout this litigation, we have been portrayed as the bad guys; as uncaring, as insensitive to the needs and aspirations of disadvantaged minority children. That we are attempting, for some unstated, but surely unworthy motive, to deny to them this golden opportunity to escape from the jungle of urban education. We have refrained from responding in kind, because we are attorneys. We believe that our job is simply to argue the law and not to debate policy. But quite frankly, we resent the role in which petitioners have cast us. We are fully aware of the educational problems that exist in cities such as Milwaukee and Cleveland and other urban centers. Indeed, in at least some cities in this country, the term "crisis" is probably not an overstatement. But these problems cannot be resolved by schemes that skim off 5,000 or 10,000 or even 15,000 students from highly motivated families and leave behind 85,000 or 90,000 other students based on the dubious theory that competition with a relative handful of private schools, coupled with fewer resources, somehow will produce a dramatic turnaround in public education. Every child, not just a chosen few thousand, is entitled to a quality education. And that goal can be achieved not by abandoning public education, but only by working within the system, by using innovative techniques like site-based management and mentoring and bringing about the necessary improvements. But my point, your Honors, is this. Even if I believed otherwise and considered voucher programs to be a viable solution to the problems of urban education, I would not change my legal argument. Because to do so, would be a disservice to this Court, to my profession, and to our system of laws.

Our challenge is not to solve the problems of urban education in any way possible. Our challenge is to solve those problems with solutions that comport with fundamental constitutional principles. I am dismayed by crime in the streets. And by the fact that I can no longer walk safely in Washington, D.C. That, too, is a crisis. And I am sure that it would help the situation if all suspected criminals were rounded up and summarily hauled off to jail. But I adamantly oppose any solution that would solve the crisis of crime in the streets by compromising our constitutional commitment to protect the due process rights of every suspected criminal. Petitioners from the outset of this litigation have emphasized the alleged educational crisis that exists in Milwaukee—as if that somehow provides a reason to loosen constitutional restraints. But they have it precisely backwards. The existence of a crisis, whether it be in the schools of Milwaukee or the streets of Washington, does not provide a reason for bending or ignoring or looking for ways around constitutional principles. To the contrary, it is in times of crisis that our commitment to these principles is tested.

During his argument two years ago, Judge Starr stated that he supported the amended choice program because he had looked into the eyes of the children who benefit from the program. I submit to you that that is a profoundly disturbing statement. It is precisely when we look into the eyes of the children and our emotions push us to simply do what we think is good for them, that we must adhere most vigorously to our fundamental principles, such as the separation of church and state. Because if we compromise these principles to solve a crisis in the short run, we pay a terrible price in the long run.[157]

Bolick recollected that Chanin's statement took him by surprise. He looked back at one of his colleagues, who "returned my wide-eyed expression," Bolick wrote in his book. "We had just witnessed something totally unexpected: *Chanin had melted down.*" And the meltdown "had exposed the first crack in his polished and eloquent veneer."[158]

In his assessment of Chanin's comments, however, Bolick was in fact mistaken. Recognizing that this would be his final appearance before the Wisconsin Supreme Court, and that if he had not already convinced a majority of the judges that the voucher program was unconstitutional he was unlikely to do so in the remaining few minutes, Chanin had made a strategic judgment to respond to the voucher proponents on their own terms. Before beginning his argument, Chanin had asked Bruce Meredith, the general counsel for NEA's Wisconsin state affiliate, who was seated with him at the counsels' table, to let him know when three minutes were left in his allotted time because he "wanted to respond to all the crap we've been listening to—to let the judges, the spectators, and the media know that we do care—that we care about kids and public education."[159]

The Wisconsin Supreme Court issued its decision on June 10, 1998. As many expected, it was a four-to-two vote to uphold the voucher program under the state and federal constitutions. The Association asked the U.S. Supreme Court to review the decision. This was the first time that a case so squarely presenting the issue of the constitutionality of a private school voucher program had made its way to the high court, and many observers expected that the justices might take it up. But they declined to do so without any comment, allowing the Wisconsin supreme court decision to stand.[160]

Meanwhile, a similar voucher case in Ohio was making its way through the courts, and before too long it would become the first test case on vouchers to be reviewed by the U.S. Supreme Court.

The Ohio case originated in 1996 when a voucher program established by the state legislature began operating in the Cleveland schools. Chanin succeeded in having the program struck down in state court, but the Ohio Supreme Court's ruling was based on the technicality that the voucher program had been enacted through impermissible "log rolling" as part of an omnibus budget bill. The legislature quickly reenacted the law in accordance with the court decision, however, putting the voucher program back in operation. New challenges were filed in federal district court on behalf of NEA by Chanin and on behalf of AFT by Marvin Frankel, a constitutional scholar and former federal judge. Applying well-established principles from Supreme Court decisions, the district court had little trouble ruling that the voucher program violated the Establishment Clause of the First Amendment. "Because of the overwhelmingly large number of religious versus nonreligious schools participating in the voucher program, beneficiaries cannot make a genuine, independent choice of what school to attend," the court said. "A program that is so skewed toward religion necessarily results in indoctrination attributable to the government."[161]

In December 2000, the U.S. Court of Appeals for the Sixth Circuit affirmed the district court's decision. Emphasizing that the overwhelming proportion of schools in the voucher program were religious institutions, the circuit court held that the program unconstitutionally promoted religion. The state of Ohio and its pro-voucher allies asked for review by the U.S. Supreme Court, and the justices agreed to hear it, making this case the long-awaited showdown over vouchers. Oral argument was scheduled for February 20, 2002.[162]

In an interview with *Education Week* several years before the Ohio case, Chanin had been asked what he thought would happen when the first voucher case made it to the High Court. "On all religion cases, the Court is going five to four," he noted.[163] "The outcome would depend on which side got the fifth swing vote."

Chanin knew for sure that at least four of the nine justices—William Rehnquist, Antonin Scalia, Anthony Kennedy, and Clarence Thomas—were solidly against NEA's position, while four—John Paul Stevens, David Souter, Stephen Breyer, and Ruth Bader Ginsburg—were likely to vote to maintain strict separation of church and state. Justice Sandra Day O'Connor had repeatedly voted to uphold public funding for religious schools in other recent cases, but she had suggested that she was not guided by ideology and that she might vote differently based on the facts in a particular case. Chanin thoroughly researched her past opinions and tailored his argument to her, believing that she was the only hope for a fifth vote against the Cleveland program.[164]

Prior to the oral argument in *Zelman v. Simmons-Harris*, there would be some infighting on the pro-voucher side, with the result that Chanin's frequent adversary in the voucher cases, Clint Bolick, would not have the chance to argue in the Supreme Court. In any event, because the program was an enactment of the Ohio legislature, its defense would have been primarily carried out by lawyers for the state. Bolick typically represented "intervening" plaintiffs in the various voucher cases—parents who stood to benefit from the vouchers but were not the main parties in the case. In numerous lower-court arguments in Ohio, Wisconsin, and other states, Bolick had received at least a short period of time to go head to head against Chanin.

Once the Supreme Court accepted review of the Cleveland case, however, the Ohio attorney general's office became less cooperative with Bolick and his intervenors. So Bolick filed a motion with the court seeking divided argument for the pro-voucher side, which would give him at least a few minutes of time to argue before the court. Bolick did not think the court would grant the motion, but he believed the tactic would force the state to let him and his group back into the discussions on strategy for the case. Chanin had filed a similar motion, proposing that he and AFT lawyer Marvin Frankel divide the argument time against the Cleveland program. The court granted the motion, and it probably would have granted Bolick's similar request, Bolick later concluded.[165]

Bolick withdrew his motion when Ken Starr, who was by now helping Ohio strategize in its defense on the Cleveland program, carved out a compromise in which Bolick and another Institute for Justice attorney would be allowed to sit at the counsels' table during the oral argument, but not allowed to argue. And Bolick, who was concerned about some of the state's decisions on arguments and strategy, was relieved when U.S. Solicitor General Ted Olson, representing President George W. Bush's administration, was granted permission to argue in support of the voucher program. Ohio would entrust its time to an assistant state attorney general named Judith French.[166]

When the Supreme Court argument finally took place, French led off her defense with an argument that the Cleveland voucher program met the various analytical tests established by the Supreme Court for evaluating whether a government program was an unconstitutional establishment of religion. The voucher program was open to all families, and parents were free to use the vouchers for either religious or non-religious schools, French noted. Most importantly, she argued, taxpayers' money was not being given directly to religious schools but to parents, who made an independent decision to give it to religious schools. "There is nothing about that benefit that suggests any sort of reference to religion," she said.[167]

Olson echoed that theory in presenting the Bush administration's argument in favor of vouchers. "It's not unlike a government check that goes to an individual who then spends it, all of it, on his church," Olson claimed. The analogy was faulty, as Chanin subsequently pointed out, because a government check may be spent for any purpose, but vouchers could be used only for private school tuition.

Under questioning from the justices, Olson acknowledged that the vouchers in Cleveland were being used almost exclusively in religious schools. He conceded that 3,700 of the approximately 3,800 students in Cleveland who used vouchers directed the state aid to religious schools.

During a colloquy with Olson, Justice O'Connor stated for clarification that "there was no attempt in the program to make sure that the money that ends up in the parochial schools is not used for religious training or teaching." He answered, "That's correct." It was not clear, however, whether O'Connor found that troubling.

It was then Chanin's turn to make his argument, followed by Frankel for AFT.

"Under the Cleveland voucher program," Chanin began, "millions of dollars of unrestricted public funds are transferred each year from the state treasury into the general coffers of sectarian private schools, and the money is used by those schools to provide an educational program in which the sectarian and the secular are interwoven." This, Chanin said, clearly violates the Establishment Clause of the First Amendment. And "regardless of the decision that individual parents may make, it is inevitable, it is a mathematical certainty that almost all of the students will end up going to religious schools that provide a religious education," he continued.

It was only a matter of moments before Justice O'Connor, who was the chief target of Chanin's arguments, began pressing him on several points.

"Well, Mr. Chanin, wait just a minute," O'Connor interrupted. "Do we not have to look at all of the choices open to the students, the community [Ohio's term for charter] schools, the magnet schools, et cetera? How is it we can look only at the ones looking to the religious schools?"

She suggested that rather than looking solely at the Cleveland voucher program, the court should perhaps analyze its constitutionality in light of other school choice programs made available to parents, namely charter schools. "If you want to look at parents' choice, then you have to look at the whole program, don't you?" she asked Chanin.

"This court has always been very program-specific in its financial-aid [to religion] cases," Chanin replied. "If public money that is reasonably attributable to the state goes to pay for religious education, it violates the Constitution."

Chanin was arguing constitutional law, but it soon appeared that, for some justices, personal opinions about public policy might have as much to do with their decision as the letter of the law. Justice Scalia, himself a product of Catholic schools, voiced his view that "studies that I'm familiar with" show that "parochial schools do a much better job than the public schools."

"I do not believe," Chanin told him, "that a crisis in the Cleveland public schools is a license to ignore the mandate of the Establishment Clause."

Chanin pointed out that the National School Boards Association had filed an *amicus* brief that identified many education reform efforts throughout the country that did not involve taking money from public schools to unconstitutionally subsidize religious education. "There are problems being solved in urban school districts all over the country without voucher programs," he told the court. "We have not said much about the educational value [or not] of voucher programs, because we don't think that this is a forum for an educational policy debate, but they are a lousy option. . . . There is no evidence that competition improves the lot for the 96 percent of the students who remain in the troubled Cleveland Public School System with less resources and even worse problems."

With that, Chanin yielded the remaining few minutes to Marvin Frankel, who was representing a separate group of challengers to the program. "We're served up with a voucher program [that] . . . is unconstitutional, and we think [the state's] effort to defend it is somewhat slap-dash, especially, for example, when they try to defend proselytization in a few hasty paragraphs, overturning 50 years of precedent, as they would hope, and saying proselytization with government money is okay, where we say that the law since 1948 has been to the contrary," said Frankel. Battling prostate cancer, Frankel delivered his argument from a wheelchair. He would die at age 81, a few weeks after the argument.

With a few minutes left for rebuttal on behalf of the state, Judith French told the court that the challengers to the voucher program "have either ignored or do not accept the last 20 years or so of this Court's jurisprudence" on the Establishment Clause.

"It seems that Ohio did it right," French said, by adopting the voucher plan in responding to the educational crisis in Cleveland. "It didn't take too much money away from the public schools, but gave enough for a limited program that is targeted to the most needy, the poorest of the poor, the low income students who would not otherwise have choice."

With that, the 80-minute argument was over. In *The New York Times* the next day, veteran Supreme Court reporter Linda Greenhouse noted that "all eyes were on Justice Sandra Day O'Connor" because of her place at the center of the court's ideological spectrum on church-state issues. "She gave away little, pressing both sides and expressing some skepticism about the answers she received."[168] *Education Week* reported that "the long-awaited constitutional showdown over religious school vouchers" had put "voucher opponents on the defensive."[169]

Bolick bounded out of the Supreme Court building to address a rally of voucher supporters, convinced that his side was headed to victory. "Everyone on our side wore huge smiles," Bolick wrote.[170]

Chanin was more reserved. He had learned long before not to predict the outcome of a case based on the oral argument. "We made the points we wanted to make, and now we have to wait and see," he thought at the time.[171]

The five-to-four decision Chanin had predicted years earlier came on June 27, 2002, the last ruling announced on the last day of the court's term. Despite his best efforts, Chanin had not won Justice O'Connor's vote, and she had joined Rehnquist, Scalia, Kennedy, and Thomas in upholding the Cleveland program under the Establishment Clause.[172]

Ultimately, Chanin encountered an adversary in the voucher wars more persuasive and powerful than Clint Bolick, Ken Starr, or Judith

French. Chief Justice Rehnquist had been, in a sense, working towards this day longer than any of the pro-voucher lawyers.

In 1973, when he was only in his second term as an associate justice, Rehnquist was a dissenter in a case in which the court struck down a New York State program of tuition reimbursement for parents whose children attended religious schools. That case, *Committee for Public Education and Religious Liberty v. Nyquist*, would be cited by Chanin many times in his arguments against the Cleveland program.

Over the next 29 years, Rehnquist would play a significant role in cases that chipped away at the *Nyquist* precedent, including writing the majority opinions in *Mueller v. Allen*, a 1983 decision that upheld a Minnesota program of state income-tax deductions for private school expenses, and *Zobrest v. Catalina Foothills School District*, a 1993 ruling that upheld the state provision of a sign-language interpreter for a deaf student attending religious school. Now, Chief Justice Rehnquist was citing these precedents in upholding the Cleveland program.

In his opinion for the majority in the Cleveland voucher case, Rehnquist said the decisions in *Mueller*, *Zobrest*, and another involving school choice in which he was not the author, "make clear that where a government aid program is neutral with respect to religion, and provides assistance directly to a broad class of citizens who, in turn, direct government aid to religious schools wholly as a result of their own genuine and independent private choice, the program is not readily subject to challenge under the Establishment Clause."[173]

In her concurrence, Justice O'Connor said she did not believe the ruling upholding the Cleveland program "marks a dramatic break from the past." She added, "The support that the Cleveland voucher program provides religious institutions is neither substantial nor atypical of existing government programs."

Justice David Souter wrote the main dissent, joined by Justices Stevens, Ginsburg, and Breyer. Reading a summary from the bench, Souter said the majority's ruling was "potentially tragic" and "a major devaluation of the Establishment Clause." He continued, "The scale of the aid to religious schools approved today is unprecedented. . . . I hope that a future court will reconsider today's dramatic departure from basic Establishment-Clause principle."

On the plaza of the Supreme Court on that hot June day, Clint Bolick beamed. "This was the Super Bowl of school choice, and children won," he said, in what seemed like a rehearsed sound bite.[174] Later, he and other pro-voucher advocates would toast each other with Dom Perignon at the Institute for Justice's offices. Chanin, meanwhile, was in Dallas that day, preparing for NEA's upcoming Representative Assembly. "There is no doubt this will give momentum to the voucher movement," he would tell a reporter. "It will energize them. But they still have to persuade those who make the decisions that it is a sound educational program that provides meaningful answers. I'm not sure this ruling helps them in that task."[175]

After a few days of reflection, Chanin had this to say: "Where do we go from here? This does not end the legal battle. It simply means we no longer have the Establishment Clause in our legal arsenal."[176]

Indeed, as time went on, it would become increasingly clear that the pro-voucher forces were clinking their champagne glasses to a Pyrrhic victory.

There was no doubt that the Ohio voucher decision deprived NEA of one arrow in its quiver. It could no longer argue that vouchers violate the Establishment Clause of the U.S. Constitution. Martin West, an education scholar sympathetic to the school voucher movement, observed in 2009 that "while the victory for private school choice in *Zelman* was real, it was also incomplete. It did not end the legal battle but rather returned it to the state court systems in which it had begun."[177]

Forty-seven states have clear language in their own constitutions forbidding government support for religion. Many state constitutions also have other provisions under which vouchers can be challenged. So Chanin turned to state courts, formulating creative arguments under state constitutions to challenge vouchers. In these arenas, voucher opponents have enjoyed much more success.[178]

Just two years after the Ohio decision, NEA took the lead in *Owens v. Colorado Congress of Parents, Teachers and Students*, a case challenging a voucher program enacted by the state for residents of Denver and several other school districts. The program required the local school districts to provide vouchers to parents of school children who were performing at an unsatisfactory level to be used to pay for private school education. The Colorado Supreme Court agreed with arguments developed by Chanin and his colleagues, finding that the program "violates the local control requirements of our state constitution because it directs the school districts to turn over a portion of their locally raised funds to nonpublic schools over whose instruction the districts have no control."[179]

An even more high-profile battle over vouchers in state courts took place in Florida. In November 1998, Jeb Bush, brother of the future U.S. president George W. Bush, was elected governor, and he promptly guided through the Republican legislature the nation's first statewide voucher program. The Opportunity Scholarship Program allowed children in public schools who received failing grades for two consecutive years to transfer to other public schools or to use vouchers to attend private schools, including religious schools. In 1999, NEA and its state affiliate, the Florida Education Association (FEA), filed a state court lawsuit, *Holmes v. Bush*, challenging the voucher program under the state constitution. The challenge was based on two arguments: First, that the voucher program violated the state constitution's religion clause, which prohibits the use of public money to aid sectarian schools or other religious institutions; and second, that it violated the education clause that requires the state to provide education through "a uniform, efficient, safe, secure, and high quality system of free public schools."[180]

The state trial court ruled in NEA's favor based on the religion clause. That decision was affirmed by a state appeals court. The state then appealed to the Florida Supreme Court, which in 2006 affirmed that the voucher program was unconstitutional under the constitution's education clause. The court's five to two ruling said the program "diverts public dollars into separate, private systems . . . parallel to and in competition with the free public schools." The court did not reach the question of whether the program violated the religion clause.[181]

Chanin described the ruling to the NEA Board of Directors a few weeks later as "an unqualified delight." The ruling tore out the heart of Governor Bush's "misguided" education reform program, he noted, and raised legal questions about other voucher initiatives in the state.

Pro-voucher advocates at the Institute for Justice and on the editorial page of *The Wall Street Journal* were "apoplectic," he said. Most importantly, the decision was important from a strategic point of view, since it proved that despite the U.S. Supreme Court ruling in *Zelman* that the federal Establishment Clause was no bar to religious school vouchers, state constitutions would provide substantial hurdles to enacting legally viable voucher programs.[182]

Undeterred, Jeb Bush then tried to make an end run around the state supreme court by amending the state constitution, even after he left office in January 2007. Both the education and religion clauses would have to be amended to revive the Opportunity Scholarship program. The traditional ways under Florida law to get amendments placed before the voters in an election was through the legislature or through a petition drive. The prospect for success with either by the next election was not good, but Bush had another option. A state entity called the Taxation and Budget Reform Commission comes to life automatically every 20 years, and, conveniently for the former governor, 2007 was one of those years. The commission has the power to propose constitutional amendments on "taxation and state budgetary matters" and put them directly on the statewide ballot. With a number of his own appointees on the commission, Gov. Bush was able to convince them to put voucher-related initiatives on the November 2008, ballot.[183]

NEA and FEA filed a lawsuit, *Ford v. Browning*, in state court challenging the move on the ground that the state commission had exceeded its authority by placing amendments on the ballot that were not primarily about taxation and the state budget. The president of FEA was the lead plaintiff, and other named plaintiffs included the presidents of the Florida School Boards Association, the Florida Association of School Administrators, and the Florida Association of District School Superintendents. In August, a state trial court ruled that, because the constitutional amendments would affect the expenditure of state money, they could remain on the ballot. The plaintiffs needed the Florida Supreme Court to act by early September to prevent the amendments from appearing on the ballot, and the court responded. It met in special session to hear the case on the morning of September 3, 2008, and by afternoon it issued a unanimous ruling that the amendments must be removed from the ballot because the commission lacked the authority to place them there. Chanin took some pleasure in seeing Jeb Bush's statement, widely quoted in the media, that the decision was "heartbreaking."[184]

In 2009, pro-voucher forces suffered another state court defeat—this time in Arizona. In 2006, the Arizona legislature adopted two voucher programs, one for children with disabilities and the other for children living in foster care homes. The Arizona Education Association was among the plaintiffs challenging both programs under the no-aid clause of the Arizona constitution, which provides that "no tax shall be laid or appropriation of public money made in aid of any church, or private or sectarian school, or any public service corporation." In March 2009, the Arizona Supreme Court ruled in *Cane v. Horne* that the program, no matter how well intentioned, violated that provision of the state constitution.[185] The ruling stymied the strategy of right-wing forces to use the programs for disabled and displaced children as a step toward a broader voucher program in the state. As the *Arizona Daily Star* reported, "The decision is a significant defeat for legislators who created the very small program in 2006 to test the legal waters. They hoped a ruling in their favor would pave the way for a full-blown voucher program, with every parent in the state entitled to use state tax money to send their children to any school they want."[186]

Chanin's legal work against vouchers contributed to winning the political battle as well, by drawing public attention to the constitutional questions raised by such programs. Although voucher programs can now be found in a few states, they are a small exception to the rule. As of 2008, vouchers or voucher-related measures had been placed before voters in 13 states and the District of Columbia a total of 22 times. Voters rejected public aid to private and religious schools every time. In all, nearly two out of three voters in those 22 elections voiced an emphatic "no" to vouchers. Even in a conservative state such as Utah, NEA won on the issue in a statewide vote in 2007. NEA and its allies were behind when the campaign began in Utah, but after voters learned how vouchers would impact public school students, they voted against vouchers by an overwhelming margin.[187]

Stopping the spread of vouchers was viewed by NEA as an historic victory, but it did not mean that school choice proponents would end their efforts to enact private school choice initiatives. Chanin gave his perspective to the NEA Board of Directors in May 2009:

> When you combine the decision in Arizona with recent decisions striking down voucher programs in Florida and other states, and our success in state legislatures in killing voucher bills, and in ballot elections in striking down initiatives to install voucher programs, it is tempting to say that the voucher movement is, in effect, dead.

> But that conclusion would to some extent miss the point. To be sure, I think the pure voucher programs that now exist in Milwaukee and in Cleveland do not appear to be going anywhere. [They have] no legs. But you must see this in the broader context.

> The motive of the voucher proponents is not simply to implement voucher programs. There is an ancillary benefit that they hope to receive from making the effort. Even when it is a losing battle, to some extent they win, because NEA and its affiliates must invest untold time and resources to beat them back, and that diverts us from using those resources and time to implement our own affirmative agenda to advance public education.

> Vouchers are a tactic in a broad strategic effort. That effort is to undermine public education by diverting public money to private schools and other private institutions, and that broader effort goes on. It will just manifest itself in other forms—in tuition tax credits, in virtual education, in privately run charter schools.

> It is good that we are beating back and maybe have killed the momentum of pure private school voucher programs, but that is not the basic issue we face. It is the diversion of public money to private education.[188]

Chapter 10

The Challenge of No Child Left Behind

A second major battle over the future of public education that became a central focus of Chanin's work in the first decade of the 21st century involved the 2001 reauthorization of the Elementary and Secondary Education Act. Commonly known as the No Child Left Behind Act, or NCLB, the law was a cornerstone of the domestic policy of President George W. Bush. It was passed with major bipartisan support in Congress, and became effective in January 2002.[189]

This coincided with a major change in NEA's leadership. Don Cameron, who had served as executive director since 1982, retired in 2000, and was succeeded by John Wilson. Wilson would help shepherd the Association through a turbulent relationship with the Bush administration over the implementation of NCLB, among other issues.

The Republican Party had long claimed to be opposed to federal intrusion into public education, following in the footsteps of Ronald Reagan, who strongly opposed creation of the U.S. Department of Education because it would increase the federal role in education policy. As Reagan's Republican platform stated, "We will respect the rights of state and local authorities in management of their school systems."[190]

Bush's platform as the Republican presidential candidate in 2000 vowed that, "instead of burdening schools with red tape and narrow government programs, we will give them maximum flexibility in using federal education . . . dollars to meet their specific needs":

> We recognize that under the American constitutional system, education is a state, local, and family responsibility, not a federal obligation. Since over 90 percent of public school funding is state and local, not federal, it is obvious that state and local governments must assume most of the responsibility to improve the schools, and the role of the federal government must be progressively limited as we return control to parents, teachers, and local school boards. . . . The Republican Congress rightly opposed

attempts by the Department of Education to establish federal testing that would set the stage for a national curriculum. We believe it's time to test the Department, and each of its programs, instead.[191]

But once Bush controlled the White House and the Department of Education, he proposed federal mandates for state and local governments that the National Conference of State Legislatures described as "more specific and far-reaching" than those imposed by any prior federal education statute.[192]

The NCLB law greatly expanded the federal role in education. Under the statute, all states initially were required to conduct annual testing in reading and mathematics for all students in grades 3 through 8, and at least once in high school. Starting in the 2007-08 school year, states were also required to test students in science at least once during their elementary, middle, and high school years. States must bring all students up to the "proficient" level on state tests by the 2013-14 school year. Individual schools must meet state "adequate yearly progress" targets toward this goal (based on a formula spelled out in the law) for both their student populations as a whole and for certain demographic subgroups. If a school receiving federal Title I funding failed to meet the target two years in a row, it must be provided technical assistance and its students must be offered a choice of other public schools to attend. Students in schools that failed to make adequate progress three years in a row must also be offered supplemental educational services, including private tutoring. For continued failures, a school would be subject to outside corrective measures, including possible governance changes.[193]

In order to help state and local governments comply with these new mandates, Congress authorized billions of dollars to implement NCLB—not enough money, but still a major increase. NEA, which supported the increased funding but questioned the wisdom of some of the law's other provisions, took no official position for or against the legislation.[194]

As the law began to be implemented, however, it became clear that the Bush administration was not going to fulfill the funding promises. Under the legislative procedures followed by Congress, "authorization" of funds to implement a new law is just the first step. Next, the funds must actually be "appropriated" as part of the budget process. Under President Bush, the federal government redirected money that was needed for education to fund the Iraq War and Bush's other priorities. By 2008, the total gap between what was originally "authorized" under NCLB and what was actually appropriated had grown to a staggering $71 billion.[195]

In addition, as the law was implemented, NEA viewed NCLB's flaws from an educational perspective as increasingly obvious. NCLB established new federal requirements that most public schools would not be able to meet, and set up a process by which schools that did not meet the requirements would then be labeled as "failing to make adequate yearly progress." School districts could then be required to provide public funds to allow students to transfer to other public schools or to private schools—thus accomplishing the goal the Right had long sought through other means, such as vouchers and tuition tax credits. In addition, NCLB defined accountability almost entirely in terms of narrow standardized tests, so teachers would have to spend the year preparing students to get good scores instead of developing learning and thinking skills to meet the rigorous demands of the 21st century.[196]

NEA and its leaders were in the forefront in their condemnation of the law. Because of this, on February 23, 2004, Rod Paige, President Bush's first secretary of education, told a White House meeting of the National Governors Association that NEA was a "terrorist organization." In the post-9/11 era, that was a highly charged statement, and Paige was quickly challenged, with some calling for his resignation. The secretary did apologize, and he tried to backtrack by saying he was not calling teachers terrorists, just their organization.[197] Although the White House rejected the calls for his removal, Paige stepped down a few months later, at the end of President Bush's first term. The Bush administration's position on NCLB remained unchanged.[198]

To generate political debate about NCLB and deal with the administration's failure to provide adequate funding, NEA leaders turned to Chanin to see if there might be a basis for challenging the law in court.[199] Chanin concluded that there was no way to strike down NCLB in its entirely, but there was, buried in the law's more than 1,100 pages, a paragraph—Section 9527(a)—that did provide the basis for a lawsuit:

> Nothing in this Act shall be construed to authorize an officer or employee of the Federal Government to mandate, direct, or control a State, local educational agency, or school's curriculum, program of instruction, or allocation of State or local resources, or mandate a State or any subdivision thereof to spend any funds or incur any costs not paid for under this Act.[200]

The language was not new to NCLB. Congress had included it in federal education legislation as early as 1994, in that year's reauthorization of the Elementary and Secondary Education Act. Thus, history suggested that lawmakers did not want the 1994 legislation, which came with a new set of accountability measures along with federal Title I aid for the disadvantaged, to force states and school districts to spend their own money on such federal mandates.[201]

Based on the inclusion of the same language in the 2001 law, Chanin decided, President Bush's Department of Education could be sued because NCLB imposed unfunded federal mandates—it required states and school districts to comply with certain requirements without providing sufficient federal funds to pay for that compliance.[202]

There was some hesitation within NEA about filing suit. For one thing, NCLB had been crafted not only by President Bush, but also by two Democratic members of Congress who were longtime allies of NEA: Senator Edward Kennedy of Massachusetts, who by that time was chairman of the Senate Health, Education, Labor, and Pensions Committee; and Representative George Miller of California, chairman of the House Education and Labor Committee. Meanwhile, NEA's strategy drew opposition from some civil rights organizations. Those groups were concerned that if NEA was successful in blocking the federal government from requiring state and local governments to spend money to comply with unfunded federal mandates under NCLB, the same legal theory could be used to block federal requirements regarding other issues, such as civil rights. Chanin explained that the civil rights laws were not vulnerable to the same challenge since they did not contain the same language barring unfunded mandates.

Meetings between NEA and its long-time civil rights allies failed to produce agreement on that issue.

The disagreement over the lawsuit was part of greater disunity among the teachers' unions and the civil rights community over NCLB. A number of groups, including the Education Trust, the Citizens' Commission on Civil Rights, the Lawyers Committee for Civil Rights Under Law, and the NAACP, had largely stood by the law amid criticism from the teachers' unions and other groups.[203]

The Citizens' Commission, a small but influential civil rights lobby in Washington, issued a report that criticized NEA and AFT's record of lobbying and rhetoric about the federal law. "Over the last decade," the 2009 report stated, "the national leaders of the National Education Association and the American Federation of Teachers have made their unions implacable foes of laws and policies designed to improve public education for disadvantaged children. . . . The unions have battled against the principle that schools and education agencies should be held accountable for the academic progress of their students. They have sought to water down the standards adopted by states to reflect what students should know and be able to do. They have attacked assessments designed to measure the progress of schools, seeking to localize decisions about test content so that the performance of students in one school or community cannot be compared with others. They have resisted innovative ways—such as growth models—to assess student performance. . . . This history is not consistent with the long record of the two unions to advance equality of educational opportunity."[204]

NEA did not see its criticism of NCLB as making it an "implacable foe" of improving public education for disadvantaged students, and eventually, NEA President Reg Weaver authorized moving forward with the lawsuit, despite the misgivings of the Association's civil rights allies.[205]

On April 20, 2005, with the Pontiac, Michigan, school district as the lead plaintiff, Chanin filed suit against the U.S. Department of Education in federal district court in Michigan. The complaint documented the shortfall in federal funding, and cited impartial studies showing that already strapped states and school districts were having to divert money from other educational priorities in order to comply with NCLB.

In support of what the plaintiffs contended that Section 9527(a) meant, the complaint quoted a speech by Education Secretary Paige as the 2003-04 school year began. He said that the NCLB Act "contains language that says things that are not funded are not required." Three months later, in another speech, Paige said that "if it's not funded, it's not required. That is language in the bill that prohibits requiring anything that is not paid for."[206]

The lawsuit asked for two remedies. First, it sought a declaratory judgment—a ruling by the court that Section 9527(a) means what it says: that states and school districts are not required to spend their own funds to comply with NCLB, and that failure to comply for this reason cannot be the basis for withholding federal funds to which they otherwise are entitled. Second, it sought an injunction prohibiting the U.S. Department of Education from withholding or threatening to withhold federal funds over non-compliance with NCLB for this reason.[207]

In addition to NEA, the plaintiffs included nine school districts: Pontiac, Michigan, an urban and largely African American district; Laredo, Texas, which had a largely Hispanic student population; and seven small, rural school districts in Vermont. The nine districts were chosen because they represented the variety of problems created by NCLB underfunding. If state and local funds had to be diverted for NCLB compliance, that meant less money for other educational programs and priorities, such as reducing class size, updating textbooks and other educational materials, and implementing curricula that have a proven track record in improving student achievement and educational quality.[208]

Nine NEA state affiliates also were chosen to be plaintiffs because studies done by the states themselves or outside education finance consultants had demonstrated the adverse impact of NCLB underfunding. The NEA local affiliate in Reading, Pennsylvania, was selected as a plaintiff because that school district had done studies of the effect of using state and local money to comply with NCLB.[209]

The U.S. Department of Education asked the federal district court to dismiss the suit on two grounds. It made the procedural argument that none of the plaintiffs had legal standing to bring the lawsuit. As to NEA and its affiliates, the department argued they could not bring suit to defend the rights of the real parties in interest—in this case, states and local school districts. In addition, the department argued that the school districts lacked standing because they did not explain in sufficient detail which NCLB requirements they were unable to meet with the federal funds they received.[210]

The Education Department also sought dismissal based on the merits of the claim itself. Section 9527(a) of NCLB, the department argued, did not prohibit NCLB from imposing unfunded mandates on states and school districts, but rather prohibited the department from imposing additional requirements beyond those specifically in NCLB, unless federal funds were provided to comply with those additional requirements.[211]

On November 23, 2005, the federal district court ruled in the plaintiffs' favor on standing but in the Department of Education's favor on the merits, agreeing with the department that Section 9527(a) of NCLB "cannot be reasonably interpreted" as the plaintiffs contended.[212]

NEA and its co-plaintiffs appealed to the U.S. Court of Appeals for the Sixth Circuit. Consistent with the practice in the federal appeals courts, the case was heard by a three-judge panel. The November 28, 2006, argument before the panel focused on the potential impact of a case that had been decided by the U.S. Supreme Court in June of that year. That case, *Arlington Central School District v. Murphy*,[213] was a special education case that on a broader level dealt with congressional powers under the Spending Clause in Article I of the U.S. Constitution. In light of the *Arlington Central* decision, the question for the Sixth Circuit panel was whether NCLB, which was enacted under the Spending Clause power, contained a "clear statement" from Congress to states and school districts that, if they took federal education funds under the law, they would also have to spend their own funds to comply with the law's provisions if federal funding fell short. Seven states and the District of Columbia filed *amicus* briefs on the plaintiffs' side answering that question "no." The states and the District of

Columbia said that when they accepted funds under NCLB, it was their understanding that they would not have to use their own funds for compliance when sufficient federal funds were not appropriated.[214]

In a decision on January 7, 2008, the Sixth Circuit panel voted two to one to reverse the lower court decision and ruled in the plaintiffs' favor. NCLB's goal of ensuring all children an equal opportunity to a quality education is laudable, the court said, but Congress has an obligation to make its requirements clear. "We conclude that NCLB fails to provide clear notice as to who bears the additional costs of compliance," the panel said. It also concluded that the plaintiffs had legal standing to pursue the suit, although that issue had not specifically been raised on appeal by the federal government.[215]

President Bush personally condemned the decision, which Chanin later described as "one of the highlights of my legal career."[216] Secretary of Education Margaret Spellings, who had succeeded Rod Paige at the start of President Bush's second term, sent a letter on January 18, 2008, to the chief state school officers stating that the Sixth Circuit's decision "undermines the efforts we have made under NCLB to improve the education of our children, particularly those children most in need. If the decision stands, it would represent a fundamental shift in practice."[217]

The Department of Education then asked for a rehearing "*en banc*," which, if granted, meant that the decision of the three-judge panel would be vacated and the case would be reheard by all sixteen judges of the Sixth Circuit. On March 8, 2008, the Sixth Circuit granted the petition for the *en banc* rehearing. Oral argument was scheduled for December 10, 2008. As a general rule, *en banc* rehearings are rare in the federal courts of appeals, but somewhat less so in the Sixth Circuit, as *The Washington Post* reported two days before the NCLB argument:

> Acting in cooperation with other Republican appointees on the court, [the Bush appointees] have repeatedly organized full-court hearings to overturn rulings by panels dominated by Democratic appointees.[218]

In what would be his last courtroom argument on behalf of NEA, Chanin presented the Association's NCLB case at the *en banc* hearing. "States and school districts are prisoners of this law. There are obligations placed on them by the No Child Left Behind Act, but the money is not enough to implement those requirements," he told fourteen of the court's sixteen judges who were present for the argument. (The other two could not be present in the ornate courtroom in Cincinnati that day, but they would participate in the decision by listening to a tape of the oral argument.)[219]

Besides addressing some of the more technical arguments in NEA's suit, Alisa Klein, the Justice Department lawyer who was representing the Department of Education, told the judges that the states and school districts could not reasonably have expected that they would not bear any costs under the education law. "No one thought Congress was going to pay the full cost of what the No Child Left Behind Act was meant to do," Klein told the court.[220]

Chanin faced a number of skeptical inquiries from the judges. If the law provided an unfunded mandate on the states, aren't the states the proper parties to be in court challenging the provision of the law, one judge wondered. (Chanin had not been able to get any states to sign on to the Pontiac case, although some had since filed *amicus* briefs on NEA's side, and the state of Connecticut was pursuing its own case against the law.) Another judge wondered why the Department of Education shouldn't be given deference on its interpretation of the unfunded-mandates provision.

By the time Chanin was ready to board his flight back to Washington, he was not feeling very confident about his case's prospects. As he put it to the National Council of Urban Education Associations, "I was not warmly received, and NEA's position was even less warmly received than I was."[221]

In January 2009, long before a ruling was expected, President Barack Obama took office. He appointed Arne Duncan, the head of the Chicago public schools, to be secretary of education. The *Pontiac School District v. Margaret Spellings* lawsuit automatically became *Pontiac School District v. Arne Duncan.*

NEA was now in the position of suing an administration it had helped elect. Chanin wondered, as he put it to the NCUEA conference in June 2009, "Who the hell are we fighting?"[222] Was it Duncan? NEA did not see eye to eye with the new secretary on every issue, but Duncan was reaching out to the Association and its affiliates, and he was expressing a willingness to work with NEA on the overdue reauthorization of the No Child Left Behind law. Was it President Obama? In a speech at NEA's Representative Assembly in 2007, Obama had sharply criticized the Bush administration's implementation of NCLB:

> Don't come up with this law called the No Child Left Behind Act and then leave the money behind. Don't tell us that you will put high-quality teachers in every classroom, and then leave the support and the pay for those teachers behind. Don't label a school as failing one day and then throw your hands up and walk away from it the next. Don't tell us that the only way to teach a child is to spend too much of a year preparing him to fill out a few bubbles in a standardized test. We know that is not true. You didn't devote your life to testing, you devoted it to teaching! And teaching is what you should be allowed to do![223]

Upon becoming president, Obama proposed an economic-recovery package that more than doubled current federal investment in education, a major step toward achieving the objective of NEA's NCLB lawsuit. Under the circumstances, Chanin recommended that NEA explore the possibility of resolving the lawsuit without further litigation. But conversations with the Education Department toward this end proved unproductive.[224]

On October 16, 2009, the full Sixth Circuit court issued its decision. As it turned out, Chanin had made much more headway with the court's judges at oral argument than he thought he had ten months earlier. But he fell one vote short of winning his case. The *en banc* court split eight to eight, resulting in an affirmance of the ruling by the lower court. For him, unfortunately, that did not mean the two-to-one Sixth Circuit panel decision in the plaintiffs' favor, which had been vacated when the rehearing *en banc* was granted, but, rather, the decision by the federal district court in Detroit that had dismissed the suit.

U.S. Circuit Judge Guy Cole Jr., who had written the panel opinion in NEA's favor, wrote an opinion in which he found that the suit was properly before the court, meaning that the school district plaintiffs had legal standing and their claims were ripe for judicial resolution. Judge Cole also concluded that the plaintiffs' suit was correct on the merits.

"NCLB rests on the most laudable of goals: to 'ensure that all children have a fair, equal, and significant opportunity to obtain a high-quality education,'" wrote Judge Cole. "Here, nobody challenges that aim. But a state official deciding to participate in NCLB reasonably could read [Section 9527(a)] to mean that the state need not comply with requirements that are 'not paid for under the act' with federal funds."[225]

Seven of the judges signed on to the part of Judge Cole's opinion dealing with the threshold standing and ripeness issues, but only six joined his conclusion on the merits. One of the seven judges believed that it was premature to decide the central issue, and would have sent the case back so the district court could have a better chance to develop a factual record in the case. Still, that added up to eight judges who were in favor of reversing and remanding the case to the district court.

A second faction on the court, totaling five judges, also ruled on the merits of NEA's suit, but reached the opposite conclusion. Judge Jeffrey S. Sutton, a rising conservative legal star and, incidentally, a former defender of the Cleveland voucher program in the Ohio courts, wrote an opinion for that faction concluding that NCLB was not at all ambiguous "when it comes to the central tradeoff presented to the states: accepting flexibility to spend significant federal funds in return for (largely) unforgiving responsibility to make progress in using them."[226] These five agreed with the other eight—for a total of thirteen—that the case was properly before the court.

A third faction made up of three judges was of the view that the suit lacked necessary plaintiffs in the form of the three states that were home to the plaintiff school districts—Michigan, Texas, and Vermont—and thus the suit should be dismissed. Added to the five judges who ruled against the plaintiffs on the merits, this meant that a total of eight judges voted to affirm the district court's dismissal of the suit.

Even though he fell short of victory, Chanin was somewhat gratified that his arguments persuaded eight judges on the Sixth Circuit to reverse the district court (and seven on the merits of the suit's central question). And that lineup played a role in a decision by NEA and other plaintiffs to seek a review by the U.S. Supreme Court. To Chanin, the arguments in favor of appeal overwhelmed those against the idea. For one thing, the Sixth Circuit had decided an important question of federal law that had immense financial implications for states and school districts. Second, the fact that the Sixth Circuit heard the case *en banc*, and disagreed sharply over 93 pages of opinions on the merits and other issues, indicated the need for Supreme Court guidance. And the case's embodiment of federalism issues and the application of the "clear statement" rule were areas that had attracted the interest of several High Court justices in recent years.[227]

There were also political and organizational considerations, Chanin argued. While Congress could remove the unfunded-mandates provision at the heart of the case, there was no guarantee lawmakers were prepared to do so, and certainly not outside of the context of a reauthorization of NCLB, which as of 2009 was already overdue, but which might not be completed for another year or two. A Supreme Court appeal could give NEA some leverage in that debate, Chanin reasoned. In any event, the Pontiac School District had already indicated that it might file such an appeal on its own if NEA did not do so. Not only was this a case for which NEA had done the heavy lifting, but it would be better for NEA to keep control of the case so that it could frame the issues before the High Court, he argued.[228]

In October 2009, the NEA Executive Committee authorized the Supreme Court appeal in the Pontiac case. A petition asking the justices to take up the case was filed in January 2010. President Obama's administration urged the Court not to take up the case. On June 7 2010, the Court turned down, NEA's appeal without comment from the justices. Such an action did not constitute a ruling on the merits of the case, but it was the end of the line for the five-year-old lawsuit.

Epilogue |

The Price of Success

Epilogue

The Price of Success

At the end of 2009, Bob Chanin retired as NEA general counsel at age 75. During his 41-year tenure in that position, he had worked with fourteen NEA presidents and five NEA executive directors—a remarkable achievement in light of the political winds that inevitably shift over time in unions and most other large organizations. It is believed that no one has ever served as general counsel for a major American labor union for anything even approaching that length of time.

In May 2009, he informed NEA of his intent to retire, and a "Tribute to Bob Chanin" took place at the 2009 Representative Assembly in San Diego. As part of the tribute, he made farewell comments to the assembly. After briefly recounting the origin and early years of his relationship with NEA, Chanin indicated how NEA has changed during that relationship and provided some advice for the future:

> In 1968, when NEA asked me to come to Washington to be its General Counsel, the decision was a no-brainer. I readily accepted, and began a relationship with NEA that has now lasted more than 40 years.
>
> Much has changed during those 40 years . . . and to me, one of the indications of this change is that I have found it increasingly necessary to spend time defending NEA and its affiliates against attacks from government agencies, conservative and right-wing groups, and unfriendly media. So much so that it brings to mind the old question, "Are we paranoid, or is someone really after us?" The answer is, we are not paranoid. Someone really is after us.
>
> During the Bush administration, for example, NEA was audited by the Internal Revenue Service. It was investigated by the Department of Labor. And it was called a "terrorist organization" by the Secretary of Education.
>
> Now that the Bush administration is history, that type

of governmental harassment will stop, but attacks by conservative and right-wing groups will continue unabated. The Landmark Legal Foundation will continue to file charges alleging that we have violated election campaign finance laws. The Right to Work Committee will continue to file lawsuits accusing us of misusing agency fees. The Heritage Foundation will continue to contend that we are guilty of financial malpractice. And other opponents will continue to argue that "paycheck protection" statutes and ballot initiatives are necessary to protect Association members from unscrupulous union bosses who are seeking to coerce them into paying for political activities that they do not want to support—when, in fact, the supporters of paycheck protection don't give a rat's ass about the rights of Association members.

And just in case any of you may not have noticed, *The Wall Street Journal*, Fox News, and *Forbes* magazine—they don't like us very much either.

Why, you may ask, is this so? Why are these conservative and right-wing bastards picking on NEA and its affiliates? I will tell you why. It is the price we pay for success. NEA and its affiliates have been singled out because they are the most effective unions in the United States. And they are the nation's leading advocates for public education and the type of liberal social and economic agenda that these groups find unacceptable.

The objective of these investigations, charges, lawsuits, statutes, and ballot initiatives is to limit the effectiveness of NEA and its affiliates by restricting our ability to participate in the political process, cutting off our sources of revenue, and diverting our energies from advancing our affirmative agenda to defending ourselves. At first glance, some of you may find these attacks troubling, but you would be wrong. They are, in fact, really a good thing.

When I first came to NEA in the early 1960s, it had few enemies and was almost never criticized, attacked, or even mentioned in the media. This was because no one really gave a damn about what NEA did or what NEA said. It was the proverbial sleeping giant—a conservative, apolitical, do-nothing organization. But then NEA began to change. It embraced collective bargaining. It supported teacher strikes. It established a political action committee. It spoke out for affirmative action, and it defended gay and lesbian rights. What NEA said and did began to matter. And the more we said and did, the more we pissed people off. And, in turn, the more enemies we made.

So the bad news, or depending on your point of view, the good news, is that NEA and its affiliates will continue to be attacked by conservative and right-wing groups as long as we continue to be effective advocates for public education, for education employees, and for human and civil rights.

And that brings me to my final—and most important— point, which is why, at least in my opinion, NEA and its affiliates are such effective advocates. Despite what some among us would like to believe, it is not because of our creative ideas. It is not because of the merit of our positions. It is not because we care about children. And it is not because we have a vision of a "great public school for every child."

NEA and its affiliates are effective advocates because we have power. And we have power because there are more than 3.2 million people who are willing to pay us hundreds of millions of dollars in dues each year because they believe that we are the unions that can most effectively represent them, the unions that can protect their rights and advance their interests as education employees.

This is not to say that the concerns of NEA and its affiliates with closing achievement gaps, reducing dropout rates, improving teacher quality, and the like are unimportant or inappropriate. To the contrary, these are the goals that guide the work we do. But they need not and must not be achieved at the expense of due process, employee rights, and collective bargaining. That simply is too high a price to pay.

When all is said and done, NEA and its affiliates must never lose sight of the fact that they are unions—and what unions do first and foremost is represent their members. If we do that, and if we do it well, the rest will fall into place. NEA and its affiliates will remain powerful, and that power will in turn enable us to achieve our vision of a "great public school for every child."[1]

The more than 10,000 delegates responded to Chanin's remarks with standing applause that lasted several minutes. But that show of appreciation and affection from the delegates was predictable, given the many close working relationships he had developed with so many leaders and members of NEA's state and local affiliates.

Some of the conservative and right-wing groups that Chanin indicated have been "picking on NEA and its affiliates" attacked his remarks, but that was also predictable. Phyllis Schlafly, president of the Eagle Forum, wrote that "Chanin is correct. Conservatives are 'after' the NEA. Since this powerful organization has effective control of the public schools, spends millions of taxpayers' dollars to indoctrinate school children, and spends millions of its own money to lobby for left-wing goals, the NEA deserves to be subjected to citizen surveillance and criticism."[2]

Mike Antonucci, a longtime NEA critic and watchdog, offered a more even-keeled assessment of Chanin's July speech and about his lifetime of work in general. "Whatever you think of Chanin," Antonucci wrote, "he is to be applauded for his clarity in an age where obfuscation is the norm in politics. We shall not see his like again."[3]

By December 2009, more than five months after that Representative Assembly, Chanin had packed up his office and sorted through 41 years' worth of files, legal papers, and memorabilia. On Saturday, December 12, the 178-member Board of Directors gathered at the Association's Washington headquarters for one of its regular business meetings. They would meet in NEA's lower-level auditorium, which would be dedicated that day in honor of the longtime general counsel. Before the dedication ceremony, Chanin delivered his final status report on NEA legal matters. A short time later, Rhoda Chanin and all of the couple's children and grandchildren would climb to the stage to hear a final farewell.

"I find it somewhat humbling to be speaking to you from the stage of the Robert H. Chanin Auditorium," he said. "It leaves me almost, but not entirely, speechless."[4]

Chanin began by making reference to his farewell speech before the RA the previous July. He reiterated his belief that NEA is the nation's most effective advocate for public education because "we have power" and that education reform goals "need not and must not be achieved at the expense of due process, employee rights, and collective bargaining."

"That is what I said at the RA," he continued. "Personally, I thought that my message was clear. But there are some people, particularly those associated with conservative and right-wing groups, who did not understand, or more likely have chosen to misrepresent what I said. Specifically, they assert that I, and by extension NEA, don't really care about children or quality public education, but instead pursue our own self-serving agenda."

He quoted a few of the critical letters he had received, and then said, "As I hope you realize, I couldn't care less about what these conservative and right-wing critics have to say about me, but the assertion that I am opposed to education reform is simply untrue. And just in case there may be some rational people who are confused about the point that I attempted to make at the RA, I would like to take this final opportunity to set the record straight."

Then, he concluded his farewell remarks with passion:

> American society is not a zero-sum game. Education employees and their associations have worked long and hard to achieve important and well-deserved rights, which we must not allow to be taken away in the name of education reform. That said, I do not believe that conflict between education reform and employee rights is inevitable. And to the extent that there is such conflict, we should make every possible effort to achieve an accommodation. Should that prove impossible, however, and should NEA be forced to make the difficult choice that it would rather not have to make, it's my hope that NEA will resist any attempt to weaken due process, employee rights, or collective bargaining. (Applause.)
>
> Some may criticize us and say that this is a self-serving and protective position, that we are, as one recent newspaper article put it, "placing union power and our members' interests above the education provided to kids." But these critics are wrong. And they are wrong because they seek

to draw a distinction that does not exist. They seek to separate the interests of education employees from the interests of their students, and this simply cannot be done.

There is a paradox here. Because it is our support for due process, employee rights, and collective bargaining that will prevent qualified people from leaving public education, and because it is our support for due process, employee rights, and collective bargaining that will attract the qualified new people that public education so desperately needs, NEA must, in the final analysis, continue to support these things if we are ever to achieve our vision of a great public school for every child.

To put the point most bluntly, what this all means is that NEA must act like a labor union. (Applause) And this appears to trouble some within our own ranks, because they are not entirely comfortable with the term "labor union." But the term is not good or bad in and of itself. The dictionary defines a labor union as "an organization of workers existing for the purpose of advancing its members' interests in respect to wages, benefits, and working conditions." This is what we do.

The critical question is not whether NEA is or is not a labor union, but whether it is a good labor union or a bad labor union. Our faults are many. We spend far too much time fighting among ourselves. Our priorities are often wrong. We are forever restructuring ourselves to do things instead of actually doing them. (Applause) Our actions do not always accord with our words, and we are guilty of the sin of hypocrisy, and we have surely not solved all the problems confronting public education and education employees. In short, we have a long way to go if we are to be all we can and should be.

But when I become depressed at the difficulty of the road ahead, I look back at what our organization was only a relatively few short years ago and I compare that to what it is today. The transformation has been truly amazing. And the accomplishments have been truly substantial. I am aware of no other organization that has done more for the people that it represents. Surely there is no other labor union that has taken so principled a position in terms of civil liberties, equal rights, and social justice. What sustains me in the final analysis is the hope that NEA can do as much for public education and education employees in the next few decades as it has done in the last few decades.

If it can, you will not have resurrected Camelot. Education employees will probably still be underpaid and underappreciated. There will probably still be student achievement gaps, and too many children will probably still drop out of school. But the world will be a little better place in which to live, and you will have the satisfaction of knowing that you did make a difference.

With that, Bob Chanin ended more than 40 years of service to the National Education Association. He, indeed, made a difference.

Acknowledgements |

Many individuals have given generously of their time to share memories of the parts of NEA history this book preserves. They include Jack Bertolino, Don Cameron, Bob Chase, Terry Herndon, Irma Kramer, Ken Melley, Jack Middleton, Dr. Joe Reed, Phillip Rumore, Jimmy Williams, Dr. Helen Wise, and Don Wollett. This story also could not have been told without transcriptions by Maureen Bridges and Kate Bridges, graphic design by Kelly J. Cedeño, legal assistance by Cynthia Chmielewski, editing by Mary Claycomb, project coordination by Roxanne Dove, publication coordination by Branita Griffin Henson, and administrative support by Kathy Williams. We are also grateful to John Wilson for initiating this project, Ann Bradley and John West for reading the manuscript and providing their insights, and to Michael Simpson for his continuing assistance and counsel. Of course, there would be no story without Bob and Rhoda Chanin, and we are indebted to them for so graciously and fully sharing their time, their stories, their papers, and indeed, their lives with us.

Selected Bibliography |

Adams, Scott J., John S. Heywood, and Richard Rothstein. *Teachers, Performance Pay, and Accountability*. Washington, D.C.: Economic Policy Institute, 2009.

Berliner, David C. and Bruce J. Biddle. *The Manufactured Crisis*. White Plains, New York: Longman, 1995.

Biskupic, Joan. *American Original: The Life and Constitution of Supreme Court Justice Antonin Scalia*. New York: Sarah Crichton Books/Farrar, Straus, and Giroux, 2009.

_____. *Sandra Day O'Connor: How the First Woman on the Supreme Court Became Its Most Influential Justice*. New York: ECCO/Harper Collins, 2005.

Bolick, Clint. *Voucher Wars*. Washington, D.C.: Cato Institute, 2003.

Califano, Joseph A., Jr. *Governing America: An Insider's Report from the White House and the Cabinet*. New York: Simon and Schuster, 1981.

Cameron, Don. *The Inside Story of the Teacher Revolution in America*. Lanham, Maryland: Scarecrow Education, 2005.

Cross, Christopher T. *Political Education: National Policy Comes of Age*. New York: Teachers College Press, 2004.

Dunn, Joshua M. and Martin R. West, editors. *From Schoolhouse to Courthouse: The Judiciary's Role in American Education*. Washington, D.C.: The Brookings Institution and the Thomas B. Fordham Institute, 2009.

Finn, Chester E., Jr., *Troublemaker: A Personal History of School Reform Since Sputnik*. Princeton, New Jersey: Princeton University Press, 2008.

Gilmore, Al-Tony. *All the People*. Washington, D.C.: National Education Association, 2008.

Gilmore, Glenda Elizabeth. *Defying Dixie*. New York: W.W. Norton, 2008.

Gray, Jerome A., Joe L. Reed, and Norman W. Walton. *History of the Alabama State Teachers Association*. Washington, DC: National Education Association, 1987.

Greenhouse, Linda. *Becoming Justice Blackmun: Harry Blackmun's Supreme Court Journey*. New York: Times Books, 2005.

Haley, Margaret. Battleground: *The Autobiography of Margaret A. Haley*. Urbana, Illinois: University of Illinois Press, 1982.

Honey, Michael K. *Going Down Jericho Road*. New York: W.W. Norton, 2007.

Ingersoll, Richard M. *Who Controls Teachers' Work?* Cambridge, Massachusetts: Harvard University Press, 2003.

Jeffries, John C. Jr. Justice *Lewis F. Powell, Jr.: A Biography*. New York: Charles Scribner's Sons, 1994.

Kahlenberg, Richard. *Tough Liberal: Albert Shanker and the Battles over Schools Unions, Race, and Democracy*. New York: Columbia University Press, 2007.

Karpinski, Carolyn. *A Visible Company of Professionals: African Americans and the National Education Association during the Civil Rights Movement*. New York: Peter Lang Publishing, 2008.

Kerchner, Charles T., Julia E. Koppich, and Joseph G. Weeres. *United Mind Workers: Unions and Teaching in the Knowledge Society*. San Francisco: Jossey-Bass, 1997.

Lieberman, Myron, and Michael H. Moskow. *Collective Negotiations for Teachers*. Chicago: Rand McNally, 1966.

Lieberman, Myron. *The Teacher Unions*. New York: The Free Press, 1997.

Murdoch, Joyce, and Deb Price. *Courting Justice: Gay Men and Lesbians v. the Supreme Court*. New York: Basic Books, 2001.

Murphy, Marjorie. *Blackboard Unions: The AFT and the NEA, 1900-1980*. Ithaca, New York: Cornell University Press, 1990.

Perry, Thelma. *History of the American Teachers Association*. Washington, D.C.: National Education Association, 1975.

Ravitch, Diane. *The Great School Wars: A History of the New York City Public Schools*. New York: Basic Books,1988.

_____. *Left Back: A Century of Failed School Reforms*. New York: Simon and Schuster, 2000.

_____.*The Troubled Crusade: American Education*, 1945-1980. New York: Basic Books, 1983.

Reuther, Victor. *The Brothers Reuther*. Boston: Houghton Mifflin, 1979.

Rosen, Ruth. *The World Split Open*. New York: Viking, 2000.

Rothstein, Richard, Rebecca Jacobsen, and Tamara Wilder. *Grading Education*. New York: Teachers College Press, 2009.

Rousmaniere, Kate. *Citizen Teacher*. Albany, New York: University of New York Press, 2005.

Rubin, David, and Steven Greenhouse. *The Rights of Teachers*. New York:

Bantam Books, 1984.

Savage, David G. *Turning Right: The Making of the Rehnquist Supreme Court*. New York: John Wiley & Sons, 1992.

Selden, David. *Teacher Rebellion*. Washington, D.C.: Howard University Press, 1985.

Stohr, Greg. *A Black and White Case: How Affirmative Action Survived Its Greatest Legal Challenge*. Princeton, N.J.: Bloomberg Press, 2004.

Toobin, Jeffrey. *The Nine: Inside the Secret World of the Supreme Court*. New York: Doubleday, 2007.

Urban, Wayne J. *Gender, Race, and the National Education Association*. New York: Routledge Falmer, 2000.

Urban, Wayne J. *Why Teachers Organized*. Detroit: Wayne State University Press, 1982.

Wertheimer, Barbara Mayer. *We Were There*. New York: Pantheon, 1977.

West, Allan. *The National Education Association*. New York: Free Press, 2000.

Wollett, Donald H., and Robert H. Chanin. *The Law and Practice of Teacher Negotiations*. Washington, D.C.: Bureau of National Affairs, 1974.

Notes |

Prologue

[1] Myron Lieberman, *The Teacher Unions* (New York: The Free Press, 1997), p. 28.

[2] Mike Antonucci, "NEA Discovers It Is a Labor Union," Education Intelligence Agency, www.eiaonline.com, July 6, 2009.

[3] Lieberman, *The Teacher Unions*, p. 204.

[4] Biographical information in this chapter is drawn from extended interviews with Bob and Rhoda Chanin, (February 2009-January 2010) as well as Chanin family papers, photographs, and memorabilia.

Part I: A Movement is Born

Chapter 1. A Wake Up Call for NEA

[1] Preamble, National Teachers Association Constitution, 1857.

[2] "Chicago Teachers Federation," *Encyclopedia of Chicago*, Chicago Historical Society, 2005.

[3] Marjorie Murphy, *Blackboard Unions* (Ithaca, New York: Cornell University Press, 1990), pp. 62-64.

[4] Kate Rousmaniere, *Citizen Teacher* (Albany, New York: University of New York Press, 2005), p. 45.

[5] Margaret Haley, Battleground (Urbana, Illinois: University of Illinois Press, 1982), p. 72.

[6] *Ibid.*, p. 81.

[7] *Proceedings of the National Education Association* (1904), pp. 145-152.

[8] *Ibid.*

[9] Joan K. Smith, *Progressive School Administration: Ella Flagg Young and the Chicago Schools, 1905-1915* (Illinois State Historical Society, 1980); "Ella Flagg Young Dies in Service to Her Country," *Chicago Tribune*, October 27, 1918, p. 9.

[10] Edgar Wesley, *NEA: The First Hundred Years* (New York: Harper, 1957),

pp. 326-327.

[11] *Ibid.*

[12] Rousmaniere, *Citizen Teacher*, p. 180.

[13] *Ibid.*

[14] Smith, Joan, *Ella Flagg Young: The Portrait of a Leader*, (Ames, Indiana: Educational Studies Press, 1979).

[15] Murphy, *Blackboard Unions*, pp. 80-86.

[16] *Ibid.*, p. 121.

[17] *Ibid.*, pp. 150-174.

[18] National Labor Relations Act, 29 U.S.C. §§ 151-169.

[19] Franklin D. Roosevelt, "Letter on the Resolution of Federation of Federal Employees Against Strikes in Federal Service," August 16, 1937.

[20] Alex MacGillis, "Union Bill's Declining Changes Give Rise to Alternatives," *The Washington Post*, March 29, 2009.

[21] Bureau of Labor Statistics, U.S. Department of Labor.

[22] *National Education Association: 150 Years of Advancing Great Public Schools* (Washington, D.C.: National Education Association, 2007), p. 63.

[23] Benjamin Fine, "Teachers' Strikes Growing in Nation," *The New York Times*, February 14, 1947, p. 23.

[24] *Ibid.*

[25] Allan M. West, *The National Education Association* (New York: The Free Press, 1980), p. 33.

[26] Ruth Rosen, *The World Split Open*, (New York: Viking, 2000), p. 20.

[27] *Ibid.*

[28] West, *The National Education Association*, p. 30; Myron Lieberman and Michael H. Moskow, *Collective Negotiations for Teachers*, (Chicago: Rand McNally, 1966), p. 192.

[29] West, *The National Education Association*, pp. 30-31.

[30] *Ibid.* pp. 32-33.

[31] Richard Kahlenberg, *Tough Liberal* (New York: Columbia University Press, 2007), p. 53.

[32] West, *The National Education Association*, p. 34.

[33] Don Cameron, *The Inside Story of the Teacher Revolution in America* (Lanham, Maryland: Scarecrow, 2005), pp. 35-39.

[34] West, *The National Education Association*, p. 67.

[35] Lieberman and Moskow, *Collective Negotiations for Teachers*, p. 56.

[36] *Ibid.* pp. 371-373.

[37] Mayor of the City of New York, *Executive Order* 49, March 31, 1958.

[38] Joseph C. Goulden, *Jerry Wurf*, (New York: Atheneum, 1982), pp. 52-54.

[39] Kahlenberg, *Tough Liberal*, p. 42.

[40] West, *The National Education Association*, pp. 54-55.

[41] Victor G. Reuther, *The Brothers Reuther*, (Boston: Houghton Mifflin, 1976), p. 367.

[42] David Selden, *The Teacher Rebellion*, (Washington, D.C.: Howard University Press, 1985), p. 29.

[43] *Ibid*. pp. 48-49.

[44] *Ibid*. p. 52.

[45] Lieberman and Moskow, *Collective Negotiations for Teachers*, p. 38.

[46] Gene Currivan, "Teachers to Vote on a Union Dec. 15", *The New York Times*, November 6, 1961.

[47] *Ibid*.

[48] Selden, *The Teacher Rebellion*, pp. 56-57.

[49] *Ibid*. p. 63.

[50] Ralph Katz, "Federation Wins in Teacher Vote," *The New York Times*, December 17, 1961.

[51] *Proceedings of the National Education Association Representative Assembly* (1962), p. 25.

[52] West, *The National Education Association*, p. 57.

[53] Interviews with Bob Chanin, February-September 2009.

[54] West, *The National Education Association*, p. 63.

[55] *Ibid*., pp. 60-61.

[56] Interviews with Bob Chanin, February-September, 2009.

[57] West, *The National Education Association*, p. 61.

[58] *Ibid*., p. 61.

[59] *Ibid*., p. 62.

Chapter 2. In the Trenches

[60] Interview with Don Wollett, February 4, 2009.

[61] Interviews with Bob Chanin, February-September, 2009.

[62] Wollett and Chanin. *The Law and Practice of Teacher Negotiations*, p. 1:33.

[63] Interviews with Bob Chanin, February-September, 2009.

[64] Goulden, *Jerry Wurf*, xviii.

[65] Michael Honey, Going Down Jericho Road (New York: W. W. Norton, 2007), pp. 1-4, 98-127, 432, 474-482, 485-492.

[66] Interviews with Bob Chanin, February-September, 2009.

[67] Cameron, *The Inside Story of the Teacher Revolution in America*, p. 45.

[68] Interviews with Bob Chanin, February-September, 2009.

[69] *National Education Association: 150 Years of Advancing Great Public Schools*, p. 65.

70 Wollett and Chanin, *The Law and Practice of Teacher Negotiations*, p. 1:9.

71 Interviews with Bob Chanin, February-September, 2009.

72 Wollett and Chanin, *The Law and Practice of Teacher Negotiations*, p. 1:9.

73 Howard L. Cherry, "Negotiations Between Boards and Teacher Organizations," *The American School Board Journal*, March 1963, p. 7.

74 "Huntington Teachers Win Landmark Cast," *The Challenger*, March 24, 1972.

75 Interviews with Bob Chanin, February-September, 2009.

76 *Ibid.*

77 *Ibid.*

78 *Ibid.*

79 *Ibid.*

80 *Ibid.*

81 Interview with Jack Middleton, February 6, 2009.

82 *Union Leader*, Manchester, New Hampshire, March 29, 1968.

83 "The Battle of Manchester," editorial in *Union Leader*, Manchester, New Hampshire, March, 1968.

84 Interview with Jack Middleton, February 6, 2009.

85 Interviews with Bob Chanin, February-September, 2009.

86 *Ibid.*

87 *Ibid.*

88 "Virtuoso at the Bargaining Table," *The Berkshire Eagle*, Pittsfield, Massachusetts, November 5, 1966.

89 Interviews with Bob Chanin, February-September, 2009.

90 *Ibid.*

91 Interview with Jack Bertolino, January 24, 2009.

92 *NEA Proceedings of the Representative Assembly* (1966).

93 Don Cameron, *The Inside Story of the Teacher Revolution in America*, pp. 81-84.

94 Interview with Irma Kramer, December 2009.

95 David R. Jones, "Militancy Sweeps Schools in U.S. as Teachers Turn to Strikes, Sanctions and Mass Resignations," *The New York Times*, June 11, 1967, p. 85; M. A. Farber, "Education Group Will Aid Strikes," *The New York Times*, July 6, 1967, p. 10.

96 *School District for the City of Holland v. Holland Education Association*, 380 Mich. 314 (1968).

97 "End-of-Millennium Report on State of Union Advocacy," Bob Chanin speech to Michigan State Staff Meeting, February 2, 2000.

98 *School District for the City of Holland v. Holland Education Association*, 380 Mich. 314 (1968).

99 Slip opinion in *Chippewa Valley School District v. Chippewa Valley*

Education Association.

[100] Digest of Education Statistics, National Center for Education Statistics, 2007.

[101] Interviews with Bob Chanin, February-September, 2009.

[102] Cameron, *The Inside Story of the Teacher Revolution in America*, pp. 93-100.

[103] *Ibid.*

[104] "Report of the Executive Secretary," *Addresses and Proceedings of the 110th Annual Meeting*, p. 13.

[105] Interviews with Bob Chanin, February-September, 2009.

[106] Jones, *The New York Times*, June 11, 1967, p. 85.

[107] Jonathan Spivak, "Militant Teachers: NEA is Trying Tougher Bargaining Techniques to Win Pay, Job Gains," *The Wall Street Journal*, June 28, 1963, p. 1.

[108] Richard J. Levine, "Militant Teachers: Many School Strikes Feared as Rival Unions Show Off Their Power," *The Wall Street Journal*, August 20, 1968, p. 1.

[109] J. Douglas Muir, "The Touch New Teacher," *The American School Board Journal*, November 1968, p. 10.

Chapter 3. General Counsel

[110] Interviews with Bob Chanin, February—September, 2009; Interview with Don Wollett, February 4, 2009.

[111] *Ibid.*

[112] Interview with Don Wollett, February 4, 2009.

[113] Interviews with Bob Chanin, February-September, 2009.

[114] Interview with Ken Melley, January 27, 2009.

[115] Cameron, *The Inside Story of the Teacher Revolution in America*, p. 88.

[116] Interview with Ken Melley, January 27, 2009.

[117] NEA Executive Committee minutes, November 1969.

[118] "History of the UniServ Program," National Education Association, 2008.

[119] Peter Brimelow and Leslie Spencer, "The National Extortion Association?" *Forbes*, June 7, 1993.

[120] Interview with Bob Chanin, November 2009.

[121] Interview with Roxanne Dove, October 2009.

[122] Wollett and Chanin, *The Law and Practice of Teacher Negotiations*, p. 1:9.

[123] Interviews with Bob Chanin, February-September 2009.

[124] Reynold Seitz, *Oregon Law Review*, Fall 1971.

[125] *Connecticut State Bar Journal*, Winter 1971.

126 "Robert H. Chanin Tribute to Don Wollett," speech, 1990.

127 Interviews with Bob Chanin, February-September 2009.

128 *Ibid.*

129 *Ibid.*

130 Susan Lowell Butler, *The National Education Association: A Special Mission* (Washington, D.C.: National Education Association, 1987), p. 50.

131 Robert H. Chanin, "The United States Constitution and Collective Negotiation in the Public Sector," *Proceedings of Eighteenth Annual Institute on Labor Law*, Southwestern Legal Foundation, 1972, p. 247.

132 NEA Board of Directors presentation, "NEA & the American Labor Movement," September 25, 2009.

133 Interviews with Bob Chanin, February-September 2009.

134 *National League of Cities v. Usery* 426 U.S. 833 (1976).

135 Interviews with Bob Chanin, February-September 2009.

136 *Garcia v. San Antonio Metropolitan Transit Authority* 469 U.S. 528 (1985).

137 Bob Chanin speech to California Teachers Association staff meeting, April 11. 1985.

138 Interviews with Bob Chanin, February-September 2009.

139 *Proceedings of the National Education Association Representative Assembly* (1980).

140 *Ibid.*

141 *NEA Educational Support Professionals Data Book*, 2007.

142 *Perry Education Association v. Perry Local Educators Association*, 460 U.S. 37 (1983).

143 *Ibid.*

144 Transcript and recording of oral argument in *Perry Education Association v. Perry Local Educators Association*, U.S. Supreme Court, October 13, 1982, available on Oyez web site, www.oyez.org/cases/1980-1989/1982/1982_81_896/argument, visited Dec. 9, 2009.

145 *Perry Education Association v. Perry Local Educators Association*, 460 U.S. 37 (1983).

146 *Ibid.*

147 *Springfield Township School District v. Knoll*, 471 U.S. 288, (1985).

148 *Wilson v. Garcia*, 471 U.S. 261 (1985).

149 *Springfield Township School District v. Knoll*, 471 U.S. 288, (1985).

150 Brief of Petitioners in *Texas State Teachers Association v. Garland Independent School District*, 1988 WL 1025563.

151 Transcript of oral argument, *Texas State Teachers Association v. Garland Independent School District*, Oyez web site. www.oyez.org/cases/1980-1989/1988/1988_87_1759/argument, (visited December 9, 2009).

[152] *Texas State Teachers Association v. Garland Independent School District*, 489 U.S. 782 (1989).

[153] New York Public Employment Relations Board, 24 PERB 3033, September 23, 1991.

[154] Phil Rumore remarks to NEA Representative Assembly, July 6, 2009.

[155] *Ibid.*

[156] *Board of Education for the City School District of the City of Buffalo v. Buffalo Teachers Federation, Inc.* 89 N.Y.2d 370, 675 N.E.2d 1202, 653 N.Y.S.2d 250 (1996).

[157] Interviews with Bob Chanin, February-September, 2009; "Stunning victory for Buffalo teachers," *NEA-NY Advocate*, January 1997, 1; "Court of Appeals Rules," Buffalo Teachers Federation Provocator, 1997; Harold McNeil, "Teachers union OKs back-pay pact," *Buffalo News*, April 11, 2000; Interview with Phil Rumore, January 15, 2009.

[158] Rumore remarks to NEA Representative Assembly, July 6, 2009.

[159] West, *The National Education Association*, pp. 228-233.

[160] Interview with Ken Melley, January 5, 2010.

[161] Interviews with Bob Chanin, February-September, 2009.

[162] *Ibid.*

[163] Myron Lieberman, "Merger of the NEA and AFT: Prospects and Consequences".

[164] Lieberman, *The Teacher Unions*, p. ix.

[165] "Union Members—2009," U.S. Bureau of Labor Statistics, U.S. Department of Labor, USCL 10-0069, January 22, 2010.

[166] Interviews with Bob Chanin, February-September, 2009.

Part II. The Pursuit of Racial Diversity

Chapter 4. Bringing Black and White Together

[1] *Brown v. Board of Education of Topeka*, 347 U.S. 483 (1954).

[2] Interview with Joe Reed, February 25, 2009.

[3] *Dred Scott v. John F.A. Sandford*, U.S. Supreme Court decision, 1857, http://memory.loc.gov/cgi-bin/query/r?ammem/llst:@field(DOCID+@lit(llst022div3)), accessed October 15, 2009.

[4] Thelma D. Perry, *History of the American Teachers Association* (Washington, DC: National Education Association, 1975), p. 45.

[5] *Ibid.*, p. 14.

[6] *Ibid.*, p. 14.

[7] *Ibid.*, p. 12.

[8] *Ibid.*, p. 173.

[9] *Ibid.*, p. 257.

[10] Al-Tony Gilmore, *All the People* (Washington, DC: National Education Association, 2008), 41-42; Mark V. Tushnet, *Making Civil Rights Law* (New York: Oxford, 1996), pp. 21-22.

[11] Gilmore, *All the People*, p. 41.

[12] President Franklin D. Roosevelt, Executive Order 8802, June 25, 1941; President Harry Truman, Executive Order 9981, July 26, 1948.

[13] *Proceedings of the National Education Association* (1943), p. 194.

[14] Gilmore, *All the People*, p. 47.

[15] *Proceedings of the National Education Association* (1950), p. 194.

[16] Murphy, *Blackboard Unions*, p. 197.

[17] *Brown v. Board of Education of Topeka* 347 U.S. 483 (1954).

[18] *Proceedings of the National Education Association* (1954), pp. 124-125.

[19] Murphy, *Blackboard Unions*, pp. 202-204.

[20] *Proceedings of the National Education Association* (1961), pp. 193-212.

[21] Perry, *History of the American Teachers Association*, p. 291.

[22] *Shelton v. Tucker*, 364 U.S. 479 (1960).

[23] Jerome A. Gray, Joe L. Reed, and Norman W. Walton, *History of the Alabama State Teachers Association* (Washington, DC: National Education Association, 1987), pp. 148-149.

[24] www.archives.gov/education/lessons/brown-v-board/timeline.html, accessed October 16, 2009; www.mississippitruth.org/pages/CRMtimeline.htm, accessed October 16, 2009.

[25] www.law.columbia.edu/focusareas/brownvboard/bvbcommemorate, accessed October 16, 2009.

[26] Tom Hayden, *Rebel* (Los Angeles: Red Hen, 2003), p. 49.

[27] www.lbjlib.utexas.edu/johnson/lbjforkids/civil_voting_timeline.shtm, accessed October 16, 2009.

[28] www.sitins.com. accessed October 16, 2009.

[29] Gray, Reed, and Walton, *History of the Alabama State Teachers Association*, p. 184.

[30] www.rubybridges.com, accessed October 16, 2009.

[31] Gray, Reed, and Walton, *History of the Alabama State Teachers Association*, 229-230; Vernon G. Smith, "African-American Male Honor Students' Views of Teaching as a Career Choice," *Teacher Education Quarterly*, Spring, 2004.

[32] Gilmore, *All the People*, pp. 51-52.

[33] *NEA 1965 Handbook*, "Desegregation in the Public Schools."

[34] www.cnn.com/2006/EDUCATION/01/31/extra.civil.rights.timeline/index.html, accessed October 16, 2009.

[35] Civil Rights Act of 1964, PL 82-352.

[36] Economic Opportunity Act of 1964, PL 88-452.

[37] www.core-online.org/History/freedom_summer.htm, accessed October 16, 2009.

[38] *Johnson v. Branch* 364 F.2d 177 (4th Cir. 1966).

[39] *Franklin v. County School Board of Giles County* 360 F.2d 325 (4th Cir. 1966).

[40] *Ibid.*, p. 55.

[41] www.nps.gov/history/nr/travel/civilrights/al4.htm, accessed October 16, 2009.

[42] Statement by President Johnson, March 9, 1965.

[43] Interview with David Rubin, July 30, 2009.

[44] www.archives.state.al.us, accessed October 16, 2009.

[45] Interview with Jim Williams, January 29, 2009.

[46] Mary Stanton, *From Selma to Sorrow* (Athens, GA: University of Georgia Press, 2000).

[47] Voting Rights Act of 1965. PL 89-110.

[48] Gray, Reed, and Walton, *History of the Alabama State Teachers Association*, p. 185.

[49] *Proceedings of the National Education Association* (1965), p. 10.

[50] Interviews with Bob Chanin, February-September, 2009.

[51] West, *The National Education Association*, p. 121.

[52] *Ibid.*, pp. 114-125.

[53] *Ibid.*

[54] Interviews with Bob Chanin, February-September, 2009.

[55] West, *The National Education Association*, pp. 131-132.

[56] *Ibid.*, 133; Interviews with Bob Chanin, February-September, 2009.

[57] Interviews with Bob Chanin, February-September, 2009.

[58] West, *The National Education Association*, p. 133.

[59] Interviews with Bob Chanin, February-September, 2009.

[60] Interview with Jim Williams, January 29, 2009.

[61] *Ibid.*; Interviews with Bob Chanin, February-September, 2009.

[62] West, *The National Education Association*, pp. 133-134.

[63] Interviews with Bob Chanin, February-September, 2009.

[64] Gray, Reed, and Walton, *History of the Alabama State Teachers Association*, pp. 227-230.

[65] Interviews with Bob Chanin, February-September, 2009; Interview with Joe Reed, February 25, 2009.

[66] Gray, Reed, and Walton, *History of the Alabama State Teachers Association*, p. 272.

[67] *Ibid.*, p. 270.

[68] Interviews with Bob Chanin, February-September, 2009.

[69] *Ibid.*; West, *The National Education Association*, pp. 147-157.

[70] West, *The National Education Association*, pp. 149-150.

[71] Interviews with Bob Chanin, February-September, 2009.

[72] West, *The National Education Association*, pp. 153-155.

[73] Interview with Jim Williams, January 29, 2009.

[74] Interviews with Bob Chanin, February-September, 2009.

[75] Interview with Jim Williams, January 29, 2009.

[76] *Ibid.*

[77] *Ibid.*

[78] Interviews with Bob Chanin, February-September, 2009.

[79] *Ibid.*

[80] Memorandum by Samuel B. Etheridge to the ATA Trustee Board, December 9, 1974.

[81] Gilmore, *All the People*, p. i.

[82] Interviews with Bob Chanin, February-September, 2009; NEA Handbook, 2008.

[83] Lieberman, *The Teacher Unions*, p. 239.

[84] Kahlenberg, *Tough Liberal*, p. 161.

[85] "Report to the NEA Board of Directors," Robert Chanin.

Chapter 5. Affirmative Action

[86] *Givhan v. Western Line Consolidated School District*, 439 U.S. 410 (1979).

[87] Brief for Petitioner, *Givhan v. Western Line Consolidated School District*.

[88] *Ibid.*

[89] *Ibid.*, p. 5.

[90] *Ibid.*, p. 6.

[91] *Ibid.*

[92] *Ibid.*, p. 8.

[93] *Ibid.*, p. 9

[94] *Ibid.*, p. 10.

[95] *Ibid.*

[96] *Givhan v. Western Line Consolidated School District*, 439 U.S. 410 (1979).

[97] David L. Hudson, Jr., "Teacher taught Miss. Schools a lesson," First Amendment Center web site, www.firstamendmentcenter.org/analysis.aspx?id=16992, accessed October 11, 2009.

[98] Interviews with Bob Chanin, February-September, 2009.

[99] Speech by Bob Chanin to National Council of Urban Education Associations, 1990; Interviews with Bob Chanin, February-September, 2009;

Kahlenberg, *Tough Liberal*, pp. 72-74.

[100] Kahlenberg, *Tough Liberal*, pp. 93-98.

[101] Quoted in speech by Bob Chanin to National Council of Urban Education Associations, 1990.

[102] *Ibid.*, p. 100.

[103] *Loving v. Virginia*, 388 U.S. 1 (1967).

[104] www.disturbingtheuniverse.com, accessed October 11, 2009.

[105] www.law.columbia.edu/fac/Jack_Greenberg, accessed October 11, 2009.

[106] Kahlenberg, *Tough Liberal*, pp. 86-87.

[107] Interviews with Bob Chanin, February-September, 2009.

[108] Kahlenberg, *Tough Liberal*, pp. 107-108.

[109] Interviews with Bob Chanin, February-September, 2009.

[110] Lyndon B. Johnson, commencement address, Howard University, June 4, 1965.

[111] Executive Order No. 11246, September 28, 1965, 30 F.R. 12319.

[112] Interviews with Bob Chanin, February-September, 2009.

[113] *Ibid.*

[114] Interviews with Bob Chanin, February-September, 2009; Interview with Irma Kramer, January 27, 2009.

[115] Interview with Irma Kramer, January 27, 2009.

[116] Interviews with Bob Chanin, February-September, 2009.

[117] *Ibid.*; Interview with Irma Kramer, January 27, 2009.

[118] *DeFunis v. Odegaard*, 416 U.S. 312 (1974).

[119] Speech by Bob Chanin to National Council of State Education Associations, December 3, 1974.

[120] Interviews with Bob Chanin, February-September, 2009; Interview with Irma Kramer, January 27, 2009.

[121] Interviews with Bob Chanin, February-September, 2009.

[122] *University of California Regents v. Bakke*, 438 U.S. 265 (1978).

[123] Kahlenberg, *Tough Liberal*, pp. 217-218.

[124] *Ibid.*

[125] Brief amici curiae, National Council of Churches et al., *University of California Regents v. Bakke*.

[126] *University of California Regents v. Bakke*, 438 U.S. 265 (1978).

[127] *United Steelworkers of America v. Weber*, 443 U.S. 193 (1979); Brief of amicus curiae, American Federation of State, County, and Municipal Employees, et al.

[128] Kahlenberg, *Tough Liberal*, p. 220.

[129] *United Steelworkers of America v. Weber*, brief of amicus curiae, American Federation of State, County, and Municipal Employees, et al.

[130] *United Steelworkers of America v. Weber*, 443 U.S. 193 (1979).

131 *Firefighters Local Union No. 1784 v. Stotts*, 467 U.S. 561 (1984).

132 *Ibid.*

133 *Proceedings of the National Education Association Representative Assembly* (2002).

134 *Ibid.*

135 Interviews with Bob Chanin, February-September, 2009.

136 *Proceedings of the National Education Association Representative Assembly* (1984), pp. 375-377.

137 *Wygant v. Jackson Board of Education*, 476 U.S. 267 (1986).

138 Interviews with Bob Chanin, February-September, 2009.

139 *Ibid.*

140 *Ibid.*

141 Kahlenberg, *Tough Liberal*, p. 242.

142 *Wygant v. Jackson Board of Education*, brief for amici curiae, National Education Association et al.; case summary prepared by Bob Chanin, November, 1986.

143 *Wygant v. Jackson Board of Education*, 476 U.S. 267 (1986).

144 Interviews with Bob Chanin, February-September, 2009.

145 Brett Pulley, "A Reverse Discrimination Suit Upends Two Teachers' Lives," *The New York Times*, August 3, 1997; Ronald Roach, "Bailing Out Piscataway School Board," www.diverseeducation.com, accessed October 11, 2009; Michael D. Simpson, "What Role Does Race Play," *NEA Today*, January 1998.

146 *Ibid.*

147 Interviews with Bob Chanin, February-September, 2009.

148 "The Use of Affirmative Action to Achieve an Ethnically Diverse Workforce," Bob Chanin speech to the State Bar of Wisconsin, May 19, 1998.

149 Interviews with Bob Chanin, February-September, 2009.

150 NEA Policy Statement Regarding the Use of Affirmative Action for Ethnic Minorities and Women in Educational Employment, adopted by NEA Representative Assembly, 1997, p. 2.

151 Michael D. Simpson, "What Role Does Race Play," *NEA Today*, January 1998.

152 Interviews with Bob Chanin, February-September, 2009.

153 *Ibid.*

154 Ronald Roach, "Bailing Out Piscataway School Board," www.diverseeducation.com, accessed October 11, 2009.

155 "N.J. District Settles Case on Race Bias," *Education Week*, November 26, 1997.

156 *Gratz v. Bollinger*, 539 U.S. 244 (2003); *Grutter v. Bollinger*, 539 U.S. 306 (2003).

[157] Interviews with Bob Chanin, February-September, 2009.

[158] Bob Chanin speech to National Council of Urban Education Associations, June 28, 2003.

[159] Brief amici curiae, National Education Association et al., *Parents Involved in Community Schools v. Seattle School District No. 1.*

[160] *Parents Involved in Community Schools v. Seattle School District No. 1,* 551 U.S. 701 (2007).

[161] Brief amici curiae, National Education Association et al., *Parents Involved in Community Schools v. Seattle School District No. 1.*

[162] *Ibid.*, pp. 8-9.

[163] *Parents Involved in Community Schools v. Seattle School District No. 1,* 551 U.S. 701 (2007).

[164] *Ibid.*

[165] *Ibid.*

[166] *Ibid.*

[167] Analysis prepared by Michael D. Simpson, NEA Assistant General Counsel, September, 2009.

[168] Interviews with Bob Chanin, February-September, 2009.

Part III: Give Me Liberty

Chapter 6. Out of the Closet and Into the Classroom

[1] "60 Minutes," CBS Television, February 25, 1973.

[2] Hawthorn, Illinois, School District dismissal notice to Jeanne Eckmann, January 18, 1982.

[3] Speech by Bob Chanin to Oklahoma Education Association Board of Directors, December 15, 1984.

[4] Brief for plaintiff-appellant, *Acanfora v. Board of Education of Montgomery County.*

[5] www.glbtq.com accessed October 12, 2009.

[6] "Discrimination Against Homosexuals," American Psychological Association, January, 1975.

[7] Interviews with Bob Chanin, February-September, 2009.

[8] www.joeacanfora.com, accessed October 12, 2009.

[9] Brief for plaintiff-appellant, *Acanfora v. Board of Education of Montgomery County.*

[10] www.joeacanfora.com, accessed October 12, 2009.

[11] Brief for plaintiff-appellant, *Acanfora v. Board of Education of Montgomery County.*

[12] *Ibid.*

[13] *Ibid.*

[14] Interviews with Bob Chanin, February-September, 2009.

[15] *Ibid.*

[16] *Ibid.*, www.usnews.com accessed October 12, 2009.

[17] Interviews with Bob Chanin, February-September, 2009.

[18] *Ibid.*

[19] *Ibid.*

[20] www.joeacanfora.com, accessed October 12, 2009.

[21] Transcript, "60 Minutes," CBS News, February 25, 1973.

[22] Jim Gallagher, "When Joe came out of the closet, I came out of the kitchen," *The News Tribune*, Woodbridge, N.J., April 12, 1973.

[23] Interviews with Bob Chanin, February-September, 2009.

[24] Brief for plaintiff-appellant, *Acanfora v. Board of Education of Montgomery County.*

[25] Testimony of Joseph Acanfora, *Acanfora v. Board of Education*, U.S. District Court for the District of Maryland, April 13, 1973.

[26] Testimony of Dr. Reginald Lourie and Dr. Felix Heald, *Acanfora v. Board of Education*, U.S. District Court for the District of Maryland, April 13, 1973.

[27] Testimony of Dr. John Money, Dr. Stanford Friedman, and Dr. William Stayton, *Acanfora v. Board of Education*, U.S. District Court for the District of Maryland, April 13-16, 1973.

[28] Memorandum and Order, *Acanfora v. Board of Education*, U.S. District Court for the District of Maryland, May 31, 1973.

[29] *Ibid.*

[30] *Acanfora v. Board of Education*, 491 F2d 498, (4th Circuit 1974).

[31] Interviews with Bob Chanin, February-September, 2009.

[32] Email from Joe Acanfora, June 17, 2009.

[33] Interviews with Bob Chanin, February-September, 2009.

[34] www.anitabmi.org, accessed October 12, 2009.

[35] *Ibid.*, www.glbtq.com, accessed October 12, 2009.

[36] Craig A. Rimmerman, *From Identity to Politics* (Philadelphia: Temple University Press, 2002), pp. 129-131.

[37] *Ibid.*

[38] www.glbtq.com, accessed October 12, 2009.

[39] www.weareca.org, accessed October 12, 2009.

[40] Ronald Reagan, "Two Ill-advised California Trends," *Los Angeles Herald-Examiner*, November 1, 1978.

[41] Craig A. Rimmerman, *From Identity to Politics* (Philadelphia: Temple University Press, 2002), pp. 129-131.

[42] Speech by Bob Chanin to Oklahoma Education Association Board of

Directors, December 15, 1984.

[43] *Ibid.*

[44] *National Gay Task Force v. Board of Education of Oklahoma City*, 729 F.2d 1270 (10th Cir. 1984).

[45] Interviews with Bob Chanin, February-September, 2009.

[46] Speech by Bob Chanin to Oklahoma Education Association Board of Directors, December 15, 1984.

[47] Interviews with Bob Chanin, February-September, 2009.

[48] *Ibid.*

[49] *Ibid.*

[50] *Ibid.*

[51] Speech by Bob Chanin to Oklahoma Education Association Board of Directors, December 15, 1984.

[52] Interviews with Bob Chanin, February-September, 2009.

[53] Brief of the National Education Association and the American Jewish Congress as Amici Curiae in Support of Appellee, in *Board of Education of Oklahoma City v. National Gay Task Force.*

[54] Transcript and audio of oral argument in *Board of Education of Oklahoma City v. National Gay Task Force*, Oyez web site, www.oyez.org/cases/1980-1989/1984/1984_83_2030/argument, (visited December 17, 2009.)

[55] Joyce Murdoch and Deb Price, *Courting Justice: Gay Men and Lesbians v. the Supreme Court*, (New York: Basic Books, 2001).

[56] Oyez site, *ibid.*

[57] *Ibid.*

[58] *Board of Education of Oklahoma City v. National Gay Task Force*, 470 U.S. 903 (1985).

[59] Interviews with Bob Chanin, February-September, 2009.

[60] Murdoch and Price, *Courting Justice*, pp. 237-249.; *Rowland v. Mad River Local School District*, 730 F.2d. 444 (6th Cir. 1984).

[61] *Ibid.*

[62] Murdoch and Price, *Courting Justice*, pp. 246-247.

[63] *Rowland v. Mad River Local School District*, 470 U.S. 1009 (certiorari denied) (Opinion of Justice Brennan, with whom Justice Marshall joins, dissenting.)

[64] Brief of National Education Association, et. al. in *Romer v. Evans.*

[65] *Romer v. Evans*, 517 U.S. 620 (1996).

[66] *Weaver v. Nebo School District*, 29 F. Supp. 1279 (D. Utah 1998).

[67] Report of the NEA Task Force on Sexual Orientation, January 14, 2002, p. 21.

[68] Resolution B-9, NEA *Proceedings of the National Education Association Representative Assembly* (1995).

[69] Gina Jarmin, "Veto Gay and Lesbian History Month," American Christian Cause, December 1995.

[70] Beverly LaHaye, "Here's an opportunity for you to protect children from homosexual propaganda in our public schools," Concerned Women for America, May, 1996.

[71] Interviews with Bob Chanin, February-September, 2009.

[72] *Ibid.*

[73] Report of the NEA Task Force on Sexual Orientation, January 14, 2002, 4.

[74] *Ibid.*, p. 19.

[75] *Ibid.*, Attachment A.

[76] *Proceedings of the National Education Association Representative Assembly* (2009), New Business Item E, "Same-Sex Couples."

[77] Phyllis Schlafly, "NEA Goes All-Out for Same-Sex Marriage," Eagle Forum, August 7, 2009.

[78] *Bowers v. Hardwick*, 478 U.S. 186 (1986).

[79] *Lawrence v. Texas*, 539 U.S. 558 (2003).

[80] *Ibid.*

Chapter 7. Gender and Other Civil Rights Battles

[81] Wayne J. Urban, *Gender, Race, and the National Education Association*, (New York: RoutledgeFarmer, 2000.); "Focus on Women: 2007," NEA pamphlet available at http://www.nea.org/assets/docs/mf_womenfocus07.pdf (visited January 5, 2010.)

[82] Analysis by Michael D. Simpson, NEA Assistant General Counsel, September, 2009.

[83] *Eckmann v. Board of Education of Hawthorn School District No. 17*, 636 F. Supp. 1214 (N.D. Illinois), 1986.

[84] "The Crimes Against Jeanne Eckmann," *Family Circle*, October 23, 1984; Speech by Michael D. Simpson, NEA Assistant General Counsel, to Idaho Education Association, August, 1994.

[85] Michael D. Simpson, "Roe v. Wade and Beyond," *NEA Today*, April 1, 1992.

[86] *Ibid.*

[87] Hawthorn, Illinois, School District dismissal notice to Jeanne Eckmann, January 18, 1982.

[88] Decision of hearing officer Sidney Mogul, Illinois State Board of Education, August 31, 1982.

[89] Steve Newton, "Jury awards Eckmann $3.3 million," *Rockford Register Star*, July 3, 1985; Jan Bone, "The Crimes Against Jeanne Eckmann," Family Circle, October 23, 1984; *Eckmann v. Board of Education of Hawthorn School District No. 17*, 636 F. Supp. 1214 (N.D. Illinois), 1986.

[90] www.filmreference.com, accessed October 13, 2009; Speech by Michael D. Simpson, NEA Assistant General Counsel, to Idaho Education Association, August, 1994.

[91] *Cleveland Board of Education v. LaFleur*, 414 U.S. 632 (1974).

[92] Brief for the National Education Association, amicus curiae, *LaFleur v. Cleveland Board of Education*.

[93] *Ibid.*

[94] *Ibid.*, p. 3.

[95] Interviews with Bob Chanin, February-September, 2009; *LaFleur v. Cleveland Board of Education*, 414 U.S. 632 (1974).

[96] www.eeoc.gov, accessed October 13, 2009.

[97] *Dike v. School Board of Orange County, Florida*, 650 F.2d 783, (11th Cir. 1981); Brief for appellant, *Dike v. School Board of Orange County, Florida*.

[98] *Ibid.*

[99] *Ibid.*

[100] *Ibid.*

[101] *Ibid.*

[102] Brief for appellant, *Dike v. School Board of Orange County, Florida*, 35.

[103] *Dike v. School Board of Orange County, Florida*, 650 F.2d 783, (11th Cir. 1981).

[104] *Littlejohn v. Rose*, 768 F.2d 765 (6th Cir. 1985); Brief for appellant, *Littlejohn v. Rose*, p. 3.

[105] *Littlejohn v. Rose*, 768 F.2d 765 (6th Cir. 1985).

[106] *Ibid.*

[107] *NEA 2008 Handbook*, C-31 Student Rights and Responsibilities, p. 255.

[108] Analysis by Michael D. Simpson, NEA Assistant General Counsel, September, 2009.

[109] *Ibid.*

[110] *Ibid.*

[111] *Safford Unified School District v. Redding*, 557 U.S. _____, 129 S. Ct. 2633 (2009).

[112] Michael D. Simpson, "Supreme Court Bars Student Strip Searches," *NEA Today*, July 30, 2009.

[113] *Lau v. Nichols*, 414 U.S. 563 (1974).

[114] *Plyler v. Doe*, 457 U.S. 202 (1982).

[115] Brief amici curiae, National Education Association and League of United Latin American Citizens, *Plyler v. Doe*.

[116] *Plyler v. Doe*, 457 U.S. 202 (1982).

[117] Analysis prepared by Michael D. Simpson, NEA Assistant General Counsel, September, 2009.

[118] NEA Office of General Counsel, "Immigration Status and the Right to A

Free Public Education," July, 2007.

[119] www.ryanwhite.com, accessed October 13, 2009.

[120] *Ibid*.

[121] *Ibid*.

[122] "Recommended Guidelines for Dealing with AIDS in the Schools," National Education Association, October 4, 1985.

[123] http://blogs.myspace.com/index.cfm?fuseaction=blog.view&friendId=277 527461&blogId=436358568, accessed October 13, 2009.

[124] www.neahin.org/ryanwhite, accessed October 13, 2009.

Part IV: Great Public Schools for Every Student

Chapter 8. The Politics of Education

[1] NEA Vision, Mission, and Values, NEA 2008 Handbook, p. 7.

[2] Robert Pear, "Education Chief Calls Union 'Terrorist,' Then Recants," *The New York Times*, February 24, 2004.

[3] Clint Bolick, *Voucher Wars* (Washington, D.C.: Cato Institute, 2003).

[4] Interviews with Bob Chanin, February-September, 2009.

[5] *Ibid*.

[6] Peter Dow, "Sputnik Revisited," www.nationalacademies.org, accessed October 13, 2009.

[7] President Kennedy, Remarks to Officers of State Education Associations and the N.E.A. November 19, 1963, www.jfklink.com, accessed October 13, 2009.

[8] Elementary and Secondary Education Act of 1965, PL 89-10.

[9] Higher Education Act of 1965, PL 89-329.

[10] Bilingual Education Act of 1968, PL 90-247.

[11] Interviews with Ken Melley, January-September, 2009; Interviews with Bob Chanin, February-September, 2009.

[12] NEA Handbook, 1956-1957, "The Teacher as a Citizen," p. 101.

[13] Minutes, NEA Board of Directors, February 15, 1969, p. 366.

[14] Minutes, NEA Board of Directors, June 28, 1970, p. 353.

[15] *Ibid*.

[16] West, *The National Education Association: The Power Base for Education*, p. 192.

[17] *Ibid*.

[18] *Ibid*.

[19] Robert W. Merry, "Teachers Group's Clout on Carter's Behalf Is New Brand of Special-Interest Politics," *The Wall Street Journal*, August 13, 1980.

[20] Marjorie Murphy, Blackboard Unions, p. 267.

[21] Robert Merry,"Teacher Group's Clout on Carter's Behalf is New Brand of Special Interest Politics," *The Wall Street Journal*, August 13, 1980.

[22] Interviews with Bob Chanin, February-September, 2009.

[23] "The Great Race," Don Cameron and Bob Chanin memorandum to NEA Board of Directors and Executive Staff, June 20, 1984.

[24] *Ibid.*

[25] *Proceedings of the National Education Association Representative Assembly* (2008).

[26] Interviews with Bob Chanin, February-September, 2009; Lieberman, *The Teacher Unions*, 75.

[27] Interviews with Bob Chanin, February-September, 2009; Gallup Poll, January 26, 1976.

[28] Interview with Ken Melley—January 2009.

[29] *Ibid.*

[30] www.presidency.ucsb.edu/ws/index.php?pid=30350, accessed October 13, 2009.

[31] *Ibid.*

[32] Joseph A. Califano Jr., *Governing America: An Insider's Report from The White House and The Cabinet* (New York: Simon and Schuster, 1981), 276; Deanna L. Michael, *Jimmy Carter as Educational Policymaker* (Albany, New York: SUNY Press, 2008), p. 96.

[33] Kahlenberg, *Tough Liberal*, p. 213.

[34] www.cato.org/pubs/handbook, accessed October 13, 2009.

[35] Kahlenberg, *Tough Liberal*, p. 214.

[36] Chester E. Finn Jr., *Troublemaker: A Personal History of School Reform Since Sputnik*, (Princeton, N.J.: Princeton University Press, 2008), pp. 77-86.

[37] *Ibid.*, 215-216; Wayne Urban, *Essays in Twentieth Century Southern Education* (New York: Routledge, 1998), p. 212.

[38] Interview with Ken Melley, January 27, 2009.

[39] Republican Party Platform, adopted by Republican National Convention, July 15, 1980.

[40] *Ibid.*

[41] www.usgovernmentspending.com, accessed March 30, 2009.

[42] National Commission on Excellence in Education, "A Nation at Risk," April, 1983, pp. 4-6.

[43] *Ibid.*, p. 9.

[44] *Ibid.*, p. 9.

[45] *Ibid.*, pp. 17-20.

[46] http://www.reagan.utexas.edu/archives/speeches/1983/42683d.htm, accessed October 14, 2009.

47 National Commission on Excellence in Education, "A Nation at Risk," April, 1983, pp. 17-20.

48 Interview with Bob Chase, January 28, 2009.

49 David C. Berliner and Bruce J. Biddle, *The Manufactured Crisis* (White Plains, NY: Longman, 1995), p. xiv.

50 National Education Association, "An Open Letter to America on Schools, Students, and Tomorrow," July, 1984.

51 NEA Professional Standards and Practice Committee, "Teacher Compensation Systems," May 2000, pp. 15-16.

52 Kahlenberg, *Tough Liberal*, pp. 275-278.

53 *Ibid.*, pp. 263-265.

54 Ronald Reagan, address to American Federation of Teachers convention, July 5, 1983, at www.reagan.utexas.edu/, accessed October 14, 2009.

55 "End-of-Millennium Report on State of Union Advocacy," Bob Chanin speech to Michigan State Staff Meeting, February 2, 2000.

56 John Brummett, "Clinton, NEA Meet Politely, Part in Firm Disagreement," *Arkansas Gazette*, January 28, 1984.

57 Lura Holifield, "Reshaping the Test for Teachers," letter to editor, *Arkansas Gazette*, 1984.

58 Jim Gallagher, "Arkansas schoolteachers up in R'ms," *Chicago Tribune*, February 5, 1984.

59 John Brummett, "Clinton, NEA Meet Politely, Part in Firm Disagreement," *Arkansas Gazette*, January 28, 1984.

60 *Ibid.*; Jim Gallagher, "Arkansas schoolteachers up in R'ms," *Chicago Tribune*, February 5, 1984.

61 John Brummett, "Clinton, NEA Meet Politely, Part in Firm Disagreement," *Arkansas Gazette*, January 28, 1984.

62 Blake Rodman, "Arkansas Union Drops Suit Over Teacher Tests," *Education Week*, November 25, 1987.

63 Susan Laccetti, "Arkansas teachers divided over state test of their skills," *Atlanta Constitution*, October 5, 1987.

64 Jane Hansen, "Critics claim teacher test racially biased, irrelevant," *Atlanta Constitution*, November 14, 1985; Susan Laccetti, "Consultants raised 'serious questions' about teacher test," *Atlanta Constitution*, August 8, 1986.

65 Kathy Scruggs, "Settlement reached in teacher test suit," *Atlanta Constitution*, March 3, 1988.

66 Interviews with Bob Chanin, February-September, 2009.

67 Peter Brimelow and Leslie Spencer, "The National Extortion Association," *Forbes*, June 7, 1993.

68 Reed Larson, Membership Alert, National Right to Work Committee, July 1993.

[69] *Railway Employes' Department v. Hanson* 351 U.S. 225 (1956); *Machinists v. Street* 367 U.S. 740 (1961).

[70] Robert H. Chanin, "The Agency Shop in Public Employment Following *Abood*," *Industrial and Labor Relations Report*, Fall 1980, p. 15.

[71] *Abood v. Detroit Board of Education*, 431 U.S. 209 (1977).

[72] Ruling by the Michigan Court of Appeals as summarized in *Abood, ibid*.

[73] Brief Amicus Curiae for the National Education Association in *Abood v. Detroit Board of Education*.

[74] *Ibid*.

[75] *Abood, ibid*.

[76] *Ibid*.

[77] "Justices Ban Forcing of Public Employees to Support Union Political Activities," *The Wall Street Journal*, May 24, 1977, p. 2.

[78] *Hudson v. Chicago Teachers Union*, 743 F.2d 1187 (CA7 1984).

[79] Brief Amicus Curiae for the National Education Association in *Chicago Teachers Union v. Hudson*.

[80] *Chicago Teachers Union v. Hudson*, 475 U.S. 292 (1986).

[81] Stephen Wermiel, "High Court Rules on Union Fees by Nonmembers," *The Wall Street Journal*, March 5, 1986, p. 4.

[82] "Collecting Agency Fees After *Chicago Teachers Union, et al. v. Hudson, et al.*" memorandum by Bob Chanin and Bruce Lerner, May 5, 1986.

[83] Brief for Respondents, *Lehnert v. Ferris Faculty Association*, U.S. Supreme Court.

[84] *Ibid*.

[85] Transcript and audio of *Lehnert v. Ferris Faculty Association*, Oyez web site, www.oyez.org/cases/1990-1999/1990/1990_89_1217/argument, (visited December 15, 2009).

[86] *Ibid*.

[87] *Ibid*. In that era, Supreme Court transcripts did not identify which justice asked a question, but it is clear from the audio in this case that Chanin's exchange on "unionism" was with Justice Scalia.

[88] Transcript and audio of opinion announcement in *Lehnert v. Ferris Faculty Association*, Oyez web site, www.oyez.org/cases/1990-1999/1990/1990_89_1217/opinion (visited December 15 2009).

[89] *Lehnert v. Ferris Faculty Association*, 500 U.S. 507 (1991).

[90] *Ibid*.

[91] *Lehnert*, 500 U.S. at 561 (Scalia, J.).

[92] Liz Schevtchuk Armstrong, "Court Allows Teachers' Union to Charge Agency Fees," *Education Week*, June 5, 1991.

[93] *Ibid*.

[94] Memo by NEA Office of General Counsel and Bredhoff & Kaiser, August 1, 1991, p. 50.

[95] Speech by Bob Chanin to the NEA-New Mexico Collective Bargaining Conference in Santa Fe, October 23, 1992.

[96] Speech by Bob Dole to Republican National Convention, August 15, 1996.

[97] Bob Chase, speech at National Press Club, February 5, 1997.

[98] The Kamber Group, "An Institution at Risk," January 14, 1997, p. 4.

[99] *Ibid.*, p. 20.

[100] Bob Chase, speech at National Press Club, February 5, 1997.

[101] Interviews with Bob Chanin, February-September, 2009.

[102] Speech by Bob Chanin, Indiana State Teachers Association, March 1, 2002.

[103] Speech by Bob Chanin to NEA National Conference, March 13-15, 1992.

[104] *Minutes*, NEA Board of Directors 1968.

[105] *Proceedings of the National Education Association*, June 30, 1972. pp. 235-249.

[106] "Policy Concerning Merger and/or the Uniting of All Educators," NEA Representative Assembly, Item 54, 1973.

[107] Harris, James A., "Address to the 1974 NEA Representative Assembly," *Proceedings*, NEA Representative Assembly, 1974, p. 19.

[108] *Proceedings of the National Education Association Representative Assembly* (1976) pp. 212-213.

[109] Cameron, *The Inside Story of the Teacher Revolution in America*, pp. 161-162.

[110] *Proceedings of the National Education Association Representative Assembly* (1993) pp. 84-100.

[111] Cameron, pp. 163-166.

[112] *Principles of Unity for a United Organization*, National Education Association, Washington, D.C., 1998, pp. 1-21.

[113] *Proceedings of the National Education Association Representative Assembly* (1998) p. 171.

[114] *Report on the 1998 Delegate Survey regarding the Principles of Unity and Merger with the American Federation of Teachers*, NEA Research, Washington, D.C., December 1, 1998.

[115] *Proceedings of the National Education Association Representative Assembly* (1998) pp. 213-240.

[116] *Minutes*, NEA Board of Directors, July 6, 2001, p. 212.

[117] *Proceedings of the National Education Association Representative Assembly* (2001) pp. 74-92.

[118] *Minutes*, NEA Board of Directors, Washington, D.C., April 30, 1999, pp. 163-164.

[119] *Report of the Secretary-Treasurer*, NEA Board of Directors, December 5, 2009.

[120] *Minutes*, NEA Board of Directors, February 7, 2007.

[121] *NEA/AFL-CIO Labor Solidarity Partnership Agreement*, National Education Association, February 27, 2006.

[122] Press Statement of John Sweeney, AFL-CIO Executive Council Meeting, San Diego, California, February 27, 2006.

[123] Report of the NEA Labor Outreach Department to the NEA Executive Committee, Washington, D.C. December 1, 2009.

Chapter 9. Chanin v. Vouchers

[124] Interviews with Bob Chanin, February-September, 2009; NEA Professional Standards and Practice Committee, "Teacher Compensation Systems," May 2000; Report of the NEA Special Committee on Charter Schools, May 2001; Report of the NEA Special Committee on Distance Education, May 3, 2002; Report of the NEA Special Committee on Early Childhood Education, April 2003.

[125] Interviews with Bob Chanin, February-September, 2009.

[126] Mark Walsh, "Public v. Private," in *Lessons of a Century: A Nation's Schools Come of Age*, (Bethesda, Md.: Editorial Projects in Education, 2000).

[127] *Ibid.*

[128] *Everson v. Board of Education of Ewing*, 330 U.S. 1 (1947).

[129] *Committee for Public Education and Religious Liberty v. Nyquist*, 413 U.S. 756 (1973).

[130] Martin R. West, "School Choice Litigation after *Zelman*," chapter in *From Schoolhouse to Courthouse: The Judiciary's Role in American Education*, Brookings Institution Press/Thomas R. Fordham Institute. (2009).

[131] *Mozert v. Hawkins County Board of Education*, 827 F.2d 1058 (1987).

[132] www.phc.edu, accessed October 15, 2009.

[133] *Mozert v. Hawkins County Board of Education*, 827 F.2d 1058 (1987).

[134] *Ibid.*

[135] *Ibid.*

[136] Brief amicus curiae, National Education Association, *Mozert v. Hawkins County Board of Education*, 827 F.2d 1058 (1987).

[137] *Mozert v. Hawkins County Board of Education*, 827 F.2d 1058 (1987).

[138] Michael D. Simpson, "Voucher Backers are in Courts of Last Resort," *NEA Today*, February, 1994.

[139] *Ibid.*

[140] Clint Bolick, *Voucher Wars, Waging the Legal Battle Over School Choice*, Cato Institute, (2003) 35 and 65; http://www.forbes.com/lists/2008/54/400list08_David-Koch_QMFE.html; http://www.forbes.com/

lists/2008/54/400list08_Charles-Koch_Z9KL.html, accessed October 14, 2009.

[141] *Ibid.*, pp. 12, 34.

[142] Interviews with Bob Chanin, February-September, 2009.

[143] Bolick, *Voucher Wars*, p. 15.

[144] *Proceedings of the National Education Association.* (1980), pp. 103-111.

[145] Speech by Bob Chanin to National Council of Urban Education Associations, 1998.

[146] *Ibid.*

[147] *Ibid.*

[148] Mark Walsh, "Bolick v. Chanin," *Education Week*, April 1, 1998, and Alison Frankel, "Blackboard Jungle," *The American Lawyer*, May 1, 2000.

[149] Bolick, *ibid.*, p. 82.

[150] *Ibid.*

[151] Mark Walsh, "Religious School Vouchers Get Day in Court," *Education Week*, March 6, 1996.

[152] Chanin speech to National Council of Urban Education Associations, *ibid.*

[153] *Ibid.*

[154] *Ibid.*

[155] *Ibid.*

[156] Mark Walsh, "Vouchers Face Key Legal Test in Wisconsin," *Education Week*, March 11, 1998.

[157] Transcript of oral argument before the Wisconsin Supreme Court in *Jackson v. Benson*, p. 266.

[158] Bolick, *Voucher Wars*, p. 122.

[159] Interviews with Bob Chanin, February-September, 2009; Mark Walsh, "Bolick v. Chanin," *Education Week*, April 1, 1998.

[160] Speech by Bob Chanin to National Council of Urban Education Associations, 1998; *Jackson v. Benson* (218 Wis.2d 835 (1998).

[161] Alison Frankel, "Blackboard Jungle," *The American Lawyer*, May 1, 2000.

[162] *Zelman v. Simmons-Harris*, 536 U.S. 639 (2002).

[163] Mark Walsh, "Bolick v. Chanin," *Education Week*, April 1, 1998.

[164] Interviews with Bob Chanin, February-September, 2009.

[165] Bolick, *Voucher Wars*, p. 170.

[166] *Ibid.*

[167] Transcript of oral argument before U.S. Supreme Court, *Zelman v. Simmons-Harris*, February 20, 2002, at www.supremecourtus.gov/oral_arguments/argument_transcripts/00-1751.pdf, accessed October 14, 2009.

[168] Linda Greenhouse, "Cleveland's School Vouchers Weighed by Supreme Court," *The New York Times*, February 21, 2002.

169 Mark Walsh, "A School Choice for the Supreme Court," *Education Week*, Feb. 27, 2002.

170 Bolick, *Voucher Wars*, p. 182.

171 Interviews with Bob Chanin, February-September, 2009.

172 Interviews with Bob Chanin, February-September, 2009; *Zelman v. Simmons-Harris*, 536 U.S. 639 (2002).

173 *Zelman v. Simmons-Harris*, 536 U.S. 639 (2002).

174 Mark Walsh, "Supreme Court Upholds Cleveland Voucher Program," *Education Week*, June 27, 2002.

175 Mark Walsh, "Advocates' Post-Ruling Choice: Bubbly," *Education Week*, July 10, 2002.

176 Mark Walsh, "Justices Settle Case, Nettle Policy Debate," *Education Week*, July 10, 2002.

177 West, "School Choice Litigation after *Zelman*," p. 170.

178 Interviews with Bob Chanin, February-September, 2009.

179 *Owens v. Colorado Congress of Parents, Teachers and Students*, 92 P.3d 933 (Colo. 2004).

180 Speech by Bob Chanin to NEA Board of Directors, September 27, 2008.

181 *Ibid.; Bush v Holmes.* 919 So.2d 392 (Fla. 2006).

182 Bob Chanin Report to NEA Board of Directors, February 10-11, 2006.

183 Speech by Bob Chanin to NEA Board of Directors, September 27, 2008.

184 Michael C. Sender, "School Tax, Voucher Questions Off Ballot," *Palm Beach Post*, September 4, 2008; Ford v. Browning, 992 So. 2d 132 (Fla. 2008).

185 *Cain v. Horne*, No. 08-0189 (Ariz. Mar. 25, 2009); Speech by Bob Chanin to NEA Board of Directors, May, 2009.

186 Howard Fischer, "AZ vouchers for schools ruled illegal," *Arizona Daily Star*, March 26, 2009.

187 Interviews with Bob Chanin, February-September, 2009; www.nea.org/home/ns/17011.htm, accessed October 15, 2009; www.nea.org/home/17956.htm, accessed October 15, 2009.

188 Speech by Bob Chanin to NEA Board of Directors, May, 2009.

Chapter 10. The Challenge of No Child Left Behind

189 Interviews with Bob Chanin, February-September, 2009.

190 Republican Party Platform, adopted by Republican National Convention, July 15, 1980.

191 Republican Party Platform, July 31, 2000.

192 Complaint for Declaratory and Injunctive Relief, *School District of the City of Pontiac v. Spellings*.

[193] Edweek.org summary of NCLB, http://www.edweek.org/rc/issues/no-child-left-behind/ Visited Nov. 18. 2009.

[194] Interviews with Bob Chanin, February-September, 2009.

[195] *Ibid.*; Speech by Bob Chanin to National Council of Urban Education Associations, 2008.

[196] Interviews with Bob Chanin, February-September, 2009; www.nea.org/home/NoChildLeftBehindAct.html, accessed October 15, 2009.

[197] Robert Pear, "Education Chief Calls Union 'Terrorist,' Then Recants," *The New York Times*, February 24, 2004.

[198] "Paige Issues Statement Announcing Resignation," U.S. Department of Education news release, November 15, 2004.

[199] Interviews with Bob Chanin, February-September, 2009.

[200] No Child Left Behind Act, PL 107-100 (2001).

[201] Bob Chanin memorandum to NEA Executive Committee, October 29, 2009.

[202] Speech by Bob Chanin, Center of Education Policy, July 14, 2005.

[203] Karla Scoon Reid, "Civil Rights Groups Split Over NCLB," *Education Week*, August 31, 2005; and Jeff Archer, "Civil Rights Groups Back NCLB Law in Suit," *Education Week*, February 8, 2006.

[204] William L. Taylor and Crystal Rosario, "National Teachers' Unions and the Struggle Over School Reform," report by the Citizens' Commission on Civil Rights, July 2009.

[205] Interviews with Bob Chanin, February-September, 2009.

[206] Complaint for Declaratory and Injunctive Relief, School District of the City of Pontiac v. Spellings.

[207] Speech by Bob Chanin, Center of Education Policy, July 14, 2005; Complaint for Declaratory and Injunctive Relief, *School District of the City of Pontiac v. Spellings*.

[208] *Ibid.*

[209] *Ibid.*

[210] Speech by Bob Chanin, Center of Education Policy, July 14, 2005.

[211] *Ibid.*

[212] Speech by Bob Chanin to National Council of Urban Education Associations, 2008.

[213] *Arlington Central School District v. Murphy*, 548 U.S.—2006.

[214] *Ibid.*, Speech by Bob Chanin to National Council of Urban Education Associations, 2009.

[215] *School District of the City of Pontiac v. Spellings*, No. 05-2708 (6th Cir. Jan. 7, 2008).

[216] Bob Chanin speech to National Council of Urban Education Associations, June 29, 2009.

[217] *Ibid.*

[218] R. Jeffrey Smith, "The Politics of the Federal Bench," *The Washington Post*, December 8, 2008.

[219] Mark Walsh, "Full 6th Circuit Weighs NEA Suit Against NCLB," *The School Law Blog of Education Week*, Dec. 10, 2008.

[220] *Ibid.*

[221] Speech by Bob Chanin to National Council of Urban Education Associations, 2009.

[222] *Ibid.*

[223] Speech by U.S. presidential candidate Barack Obama to National Education Association Representative Assembly, July 5, 2007.

[224] Interviews with Bob Chanin, February-September, 2009.

[225] *School District of the City of Pontiac v. Secretary of the U.S. Department of Education*, (en banc decision, Oct. 16, 2009).

[226] *Ibid.*

[227] Bob Chanin memorandum to NEA Executive Committee, October 29, 2009.

[228] *Ibid.*

Epilogue: The Price of Success

[1] Speech by Bob Chanin, NEA Representative Assembly, July 6, 2009.

[2] Phyllis Schlafly, "Furor as NEA's General Counsel Blasts 'Right-Wing Bastards'," Eagle Forum, August, 2009.

[3] Mike Antonucci, "NEA Discovers It Is a Labor Union," www.eiaonline.com, July 6, 2009.

[4] Speech by Bob Chanin, NEA Headquarters Auditorium Dedication, December 12, 2009.

Index |

~B~

~C~

~D~

~G~

~H~

~I~

~O~

~S~